DATE DUE	
NOV 0 6 1990	
NOV 2 8 1990	
APR 3 0 1991	
DEC 2 3 1991	
JAN 2 8 1993	
APR 1 4 1994	
NOV 01 1996	
NOV 01 1996	
ILL 2·19·99	

ORIGINS OF HUMAN AGGRESSION

ORIGINS OF HUMAN AGGRESSION
Dynamics and Etiology

Edited by

Gerard G. Neuman, Ph.D.

*Institute for Psychodynamics and
Origins of Mind
La Jolla, California*

HUMAN SCIENCES PRESS, INC.
*72 FIFTH AVENUE
NEW YORK, N.Y. 10011-8004*

Printed in the United States of America
987654321

Library of Congress Cataloging-in-Publication Data

Origins of human aggression.

   Papers presented at a symposium sponsored by the
Institute for Psychodynamics and Origins of Mind,
held in New York City, Dec. 1984.
   Includes index.
   1. Aggressiveness (Psychology)—Congresses.
2. Violence—History—Congresses. 3. Genetic
psychology—Congresses. I. Neuman, Gerard G.
II. Institute for Psychodynamics and Origins of
Mind (U.S.)
BF575.A3075   1987   302.5′4   86-15370
ISBN 0-89885-324-9

CONTENTS

CONTRIBUTORS

Kent G. Bailey, Ph.D., professor of Psychology, Virginia Commonwealth University, Richmond, VA. Clinical psychologist and specialist in psycho-biological regression, as developed in his forthcoming publication, *Human Paleopsychology: Aggression and Pathological Processes.*

Lloyd deMause, author of *Foundations of Psychohistory,* an introduction to the field. Director of the Institute for Psychohistory and founder of the International Psychohistorical Association, *The Journal of Psychohistory,* and *The Journal of Psychoanalytic Anthropology.*

Judith S. Kestenberg, M.D., psychoanalyst and teacher, and

Milton Kestenberg, L.L.D., attorney and research historian. Founding members of the Group for the Psychoanalytic Study of the Effect of the Holocaust on the Second Generation and of the Jerome Riker International Study of Organized Persecution of Children, sponsored by Child Development Research. Contributors to *Generations of the Holocaust,* edited by M. S. Bergmann and M. E. Jucovy.

Paul D. MacLean, M.D., chief, Laboratory of Brain Evolution and Behavior, National Institute of Mental Health, Bethesda, MD. In his innovative neurobiological and behavioral research, he has described and given the names to the "triune brain," the "limbic system," and the "R-complex," and revealed the possibilities within man's developing neocortex.

Robert S. McCully, Ph.D., professor, Department of Psychiatry, Medical University of South Carolina, Charleston, SC. Author of *Rorschach Theory and Symbolism.* His interest in the origins of symbol-formation has taken him into the field and methodology of research in prehistoric cave paintings, prehistoric religions, and prehistoric artifacts.

Gerard G. Neuman, Ph.D., clinical psychologist in private practice. Diplomate in Clinical Psychology (ABEPP). Founder and Director of the Institute for Psychodynamics and Origins of Mind (IPOM).

Robert Rousselle, Ph.D., specialist in Greek and Roman history. Contributing editor to *The Journal of Psychohistory.* Independent historical research, West Hempstead, NY.

Howard F. Stein, Ph.D., professor in the Department of Family Medicine, University of Oklahoma Health Sciences Center, Oklahoma City, OK. Editor of *The Journal of Psychoanalytic Anthropology.* Author, editor, and consultant in analytic study of contemporary society as a psychoanalytic anthropologist and psychohistorian.

ACKNOWLEDGMENTS

It is easy to thank individuals at a distance; it is difficult to thank individuals empathically close. The interactive process leading to combined growth makes the expression of thanks almost trivial.

Nevertheless, I shall try to provide some sense of this interaction. The book originated at a symposium, "Slaying Mankind's Most Pernicious Dragon," sponsored by the Institute for Psychodynamics and Origins of Mind, in December, 1984, in New York City. The contributors for the symposium were selected because they could best represent the emerging new approaches on the frontiers of thinking and research on aggression, as well as in the expectation that they could advance the subject matter through interaction and planning.

The development of my own thinking about aggression goes back to my first discovery of the works of Dr. Karl A. Menninger whose books, *The Human Mind, Man Against Himself* and *Love Against Hate,* inspired me to come to Topeka, Kan. to learn. First and foremost I want to acknowledge all that I received from his integrative concepts, his enthusiasm for actively correcting the problems he perceived, and his use of all relevant team members to achieve the broadest and most intensive solutions to the problems at hand. In addition, the epilogue's title itself was suggested by a presentation Dr. Menninger recently gave at the Smithsonian Institution in Washington, D.C.

For many years I listened to the fantasy and dream material of my patients, observed their at times unexplainably irrational behavior, had interpreted the content in terms of "archaic part objects" but could not under-their origin. I also had to admit to myself that I did not have any more success with the very sick, orally regressed, addictive or otherwise pre-oedipally acting patient than the next therapist, which left me with a sense of needing to learn more.

Almost 10 years ago, I believed I could obtain additional knowledge about the human personality if I better understood its developmental origins and the factors that made specific ways of human adaptation necessary. Drawn by a layman's curiosity, but having no real knowledge of prehistory, I searched for a teacher. I chose Professor Freeman of the University of Chicago. When I first talked with him, we both knew that we could gain from one another if we found a way of structuring the cooperation. After establishing that the level of *Homo erectus* with his initiation of the use of fire was a good place to start, he explained that although archeologists could approximately date the artifacts of early man, there was no good understanding of what they meant or how they fitted into the life of prehistoric respondents who could not respond now. Showing me various artifacts such as tools, sculpture, and paintings, he wondered whether my experience in interpreting children's drawing might be of help in discovering their meaning.

In the chapter, How We Became (In)human, much of my interpretation is based on primary and secondary sources of archeological material which I have integrated in my reading over the last 10 years. Discriminating the specifics of references is often difficult. The books, *Humankind Emerging* by Bernard G. Campbell and *Ascent to Civilization* by John Gowlett, proved most helpful in maintaining a simple structure for the final presentation of a few sections of this chapter.

In my own professional activities, I began to impart my newly acquired enthusiasm for prehistoric roots to students, patients, and colleagues. One of them was Allan Laughlin, who had intuitive insight into what Les Freeman and I were talking about. His own interest in Object Relations Theory, especially as developed by the English School, seemed to relate directly to the "objects" we were looking at. In weekly meetings with Allan, even minute imprints on rocks or details of sculptures and paleolithic wall paintings took on psychodynamic life. The prehistoric material tied down some of the more free-floating theories that we spun. It occurred to us many times that philogenetic prehistory had a counterpart in individual ontological prehistory.

Two outstanding men in their own fields proved of help with that. Long before I had the opportunity to meet him, I had been impressed with Paul MacLean's Triune Brain approach. Paul's combination of the dynamic origins of his professional career with the concept of biological evolution allowed for an explanation of many previously unclear phenomena. He graciously has helped in the development of my thinking in our personal contacts and has given the dimension of a psychobiological root to our concepts. Kent Bailey, in his desire to understand aggression and to develop his unique regression hypothesis, had also drawn from similar sources. Reading his articles led to personal interchange of ideas. Although our backgrounds have been some-what different, as he came through the more academic ranks in psychology and I through the more depth dynamics approach, we have continued working on this problem in the same direction, assisting one another when-ever possible.

For many years I had been interested in developing the interpretation of the Rorschach test into a depth psychological tool for increasing our un-derstanding of an individual's prehistory. That led to my discovery of Rob-ert McCully's brilliant *Rorschach Theory and Symbolism—A Jungian Approach to Clinical Material.* Even though I do not carry a Jungian membership card and have differences with a number of Jung's basic ideas, I was struck by the similarity in our approach to the Rorschach, prehistory, and human person-ality. We have continued to work together, while each developing our own material.

To this phylogenetic approach, which included the prehistoric archeo-logical and psychobiological roots, Lloyd deMause, founder of the Institute for Psychohistory, added the ontogenetic root of fetology. In addition to in-terpreting historical events and the psychobiographical implications of his-torical personalities based on his explorations of child-rearing through the ages, he is anchoring his work in the earliest origins of individual man, namely the fetus in the womb.

A new world opened up for me. Many fantasy and dream expressions of my patients, especially the most ill ones, were trying to deal with hurts they had experienced in the womb. At first, I thought the patients could not emotionally reach such early levels, but found that visualizations and touch-ing on the problem intellectually made a decided difference.

Turning to the study of aggression in events of more recent history, I discovered the body of work by Judith and Milton Kestenberg in Holocaust research. I already had learned much from Judith's work as a pioneer psy-choanalyst dealing with oedipal and pre-oedipal developments of parent and child, especially girls, which are still so poorly understood. Her work in cre-ative motion research and her chapter in a publication devoted to Winni-cott's work (*Between Reality and Fantasy,* edited by Simon A. Grolnick and Leonard Barkin) builds important new bridges between biology and depth psychology.

Howard Stein, anthropologist, and Robert Rousselle, historian, have both been of great help in developing my further understanding of aggression in historical and more recent times.

Others are all the professionals, teachers, students, patients and artists, too numerous to mention, who have not written for this book specifically but come to mind as I am thinking of the developmental processes of our team approach over the past 10 years. I hope that as they read the book they will experience our thanks, as the contribution of each one of them became part of the ever-developing tapestry. They, and the spiritual forebears who in-spired our team, deserve our deeply felt gratitude.

Professional and spiritual contributions alone do not bring a book to the reader, however. This book could not have been produced without the literally hundreds of hours and constant cooperation and concern of my wife, Sophie. She has made contributions in all areas—sounding board, professional advisor, assistant editor, and typist.

Another important individual is Norma Fox, a most creative editor. Her interest and encouragement have provided the ego support to stay on the job through many trying hours. In addition, her suggestion led to the chapter on terrorism.

There are many, many others who have contributed. This book has been truly a labor of love on the part of the contributing authors and those helping with the production.

Gerard G. Neuman, Ph.D.

INTRODUCTION

After reviewing the literature on aggression in the first chapter, we proceed with giving one of the roots of our new understanding of its origin and development, the basic biological root.

MacLean's material on the Triune Brain is well-known and repeatedly quoted in physiological and brain research circles. It seemed important to include it here as basic introductory material, as many social scientists may not be familiar with the possibility of seeing the evolutionary logic of moving from the reptilian through the mammalian to the human brain. In his own analogy of "separate drivers of the same car" to the degree that they "get along," or, as the scientist would say, can be "integrated," we are mature, healthy, and have things under control. To the degree that cannot be achieved, the various forms of symptomatic malfunctioning come to the fore—uncontrolled aggression being one of them. As a brain researcher, he can show us important pathways and synoptic connections and give us a picture of the "basic hardware" which makes human functioning possible with its unprecedented scope. Although the specific contents of behavior do not always make sense, the physiological basis for their occurring now finds a meaningful overall integrative structure.

We follow with Bailey's all-inclusive regression hypothesis, which is largely based on MacLean's findings. Here, we can see what happens when the so laboriously developed internalized evolutionary order unravels, so that we gain a better understanding of the specificity of behaviors arising out of the interactions of stress and reaction to it. The integrative power of his theory is truly impressive, giving us hope of finding the specific landmarks for a re-building process.

The new root of fetology is represented by Lloyd deMause in the next chapter. His book, *Foundations of Psychohistory,* contains the development of his basic ideas. Psychoanalysts generally have not and are still not including this root, so obvious in clinical fantasy and dream material.

As we believe that we can better understand human behavior through knowing the historical roots of its origin and development, I have tried to sketch the inner human side of our prehistory, based on the existing exter-nal evidence of archeology. Since many conjectures need to be based on in-ferences, it is likely that many aspects of the presentation will need to be changed as additional finds may throw new light on previous formulations and theories. Although a number of conjectures may prove controversial, they offer a framework to which future finds can be related. We are very early in the development of the field of psycho-prehistory.

Chapters six and seven give examples of case studies in prehistory, showing the restitutional approaches to early handling of aggression and demonstrating the possibility of interpreting archeological finds in terms of human motivation and growth.

McCully, in his chapter, gives us the flavor of a matriarchal world un-derlying the artistic creativity of paleolithic times. Jung and his followers had developed meaningful structural concepts such as the archetypes and other phenomena, assisting in the understanding of man's inner experience of the developing world, as well as the meaning he gave to the world around him. In addition to showing us forms of integrating the "terrible mother" aspects as projections of the previously internalized aggressive fears, he paints a beautiful picture doing it. He is the guide on a depth psychological trave-logue, taking us not only to paleolithic sites, but into the deeper layers of ourselves.

Moving on from the pre-historic to historic and more recent times, we included Rousselle's chapter to show that cannibalism is not just found in New Guinea and the primitive wilds of Africa, but presents an internalized layer even in historical times, and remained in the depth of the psyche of every one of us. As Rousselle shows, during Greek and early Christian times, can-nibalistic fantasy wore a still thin cover. Much as we try to separate ourselves from our deeper past, our myths, fantasies, and dreams keep us integra-tively related. These structures represent the means we have invented to keep ourselves in one piece, to avoid the splits and separations that cause illness, acting out, or the various forms of psychological symptomatology.

The next three chapters carry us into present time. The events of the Holocaust, having occurred almost half a century ago have still not been in-tegrated and still leave the participant with an unintegratable past and the observer with the puzzle of horror; how is man capable of such sadistic be-havior? The Kestenbergs try to help us understand. It is a most valuable help, although it will take uncountable chapters and books to really come to terms with it. Too many clinicians and social scientists in dealing with this severely aggressive material separate themselves from it by building a schizoid academic wall of objective "rationality." The Kestenbergs have the courage and wisdom to face it and, thus, lead the rest of us into examining our own relationship to it.

Stein's chapter analyzes the ingredients of the most important international relationship of our times, namely the one between two superpowers, the United States and the Soviet Union. Can a better understanding of the intro- and projective perceptions we have of each other help prevent another holocaust, a holocaust which may be so global that none of us may be left to analyze the causes?

Neuman's chapter on terrorism adds a dynamic view of a newer, contemporary form of aggression which seems to know no containing force nor recognizes previously established bounds and boundaries. Terrorism approaches the almost ultimate representation of "evil" for which men may not be able to find "rational" answers.

The final summaries offer more theoretical possibilities for understanding the root causes of aggression and the means of restitution.

Although we tried to structure the sequence of the material in a developmental manner, there is no real reason why the chapters cannot be read for their individual content or in any order chosen. In fact, the reader may find the reading of later chapters a help in better understanding earlier ones and *vice versa*. Each chapter reread may offer new aspects of understanding not available during a first reading.

Chapter 1

PAST AND PRESENT THINKING ON AGGRESSION

An Introductory Overview

Gerard G. Neuman

There are between 20,000 and 30,000 scientifically sound references on the subject of aggression. Our review of them, therefore, will have to be a "Cook's Tour of a Cook's Tour" in this chapter which we hope will open doors to current cultural, neurophysiological, and personality research.

We can divide the past approaches into the various schools of thought such as psychophysiology, evolutionary physiology, ethology, sociology, human learning theory, social and cultural anthropology, Gestalt psychology, descriptive abnormal psychology, and the various schools of psychoanalysis from the orthodox Freudian, the Jungian, Kleinian, and Object Relations approach, and offshoots from all of them.

Although all start with what they conceive of as a valid frame of reference, the leaders of all the schools generally agree that their view only covers a very special aspect of the problem, with the main determinants still remaining unexplained.

Meanwhile, we look every day at the shocking results of aggression—uncontrolled greed and criminality, destruction of the earth and its resources, and more powerful weapons with seemingly less and less control of them. Historically, more people were killed in the last hundred years than have existed from the beginnings of mankind up to the last century. A total of 20 million men and women were killed on the battlefields of World War II and an equal number as a consequence of the wars off the battlefield. Volumes have been written on family, community, tribal, religious, national and international violence, all leading to the conclusion that man, without doubt, is the most destructive creature on earth, unmatched in his volume or motivation by any other animal group.

Neither the legal system of any country nor any religious, educational, or therapeutic approach has had any significant impact on improving the tottering status quo. What are we to do? We find no answer, see the problem as overwhelming, get frightened for a while, then, considering the problem too big for any one of us individually or all of us collectively, shrug our shoulders and go on, knowing that the time bomb is ticking.

Now, in my Cook's Tour, I shall assume that you are familiar with the major aspects of each school of thought. A selected bibliography can fill you in and, if any part stimulates you further, each of the references has more references, so you will not have any difficulty familiarizing yourself with the background. I will use my limited space here to point out the shortcomings of each approach, putting myself in the hazardous position of appearing at best, arbitrary, superficial, and at the worst, arrogant. My aim, however, is to lay the groundwork for the points made in the following chapters of this book.

Another disclaimer should be added at this point. The sophisticated reader will probably sense that we have not come closer to the understanding of the problem because deep down, we would find it too uncomfortable to find out, and that we put up many forms of resistance to somehow hide the discomforting truth from ourselves and our neighbors. I will not endeavor to do any unveiling at this introduction but we may all come to more poignant conclusions as the multifaceted story unfolds in the book, and the need for these resistances may be more understandable by the time we draw our conclusions.

Before starting with the major approaches to aggression, there is one other important limitation. We all look for simple, basic answers. Just as there is no *one* form of cancer or schizophrenia, so there is no *one* form of aggression. Homicidal aggression, for instance, has different variables than rape or burglary. Atomic warfare has different variables than the power plays on the board of a corporation.

There are three major directions aggression can take:
- It can be acted out. This is primarily the subject matter of this book.
- It can be "acted in," which produces many of the forms of physical illness.
- We can escape the field through strong emotional defenses leading to the various forms of psychoses, depressions, manias, schizophrenias, or neuroses.

Aggression, violence, and death have been of human concern ever since mankind began to use symbolic thought. The modern study of human behavior, whether individually or in groups, society, politics and all related fields, starts with Darwin's monumental discoveries in the field of evolution during the middle of the last century (1852). From then until the 1930s, the people who believed that aggression was an inborn fact of evolutionary nature carried the field. A change occurred in 1939 when a monograph by

Miller and Dollard, titled *Frustration and Aggression,* shifted the argument from inborn roots to learned phenomena. The nature-nurture argument of the old days was updated to the inborn-learned level. We have found that any time there is a bipolar argument, neither pole can be completely the answer, as each implies the other, and integration on a different level is usually required. Their approach still represents the major plank in present day social science research in the field of aggression. The basic postulate is: aggression is always a consequence of frustration. It does not always show itself in pure form but can be delayed, repressed, displaced, changed in form, deflected, etc.

The social scientist using this approach deals in the following variables:
- Attempts to define the "instigator" of the frustration producing situation,
- Predicts sequences of responses to the frustration,
- Substitutes avenues for expressing the aggression aroused by frustration. These include deflection, inhibition induced through threats or punishment, catharsis in therapy, substitute activity, transfers to bodily expression or to symbolic behavior.

Thousands of experiments have been and are being conducted with these principles in mind. Why doesn't something that sounds so reasonable work in practice?

It is our belief that it is too reasonable. It usually works in reasonable settings such as group solutions for problems among individuals, more obvious social conflicts, and behavior science laboratories which make use of these concepts. As Dollard found out in his own research in the late 1940s and early 1950s, it could not provide answers for racial problems in the South, it did not have good answers for the field of criminology where minor deterrence worked for reasonable situations, but the death penalty and other more severe deterrence did little for homicide and rape, and answers for intergroup wars of a more deep-seated nature were as far away as ever.

Most people I consulted in the criminology field admitted that they have no real answers for the more serious problems. One ray of light is the work of M. Wolfgang and F. Ferracuti (1967) who found that violence is best understood in terms of deep feelings of revenge, as detailed in their book, *Subcultures of Violence.*

The social learning theory did contribute to the knowledge that children learn from parents and that aggressive children are likely to come from aggressive, unstable, and frustrating families, but then, even the Babylonians and the Greeks knew that. The real goal remains to find ways to better classify overt behavior and to relate it to the more deep-seated roots within individuals and groups, a task we hope to advance in the following chapters.

Turning away from the social scientist's approach, how about the fields of neurology, physiology, and biology? I went through myriad research studies of animals, usually showing that the male of the species is the more aggressive, and that the invasion of territory or competition for mating cause aggressive reactions. In the higher species, centers for inhibitions of aggression were built into the brain of the sub-human animal in order to preserve the species. This makes a pecking order in the group formation possible. Most of the research has been aimed at identifying physiological or neurological origins of aggression. It has, however, become evident that aggression in the animal is a normal ecological component for the protection of the individual and the species.

Recognizing the insufficiency of having animal behavior explained in purely mechanistic ways, the ethologists such as Lorenz (1963) and his colleagues and students, Tinberger (1965) and Eibl-Eibesfeldt (1971) try to explain not only evolutionary physical change, but to include rituals and motivational elements as part of the evolutionary process. They show how motivation and expression of aggression are ritualized by the individual species.

Lorenz and his later adherents such as Ardrey (1961) and Morris (1967) apply facts learned from animals to the human species. In comparing the human with the animal, Lorenz suggests that, unlike nonverbal animals, man's rapid technological development has outstripped the slower evolution of innate inhibitions against the expression of his aggressive instincts. As solutions, he suggests providing men with opportunities to discharge their aggressive instincts through participation in sports and other harmless competitive activities.

If the human species is just a continuation of the evolutionary process, how does it happen that the human, who split off from the higher ape, is the first species in evolution that could not solve its own problems? As much as Ardrey with his "territorial imperative" and Morris with his "naked ape" have tried, they still could not come up with an explanatory model for the transition from humanid to humanoid to homo sapiens.

As we have seen, many social scientists and anthropologists insist that nature and biology have nothing to do with human behavior, while most evolutionists see the human as just an extension of the evolutionary animal series.

Before leaving the field of ethology and biology, I should like to call attention to one idea in the study of aggression which seems to tie the animal to the human field. This is the pathology introduced by "isolation induced aggression" (usually isolation from the maternal animal, Valzelli, 1981) which occurs as soon as two or more previously isolated subjects (mice or rats) are put in contact with each other. Fierce compulsive and repetitive fighting begins immediately and continues until the participants are exhausted. (Here we seem to witness the regression from the mammalian to the reptilian level, so well discussed by MacLean in a later chapter.) In the absence of any prior relevant or explicit training to fight, and in the absence of territorial, sexual, or food cues, the fighting occurs.

As with mice, rats subjected to maternal isolation or even other socio-environmental deprivation (derived trauma) often demonstrate either behavioral or neurochemical and neurophysiological alterations which serve as the basis for the isolation syndrome, often leading to mouse-killing behavior or pup-killing (Moyer & Kern, 1965; Paul & Kupferschmidt, 1975). Normally, rats do not kill mice. In nature, frogs and turtles elicit aggression in nearly 100 percent of rats, whereas mice elicit aggression in only 15 percent of rats. Mouse killing by rats, regardless of whether surgically or environmentally induced, has so far been the only phenomenon that can be used to seemingly change the behavior of a species over generations, as mouse killing activity is self-reinforcing and punishment only temporarily inhibits, rather than eliminates, mouse killing by rats.

The neurochemical transmitters' correlates have been studied extensively in the mouse and rat, and sometimes are found somewhat comparable to the human. It was found that with the same distress, the behavior of mice differed considerably from the behavior of rats. How can we then be asked to make direct comparison between the simpler mammal and the human?

The various isolation experiments with rats and mice do not make clear whether we are dealing with merely "isolation" or maternal isolation. The fact that pup-killing appears in response to isolation seems to make the maternal hypothesis more likely. Harry Harlow (1979) studied specifically maternal isolation in higher forms, namely, monkeys.

Harlow found that the various forms of aggression and depression are very close to human reactions as described by Freud, Melanie Klein, and Winnicott. There is still much that we can learn, however, from comparative ethology if some of the avenues suggested by these early pioneers could be elaborated in more research.

What can we learn about aggression from social and cultural anthropology? Many of the early experts in the field, such as Margaret Mead (1930), Ruth Benedict (1934), Malinowski (1927), and Kardiner (1945) were intent on making anthropology a true social science divorced from biology. Some of them were influenced by social learning theory; child-rearing practices were the touchstone for people influenced by Kardiner; and some went deeply into Freud, such as Geza Roheim (1930) and George Devereux (1966). One of their early concepts employed the word "functional"; i.e., a society establishes its institutions in terms of what proves functional for its members. Looked at more closely, however, this does not add much to the understanding of human behavior. It begs the question since what is functional for the group is what exists. Kardiner added the concept of the health of a society. He stated that wherever the institutional forms were closer to the actual behavior of the group, the society was healthier. Since the spiritual life and other cultural forms are compensating for unfulfilled realities, as they move further away from the tribe's reality, the mental health level of the tribe is lower. Direct expression of aggression in the Sioux or Pueblo Indians seemed healthier to him than their substitute in sand painting as in the Navahoe, for instance.

Ruth Benedict's *Patterns of Culture* (1934), although still a great oversimplification of the cultures discussed, suggests a certain dynamic depth for each. We can see in the religion and "men's clubs" of the Kwakiutles of America's Northwest coast a relatively primitive defense system against the fear of the cannibalistic mother.

In my own analysis of the cultural system of a number of other tribes, I discovered a dynamic depth in all of them, leading to the aggressive cannibalistic understructure which influenced the development of their culture considerably more than their everyday "functional" need. It made their group organization, family organization, sibships, religious practices, etc. much more understandable.

Social anthropologist, Ashley Montagu in particular, believes that aggression is a learned behavior and violently attacks the "instinctual" theorists, Lorenz, MacLean, Freud, and Ardrey.

We analyzed some of the cultures mentioned by the most highly vocal anti-aggressive social learning theorist, Ashley Montagu (1974, 1976), who believes that man is basically not aggressive and that all aggressive behaviors are learned and can be unlearned. Among Montagu's proofs are the "peace loving" Arapesh, first visited by Margaret Mead (1968) and described by her in a number of her now famous publications. It turns out that the natives of that area have a hidden lifelong religious system almost unmatched in violence. The analysis of it would take us too far at this point, but it is described by Donald F. Tuzin (1980) of the University of California in San Diego in *The Voice of the Tambaran*. The study of this South Sea area has been his life work. He and his colleagues and students were able to talk to informants about the "real" mothers, subjects which had not been discussed with previous anthropologists, and, thus, these cultures prove to be far from the idealized paradise our earlier romanticized idealism was seeking.

As a matter of fact, the more aggression experienced, the more beautiful the restitutional picture needs to become. We have learned that the more intricate the art or the more detailed the religious practices, the more early trauma and fear had to be turned around into a reaction formation first and then defended with more layers so as to really defend from the original panic.

There seem to be only a handful of social anthropologists who openly discuss the basic issues of aggression. Foremost is George Devereux (1966), who sees culture as a defense against the parents' cannibalistic and incestuous drives. Geza Roheim (1930) finds the same picture in Australian primitives, as well as Derek Freeman (1963) more recently. Freeman takes the more historical approach in a paper, "Human Aggression in Anthropological Perspective," given at a symposium on the Natural History of Aggression in London in October, 1963. In his description of more recent historical events, he refers to a source on the Middle Ages, when "Basil II (1014) could blind 15,000 Bulgarians, leaving one eye to the leader of every hundred, it ceases to be a surprise that the Greeks in the time of Malek Shah (1106–1116) should drown Turkish children in boiling water or that a crusading Prince of Antioch (1097) should cook human beings on spits to earn for his men the terrifying reputation of cannibalism." After reviewing other similar atrocities, he also concludes "that no group of animals is more aggressive or ruthless in their aggression than the adult members of the human race."

Going over the map of the world, it can be seen that with very few exceptions, graphic evidence shows warfare among primitive people to have been endemic and, on occasion, internecine. Some neighboring tribes live in an unending round of death and revenge. Freeman quotes the psychologist William James (1911) who saw the human beasts of prey as being the only ones who prey systematically on their own species. He points to cannibalism, which has been reported in almost all parts of the world and, on the evidence of paleoanthropology, probably was once a universal practice. This will be developed in greater detail in the chapter on prehistoric man.

I have left the psychoanalytic contribution on aggression for the last as it is the field that has studied human aggression most intensively.

The giant that Darwin became for scientific thinking, Freud (1946) became for the study of the dynamics of human behavior. What do we learn from him about human aggression? The first thing that comes to mind is his global theory about the Death Instinct. Thanatos was seen by him as an inborn impulse to destroy, balanced by Eros, the impulse to sustain and advance life. Many analysts after Freud could not accept the death instinct. To the ones who translated it for the clinicians belong Karl Menninger, who stated in *Love against Hate* (1942), "Man's chief fears are not of the immensity of the universe but of the malignity of his own aggressive instincts." Frieda Fromm-Reichman in *Principles of Intensive Psychotherapy* (1950), echoed Menninger's sentiments. Freud started with studies in the 1880s and 1890s and concluded that the un-analyzed child, either seduced or more often wishing to have been seduced, resolves its conflict by identifying with the aggressor and finally becoming the aggressor. Freud noticed at the same time in his analyzed dreams that the dreamer, child and adult alike, experiences death wishes but he attributed these phenomena to wishes rather than basic aggressive instincts and interpreted them as such.

Paul Stepansky (1977) in his study, *A History of Aggression in Freud,* reviews the ways in which Freud dealt with the problem of aggression at different times. Eventually, motivation related to sex became the moving apparatus of Freud's personality theory. We recently reanalyzed all of Freud's dreams and came to the conclusion that there was a basic aggressive layer below his own interpretations, of which he seemed at times aware, but which he almost consciously avoided. To discuss the reasons for this avoidance would take us too far afield and can be found in the numerous biographical studies of Freud by Ernest Jones (1953), Max Shure (1972), and others. Most people read the early Freud where, for personal reasons, he avoids giving aggression an independent position. In his later revisions of his thinking and his theory, however, aggression takes a more important role. The impact of World War I and his own reading in anthropological and archeological material led him in 1915, in his essay *Totem and Taboo*, to give aggression philogenetic precedence.

Freud never allowed himself to experience the underlying aggression toward mother, which was part of the content of a dream he had when he was nine years old. The dominant impact on him, he believed, was his father. *Totem and Taboo* speaks about parricide as the primal crime, the restitution of which produces religion, ritualistic societal restitutions, and, in individuals, neurosis. By 1919, in a letter to a Dutch psychopathologist Van Eeden, he wrote . . . "the primitive, savage and evil impulses of mankind have not vanished in any individual but continue their existence, although in a repressed state—in the unconscious as we call it in our language—and they wait for the opportunities to display their activity."

Freud, however, was still not metaphysically able to accept aggression, and he reclassified it as a "perversion." This inability to integrate aggression caused him to resolve a period of depression constructively by giving us *Mourning and Melancholia,* the basic contribution on the phenomenon of depression, so closely related to the problem of aggression. Here too, however, Freud carefully chose not to slip down to the more basic roots of depression.

Freud continued to make a clear distinction between the treatability of the psychotic and neurotic process. He did not think that psychoanalysis could treat schizophrenia or psychoses. Even in his descriptions and dynamic formulations of the Schreiber case (the first psychoanalytic case study of psychosis), he does not discuss the origins of the content of the "mad man's" delusions, but neither do any other analysts, as to what in the crazed brain produces the dragons and bulls and catastrophes which none of the patients had ever experienced or read about. Freud, and all the other analysts following him, saw human pathology as arising from post-natal experiences of the child, not making connections with the philogenetic roots or their own fetal experiences. What Freud *did* give us, however, was a new way of analyzing the underlying motivation for human behavior, which has radically changed mankind's thinking.

Adler (1917), before his break with Freud, like Freud, had seen the polymorphically aggressive child as reacting to frustration but formulated an aggressive drive, developing into a "masculine protest." He spoke of organ inferiority as producing the frustration that led to this aggression. The difference of opinion between Freud and Adler became most obvious around the "little Hans" case and led to the break between the two analysts.

Adler was the first and only analyst who discussed the necessity of finding compensation for inferior organs and situations, thereby giving ontological expression for the philogenetic trauma mankind experienced. Unfortunately, he became sidetracked into simplified social solutions, becoming caught up in the political tenor of his times, and thereby compromised the depth of the dynamics of the "unconscious." It is unfortunate that the competitive male-male shortcomings Freud, Adler, and Jung exhibited did not allow for an integration of their respective theories, which would have made an even richer dynamic beginning of the early psychoanalytic theory of man's personality.

What were Jung's (1952) contributions to the concept of aggression? In the concept of the "Shadow" the non-accepted negative (evil) part in ourselves, he partially anticipated the English School of Object relations, which we will discuss below. In his archetypes, he does discuss the "terrible" aspects of the Great Mother, which is handled in greater detail in one of the later chapters.

Searching through the indices of Jung's and his followers' writings, the word aggression rarely appears. Although the adjective is used two or three times in superficially behavioral descriptions of a case study, it never appears as a concept in itself. Why?

After his break with Freud and a period of fundamental emotional regression in service of the new Jungian ego, Jung created a personality theory which is a total reaction formation to final ambivalences in the basic make-up of the psyche itself. His theory implies that the unconscious, left to its choices, will find a creative self-enhancing "individuation." The dualities are problems along the way to be transformed into psychic gold. Why this almost extreme suppression of aggression?

A very early childhood dream gives us a clue. When only three years old, he dreamed of a large phallus seated on a throne in an underground chamber. He hears his mother call out, "Yes, just look at him. That is the man-eater." (Jung, 1963). With this fear of a phallus as the executor of mother's unconscious infanticidal and cannibalistic wishes, is it any wonder that both sex and aggression had to be totally suppressed, repressed, and transformed into religious themes, father being a minister? Being almost conscious of it at three, he had to erect a lifelong defense against being devoured. Needing a stronger father, there was almost a danger of this happening in relation to Freud. But as much as both men tried to avoid it, both men's basic defensive needs were greater than the cooperative structure could contain.

The analyst who seemed to have no real difficulty with looking aggression in the face was Melanie Klein (1954). Daughter of an unsuccessful Viennese doctor, and essentially a lay person, she went into analysis with Ferenczy in Budapest. He later sent her to continue her analysis with Abraham in Berlin. She impressed the head of the London Institute so greatly, that he invited her to come to London, where she, in her own uncompromising fashion, started the English School of Object Relations.

Specializing with children in her work, she traced their problems of aggressive behavior to pre-oedipal origins by studying their uncontrolled fantasy life in play therapy and dreams. Out of her work grew the important concepts of introjection and projection and the child's transition from the first year's schizoid and paranoid to the depressive position. She regards this stage as the central one for development. It is the stage where concern for others begins to arise, as the child can now see a "whole object," a whole good breast, rather than splitting mother into the sustaining and the destructive breast. As elaborated by Winnicott (1951), mother has sustained the murderous fantasies of the infant and having survived as a good and strong introject can now become an object of "love." It is an endopsychic process not requiring external "sublimation" but leading to healthy productive and, eventually, creative adjustment on the outside. In other words, although basically not addressing the roots of aggression in man, the object relations theorists offer us a model for transforming aggressive roots into creative and empathic behavior which can implement the good of all of us.

D. W. Winnicott (1951), with his concepts of the "transitional object," later "transitional space," showed us mechanisms whereby we can invest things, people, ideas and cultural concepts with the qualities of the good mother so as to make them introjectable. We will have more to say about him in the material on "the elemental space" in the concluding chapter.

These dynamic formulations of the English School have carried the understanding of the dynamics of aggression further than any previous theorist or analyst had been able to achieve.

We have reached the end of our Cook's Tour. We are left with the impression that there has been a great effort toward understanding, but we seem to have come no nearer to the truth. Implicit in most of the work is the assumption that aggression is something which enters from the outside—that mankind and, we as individuals, lived in a paradise of peaceful union with nature, and that we as individuals are born without blemish until aggression (evil) entered us. We deal with aggression as though it were an illness, and that if we could only learn the cause, we would find the cure.

It is my belief that our multileveled defenses against recognizing our own aggression still prevent us from dealing with the real questions. A study of our philogenetic and ontological origins, however, shows a specific pattern in the general story of how the tensions and uncontrolled forces of violence in nature have been held in check by repeated processes of differentiation, alternating with processes of integration toward more abstract forms. The human species went through unique forms of integration during its beginnings, making mankind, though still part of the evolutionary process, a new and separate species. Our special form of anxieties and fears made special defense mechanisms necessary, which, so far, have also proved inadequate.

Based on the additional knowledge gained from philogenetic pre-history, ontological pre-birth history, neurobiology, and the history of man's aggression and his defensive attempts, a new integration may become possible.

<h2 style="text-align:center">REFERENCES</h2>

Adler, A. (1917). *Study of organ inferiority and its psychical compensation*. (S. Jelliffe, trans.) New York: Nervous and Mental Disease Publishing.

Ardrey, R. (1961). *African genesis*. New York: Atheneum.

Benedict, R. (1934). *Patterns of culture*. Boston: Houghton Mifflin.

Darwin, C. (1952). The origin of species and the descent of man. In *Great books of the western world*. Chicago: Encyclopaedia Britannica. (Original work published 1859.)

Devereux, G. (1966). The cannibalistic impulses of parents. *The Psychoanalytic Forum. I* (1), 114.

Dollard, J. (1949). *Caste and class in a southern town*. New York: Doubleday.

Dollard, J., Miller, N.E., et al. (1939). *Frustration and aggression*. New Haven: Yale University Press.

Eibl-Eibesfeldt, I. (1971). *Love and hate*. New York: Holt, Rinehart & Winston.

Freeman, D. (1963). *Human aggression in anthropological perspective*. Speech given at a symposium on the Natural History of Aggression, London.

Freud, S. (1946). *Collected papers*. Vols. 1–5. New York: International Psychoanalytic Press.

Fromm-Reichman, F. (1950). *Principles of intensive psychotherapy*. Chicago: University of Chicago Press.

Harlow, H. F. & Mears, C. (1979). *The human model: primate perspectives*. Washington, D.C.: V. H. Winston & Sons.

James, W. (1911). *Memoires and studies*. London: Longman, Green.

Jones, E. (1953). *The life and work of Sigmund Freud*. New York: Basic Books.

Jung, C. G. (1952). *Collected works*. New York: Pantheon Books.

Jung, C. G. (1963). *Memories, dreams, reflections*. Recorded and edited by A. Jaffee. (R. Winston and C. Winston, trans.). New York: Pantheon Books.

Kardiner, A. (1945). *The psychological frontier of society*. New York: Columbia University Press.

Klein, M. (1954). *The psychoanalysis of children*. London: The Hogarth Press.

Lorenz, K. (1963). *On aggression*. New York: Harcourt, Brace & World.

Malinowski, B. (1927). *Sex and repression in savage society*. New York: World Publishing.

Mead, M. (1930). *Growing up in New Guinea*. New York: William Morrow.

Mead, M. (1968). *The mountain Arapesh*. New York: Natural History Press.

Menninger, K. (1942). *Love against hate*. New York: Harcourt, Brace.

Montagu, A. (1974). *Man and aggression*. New York: Oxford University Press.

Montagu, A. (1976). *The nature of human aggression*. New York: Oxford University Press.

Morris, D. (1967). *The naked ape*. New York: McGraw-Hill.

Moyer, K. E. & Kern, J. H. (1965). Behavioral effects of isolation in the rat. *Psychonom. Science, 3,* 503–504.

Paul, L. & Kupferschmidt, J. (1975). Killing of conspecific and mouse young by male rats. *Journal of Comparative Physiology and Psychology 88,* 755–763.

Roheim, G. (1930). *Animism, magic and the divine king*. New York: International Universities Press.

Shure, M. (1972). *Freud living and dying*. New York: International Universities Press.

Stepansky, P. E. (1977). *A history of aggression in Freud*. New York: International Universities Press.

Tinberger, N. (1965). *Animal behavior*. New York: Time-Life.

Tuzin, D. F. (1980). *The voice of the Tambaran*. Berkeley: University of California Press.

Valzelli, L. (1981). *Psychobiology of aggression and violence*. New York: Raven Press.

Velikovsky, I. (1982). *Mankind in amnesia*. New York: Doubleday.

Winnicott, D. W. (1951). Transitional object and transitional phenomena. In *Through pediatrics to psychoanalysis*. New York: Basic Books, pp. 204–218.

Wolfgang, M. E. & Ferracuti, F. (1967). *The subculture of violence*. London: Tavistock.

Chapter 2

ON THE EVOLUTION OF THREE MENTALITIES OF THE BRAIN[1]

Paul D. MacLean

Introduction

The human brain evolves and expands along the lines of three basic patterns characterized as reptilian, paleomammalian, and neomammalian.

Thus the relevance of work on animals to human affairs becomes apparent. Figure 2–1 suggests how the three evolutionary formations built on one another—the reptilian formation in black, capped by the paleomammalian (the shaded area), and, finally (biggest and topmost) the neomammalian in white. Radically different in chemistry and structure, and in an evolutionary sense countless generations apart, we have, so to speak, a hierarchy of three-brains-in-one, or what may be appropriately referred to as a *triune brain*.

What this situation implies is that we are obliged to look at ourselves and the world through the eyes of three quite different mentalities. To complicate things further, there is evidence that the neural machinery underlying the two older mentalities lacks the capacity for verbal communication. But to say that they lack the power of speech does not belittle their intelligence, nor does it relegate them to the realm of the unconscious.

Stated in present-day terms, one might imagine that our brain repre-

[1]From a paper prepared for the Louis Leakey Memorial Symposium, *In Search of Man*, 1975.

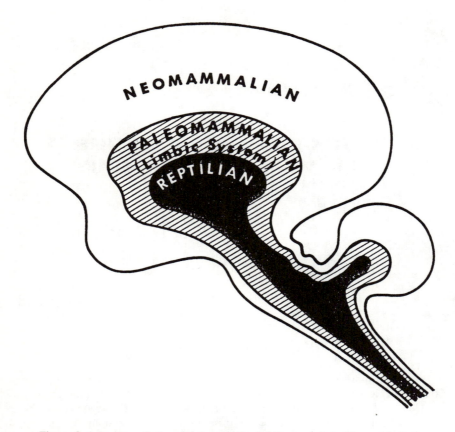

Figure 2–1. In its evolution, the human forebrain expands in hierarchic fashion along the lines of three basic patterns that may be characterized as reptilian, paleomammalian, and neomammalian. (From P. D. MacLean, *Journal of Nervous and Mental Disorders, 144,* 374–382, 1967.)

sents an amalgamation of three biological computers, each with its own special intelligence, subjective sense, sense of time and space, memory, motor, and other functions. What seems notably lacking is a neural code for intersignaling in verbal terms.

Although my proposed subdivision of the brain may seem simplistic, recent anatomical, physiological, and histo-chemical findings reveal the three basic formations in clearer detail than ever before.

Before characterizing each of the three mentalities, I should point out that the basic neural machinery required for self-preservation and the preservation of the species is built into the lower brain stem and spinal cord, as shown in Figure 2–1. This neural chassis might be compared to the chassis of an automobile or other vehicle requiring a driver.

The odd situation that we must consider is the evolution of three different drivers for the same vehicle, all of different minds, and all located in the forebrain above the neural chassis.

Let us look first at the reptilian driver. *In the search for man and woman* we must go back to the age of reptiles and consider how these animals, which never learned to talk, began to creep into our nervous systems. Each one of us has a large fist of ganglia in our forebrain which conforms in organization and chemistry to a nuclear mass in reptilian brains. Since these structures have several names attached to them, here, they are referred to as a whole—the reptilian complex—or, for short, the R-complex. Figure 2–2 shows how a stain for cholinesterase sharply demarcates "the big fist" in the monkey's brain, as well as how this same stain demarcates the R-complex in animals ranging from reptiles to man. The black areas show the selective chemical staining of the R-complex.

When we apply the fluorescent technique of Faulk and Hillarp, the bulk of these structures glows a bright green because of large amounts of dopamine, a neural sap that seems to be a prime energizer.

From the standpoint of evolution, it is curious that ethologists have paid little attention to reptiles, focusing instead on fish and birds. Some authorities believe that, of existing reptiles, lizards would bear the closest resemblance to the mammal-like reptiles believed to be the forerunners of mammals. At all events, lizards and other reptiles provide illustrations of complex, prototypical patterns of behavior commonly seen in mammals, including man. It is easy to list more than 20 such behaviors that may primarily involve self-preservation or survival of the species. Table 2–1 shows such a list. First and foremost are all those activities that involve the establishment and defense of territory.

The *will-to-power* was at the heart of Nietzsche's philosophy. He regarded the will-to-power as the basic force of the entire universe. "Thus life taught me," he wrote. Nietzsche's writing on this subject may yet earn him recognition as a foremost ethologist and authority on human reptilian behavior!

One will find the will-to-power dramatically expressed in the behavior of some lizards. To see two rainbow lizards striving for dominance is like returning to the days of King Arthur. These animals have beautiful colors and like many lizards, use head bobbing and pushups in assertive, aggressive, courtship and greeting displays. In a contest, once the gauntlet is thrown down, the aggressive displays give way to violent combat, and the struggle is unrelenting. In defeat they lose their majestic colors, lapse into a kind of depression, and die two weeks later.

As yet, few experiments have been conducted on reptiles in an attempt to identify forebrain structures involved in species-typical, prosematic forms of behavior.

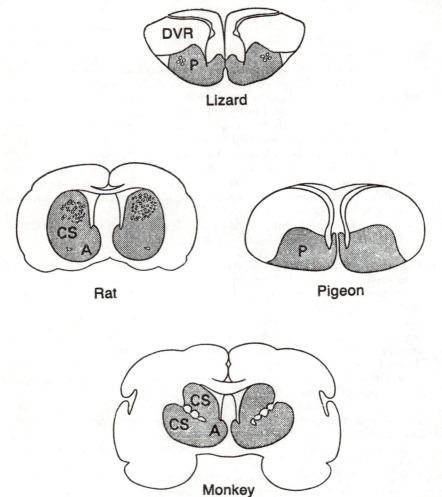

Figure 2–2. Shaded areas indicate how a stain for cholinesterase demarcates the greater part of the R-complex in animals ranging from reptiles to primates. With the fluorescent technique of Faulk and Hillarp, the same areas shown above glow a bright green because of the high content of dopamine. No existing reptiles represent the forerunners of mammals. Birds are an offshoot from the Archosauria ("ruling reptiles").

Table 2-1

Prototypical Patterns of Behavior

(1) selection and preparation of homesite
(2) establishment of territory
(3) trail making
(4) "marking" of territory
(5) showing place-preferences
(6) ritualistic display in defense of territory, commonly involving the use of colora-
     tion and adornments
(7) formalized intraspecific fighting in defense of territory
(8) triumphal display in successful defense
(9) assumption of distinctive postures and coloration in signaling surrender
(10) routinization of daily activities
(11) foraging
(12) hunting
(13) homing
(14) hoarding
(15) use of defecation posts
(16) formation of social groups
(17) establishment of social hierarchy by ritualistic display and other means
(18) greeting
(19) "grooming"
(20) courtship, with displays using coloration and adornments
(21) mating
(22) breeding and, in isolated instances, attending offspring
(23) flocking
(24) migration

With Greenberg and Ferguson, I have performed some pilot experiments on the effects of destruction of the R-complex on the display behavior
of the green Anolis lizard. Because the optic nerves are almost entirely
crossed, we can eliminate the R-complex in one hemisphere and then test the
animal's display with either eye covered. When looking with the eye projecting to the deficient hemisphere, the animal shows no interest in a rival lizard. But allow him to see his rival with the good hemisphere and the
aggressive display behavior returns immediately in full force.

In contrast to reptiles, the R-complex of mammals has been subjected to
extensive investigation. It cannot be overemphasized, however, that 150 years
of experimentation have revealed little specific information about its functions. The finding that large destructions of the mammalian R-complex may
result in no impairment of movement, speaks against the traditional clinical
view that it subserves purely motor functions. As with reptiles, we are con-
ducting experiments on mammals, testing the hypothesis that the R-complex
plays a basic role in species-typical, prosematic behavior.

Thus far, crucial findings have turned up in the work on squirrel monkeys. It is a remarkable parallel that as in some reptiles and lower forms, squirrel monkeys perform the same kind of display in courtship, as in the show of aggression. In each situation, the male vocalizes, spreads one thigh, and directs the erect phallus toward the female. Ploog's observations have shown that it is an unlearned form of behavior. The display is also used as a form of greeting, and I have described one variety of squirrel monkey that will regularly display to its reflection in a mirror.

I have used the mirror test as a means of learning what parts of the brain may be involved in display rituals. Monkeys are tested twice a day, and we record the latency and magnitude of the erection, as well as other components of the display, including vocalization, spreading the thigh, scratching, and urination. We then compare the baseline performance with the performance after removal of specific brain structures. This work has involved more than 36 monkey-years of observation.

Thus far, I have made observations on more than 100 animals. I have found that extensive removals of parts of the neomammalian and paleo-mammalian formations may have no effect, or only a transitory effect, on the display.

Lesions, however, of the main outflow nucleus of the R-complex, or interruption of its pathways, resulted in a profound alteration or elimination of the display.

This latest series of experiments, involving more than 40 animals, are highly significant because they demonstrate for the first time in a mammal that the R-complex is involved in complicated, species-typical behavior.

Since the mirror display also involved "imitative" factors—or isopraxic factors—the results also indicate that the R-complex is implicated in natural forms of isopraxis. Isopraxic refers to behavior in which two or more individuals engage in the same kind of activity. It cannot be overemphasized that isopraxis is basic to maintaining the identity of a species or a social group.

Isopraxis is one of a pentad of important interoperative behaviors seen in reptiles and higher forms. The four other behaviors may be denoted as perserverative, re-enactment, tropistic, and deceptive. Without defining them, I shall simply say that in human activities they find expression in obsessive-compulsive behavior; personal day-to-day rituals and superstitious acts; slavish conformance to old ways of doing things; ceremonial re-enactments; obeisance to precedent, as in legal and other matters; responding to partial representations, whether alive or inanimate; and all manner of deception.

No one would argue that instincts, as generally understood, play a significant role in human behavior. But how are we to characterize proclivities of the type I have just mentioned? If as many claim, all human behavior is learned, why is it that in spite of all our intelligence and culturally determined behavior, we continue to do all the ordinary things that animals do?

It is easy to draw parallels between reptilian and mammalian patterns of behavior. I'll illustrate only one important one—deception, first saying that we know almost nothing about brain mechanisms of predatory and deceptive behavior, but that if we keep looking, we may find the basic, neural circuitry built into the reptilian formation.

In the attempted assassination of presidential candidate George Wallace, Arthur Bremer stalked his victim for days at a time. Resorting to reptilian rhetoric, we might ask, "Did Arthur Bremer learn to do this by reading Auffenberg's account of the predatory and deceptive behavior of the giant komodo lizard?" These animals, growing up to 10 feet in length, will relentlessly stalk a deer for days at a time, or wait in ambush for hours, activities requiring a detailed knowledge of the terrain and a good sense of time. Waiting for just the right moment, the huge lizard will lunge at the deer, cripple it with a slash of the Achilles tendon, and bring it to an agonizing death by ripping out its bowels.

This mention of a deceptive behavior of lizards is a reminder that white collar criminality has never been so much in the news as during the past few years. If we have learned through our culture that "honesty is the best policy," why is it that so many people are willing to take such enormous risks to practice deception? Why do the games that we teach our young place such a premium on deceptive tactics and terminology of deception?

THE PALEOMAMMALIAN BRAIN

We go upstairs now to the next mentality! Reptiles have a perfect memory for what their ancestors have learned to do over millions of years, but there are behavioral indications that the reptilian brain is poorly equipped for learning to cope with new situations! The reptilian brain has only a rudimentary cortex. In the lost transitional forms between reptiles and mammals—the so-called mammal-like reptiles—it is presumed that the primitive cortex ballooned out and became further refined. The primitive cortex might be imagined as comparable to a crude television or radar screen, providing the animal with a better means of viewing the environment and learning to survive.

Imagine this old cortex expanding from the brainstem like a balloon and forming what Broca called the limbic lobe because it surrounds the brain stem. The limbic lobe is shown in Figure 2–3 in black. It illustrates that the limbic cortex is found as a common denominator in the brains of all mammals. The limbic cortex, together with its brain stem connections, comprises the limbic system, terminology I suggested in 1952. It must be emphasized that this limbic system represents an inheritance from lower mammals. Animal and clinical research of the past 40 years suggests that this old limbic system derives information in terms of emotional feelings that guide behavior required for self-preservation and the preservation of the species.

Clinical findings provide the best evidence that the limbic system is involved in emotional experience and behavior. Epileptic discharges in or near the limbic cortex may be accompanied by a wide variety of vivid emotional

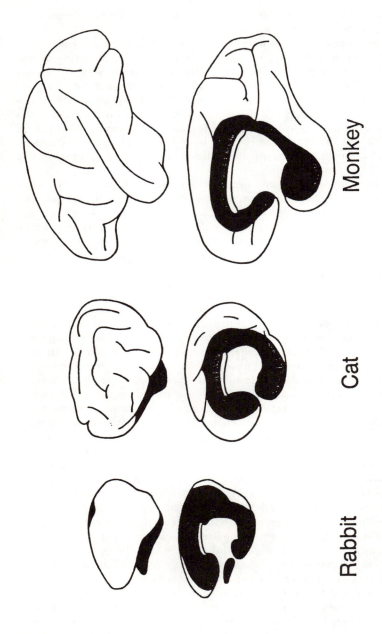

Rabbit

Cat

Monkey

Figure 2–3. The limbic lobe of Broca (shaded) is found as a common denominator in the brains of all mammals. It contains the greater part of the cortex representative of the paleomammalian brain. The cortex of the neomammalian brain (shown in white) mushrooms late in evolution. (After P. D. MacLean, *Journal of Neurosurgery, 11,* 29–44, 1954.)

feelings, ranging from intense fear to ecstasy. It is one of the wonders of the brain that epileptic discharges arising in the limbic cortex tend to spread in and be confined to the limbic system. Elsewhere, I have referred to this condition as a "schizophysiology" and have suggested that the underlying factors may contribute to inexplicable conflicts between "what we feel" and "what we know."

It is of special interest that at the beginning of a limbic discharge a patient may have an intense feeling of what is real, true, and important, or experience eureka feelings like those associated with discovery, a feeling of "this is it, the absolute truth." There may be oceanic feelings like those occurring in mystical revelation or under the influence of psychedelic drugs. It is difficult to imagine anything of greater epistemological significance than that the ancient limbic system has the capacity to generate strong, affective feelings of conviction that we attach to our beliefs, regardless of whether they are true or false.

Except for the crocodilia, reptiles show no interest in their young, which come into the world prepared to do everything that they have to do except procreate.

The evolution of mammals includes the progressive attention and care that they give to their young. This care amounts psychologically to love which, in turn, means being loved. It is this capacity, one might say, that makes mammals so lovable!

The evolution of parental care seems to be correlated with the development of three subdivisions of the limbic system. The two older divisions are closely related to the olfactory apparatus (marked *1* and *2* in Figure 2–4). Experimental work has shown that the subdivision marked *1*, and connected with the amygdala, primarily is concerned with feeding, fighting, and self-protection; whereas the division just across the way in the septal region, the one marked *2*, is concerned with genital and procreational functions. Hormonal effects on this region occurring early in development determine whether the individual will be male or female.

The close relationship of oral and genital functions in this part of the brain is apparently due to the olfactory sense which, dating far back in evolution, plays a primary role in both feeding and mating. By electrical stimulation, we have traced neural circuits involving the mouth and genital lying side-by-side right down through the brainstem. Activity in one spills over into the other, and both may be elicited in angry, combative responses. We therefore can see here a close tie-in of oral and sexual functions in aggression.

You will note that the major pathway to the third subdivision, *3*, bypasses the olfactory apparatus. This third subdivision progressively becomes larger in higher primates and reaches its greatest development in the human brain. There is experimental evidence suggesting that the great development of this division reflects a shift in emphasis from olfactory to visual influences in socio-sexual behavior. There also are indications that this subdivision may be implicated in the evolution of empathy.

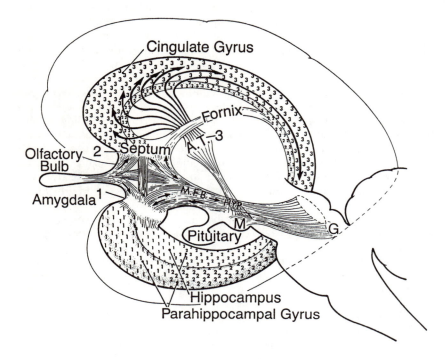

Figure 2–4. Diagram of three main subdivisions of the limbic system and their major pathways. See text for summary of their respective functions. Abbreviations: AT, anterior thalamic nuclei; HYP, hypothalamus; MFB, medial forebrain bundle; PIT, pituitary; OLF, olfactory. (After P. D. MacLean, *American Journal of Medicine*, 25, 611–626, 1958.)

THE BASIC PERSONALITY

In mammals, the major pathways to and from the reptilian and limbic formations pass through the hypothalamic and subthalamic regions. If the majority of these pathways are destroyed in monkeys, the animals are greatly incapacitated, but with careful nursing, they recover the ability to feed themselves and move around. They retain, of course, the great motor pathways from the neocortex to the neural chassis. The most striking characteristic of these animals is that although they look like monkeys, they no longer behave like monkeys. Almost everything that one would characterize as species-typical, simian behavior has disappeared. These large connecting pathways between the reptilian and limbic formations provide the avenues to the more permanent features of the basic personality.

There is now much evidence that it is the special chemistry of the limbic and reptilian formations that make many of the psychotropic drugs selectively effective in various neurotic and psychotic disorders.

I should emphasize with respect to the basic personality that signals reaching the *reptolimbic* formations from both the outside and inside worlds are essential for a feeling of personal identity and individuality. For example, during a limbic seizure when the limbic system is knocked out of commission, the new brain may continue to function, and the patient will go about his-or-her business like a disembodied spirit, having no recollection of what transpired.

THE NEOMAMMALIAN BRAIN

There are indications that insistent signals from the inside world make it difficult for the organism to make cold, reasoned decisions required for survival. In the evolution of the neocortex, nature apparently attempts to remedy this situation, and to see how, we must climb a second flight of stairs to consider our third mentality.

The neocortex culminates in the human brain, affording a vast neural screen for the portrayal of symbolic language and the associated functions of reading, writing, and arithmetic.

For solutions of situations that arise in the external world, nature designs the neocortex so that it receives information largely from the eyes, ears, and body wall (signals, incidentally, that, unlike taste and smell, lend themselves to amplification and radiotransmission). As such, the neocortex develops, at first, as a coldly reasoning, heartless computer. It is a type of computer that makes it possible for monkeys to scheme their way like gangsters into another troop, polish off the dominant males, and perform infanticide before the distressed mothers.

Now, for some inexplicable reason, nature must have concluded that a genie had been let out of the bottle that could become a veritable Frankenstein. I say "inexplicable" because nature, herself, seems to have given its blessing to the paradoxical principle of the-need-to-die-in-order-to-live.

Have you seen the heron swallow live fish after live fish? Have you seen the fish squirm and wiggle in the heron's crop as it is slowly peeled away by burning juices? Have you heard birds cough themselves to death from airsacculitis? Have you risen in the night to give them cough syrup? Have you seen the cat play with the mouse? Have you seen cancer slowly eat away or slowly strangle another human being? Are we this very day watching millions of people dying of famine? This has been nature's way for millions of years. The misery piles up like stellar gases tortured by a burning sun.

Then, why slowly, but progressively, has nature added something to the neocortex that for the first time brings a heart and sense of compassion into the world? Why suddenly did this feeling of compassion become verbalized 2,000 years ago, and then almost explode with the humanitarian movement of the past two hundred years? Altruism and empathy are almost new words!

Figure 2–5 shows the gradually evolving neocortex of the frontal lobe which reaches its greatest development in the human brain. This is the only neocortex that looks inward to the inside world. Note how its circuits tie in with the great third subdivision of the limbic system. Clinically, there is evidence that this frontal cortex, by looking inward, so to speak, obtains the insight required for identifying with another individual.

It is a new development that makes possible the insight required for the foresight to anticipate and plan for the needs of others as well as the self, to use our knowledge to alleviate suffering everywhere. It shows that Nietzsche's claim that there is no inherent human goodness is a lie. Rather for him, the instinct for the will-to-power was the supreme and highest instinct. The good, the true, the beautiful was that which served one's own selfish advancement. Pity and compassion were weaknesses. He saw a social structure fostering the

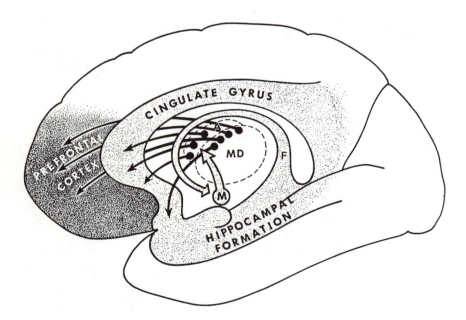

Figure 2–5. Diagram of the human brain, indicating the evolutionary tie-up of the limbic system with the prefrontal cortex, one of the most recent developments of the neomammalian brain. (From P. D. MacLean, *Journal of Nervous and Mental Disorders, 144,* 374–382, 1967.)

rise of supermen—supermen who should be allowed to trample on persons weaker than themselves. This is how we see the will-to-power work among ordinary reptiles. In our lifetime, we have seen present day supermen, the superreptiles, trample upon millions upon millions of innocent citizens. But our knowledge of the brain assures us that we do not have to accept the cynical, big-sell of their will-to-power.

If we read nature correctly, if we correctly sense its turnabout, its conversion, that finds expression in us as human beings, then perhaps we should speed up the search for man and also look for angels. As human beings, we seem to be acquiring the soft brain stuff of which angels are made. Perhaps it's time to take a fresh look and begin again to behave a little more like angels.

The royal mantle of responsibility falls on each one of us. Once you discover the wonders of the brain, you can never look at yourself the same way again.

BIBLIOGRAPHY

MacLean, P. D. (1973). A triune concept of the brain and behaviour. Lecture I. Man's reptilian and limbic inheritance; Lecture II. Man's limbic brain and the psychoses; Lecture III. New trends in man's evolution. In T. Boag & D. Campbell (Eds.), The *Hincks Memorial Lectures*. Toronto: University of Toronto Press, pp. 6–66.

Chapter 3

BRAIN ROOTS OF THE WILL-TO-POWER[1]

Paul D. MacLean

In looking for the origins of the will-to-power, we must, as in the case of other psychological matters, turn our attention to the anatomy and functions of the brain. After reviewing some recent developments regarding the evolutionary brain roots of power, I will briefly discuss the question of why we, as mammals, seem to lack the safeguards, particularly in large groups, against a primitive regression to the irrational and violent use of power. As Arthur Koestler (1968) reminds us, we have more to fear because of collective violence than violence of individuals, especially when we are swayed by demagogic leaders who use the masses to satisfy their own driving needs for power.

Our experimental work indicates that the deepest roots of power can be traced to the reptilian formation, which, for short, I will refer to as the R-complex (MacLean, 1973a). The later developments (the paleo- and neo-mammalian formations) greatly extend the options for the use of power and the expression of power.

A study of the fossil record has made it possible to trace back our genealogy to the therapsids, the mammal-like reptiles living 250 million years ago, a duration of time equivalent to 10 million human generations. These therapsids existed long before the dinosaurs. They populated the earth in large numbers when it was but one continent, Pangaea, including the part that later broke off as Antarctica (Colbert, 1972). Some species had a likeness to dogs and wolves. In body carriage and in structure of the jaws and teeth, the

---

[1]Portions of this chapter are reprinted from *Zygon,* December 1983, Volume 18, No. 4. Used by permission.

advanced forms closely approached the condition of mammals (Colbert, 1969; Romer, 1966).

For comparative studies, it is unfortunate that there are no existing reptiles directly in line with therapsids. Of existing types, lizards would probably bear the closest resemblance to the mammal-like reptiles, with the giant Komodo dragon perhaps being the best prototype (MacLean, 1978a), as seen in Figure 1.

In analyzing the behavior of lizards, one can identify more than 25 forms of behavior that are also characteristic of mammals (MacLean, 1978a). Those notably lacking in lizards are nursing in conjunction with parental care, play, and audiovocal communication (except notably geckos). This behavioral triad characterizes the evolutionary dividing line between reptiles and mammals. It commonly is assumed that all four-footed vertebrates vocalize, but this is not so for most lizards, and the same may have been true of the mammal-like reptiles. In our carnivorous therapsid ancestors, two small bones of the jaw joint were gradually becoming smaller, but they had not yet migrated to become the malleus and incus of the highly tuned mammalian ear (Colbert, 1969; Romer, 1966). Hence, there is evidence that the therapsids were hard-of-hearing and were possibly mute like most existing lizards. Consider, here, a great difference between reptiles and mammals. The isolation call appears to be characteristic of all mammals. It may be the most basic vocalization because it served originally to maintain maternal-offspring contact and, later on, contact of members among a social group (MacLean, 1982). Separation of a suckling from its mother is calamitous. Contrast this situation with that of lizards which may cannibalize their young. The young of the Komodo dragons, for example, must escape to the trees for the first year of life in or-

Figure 3–1. Display of a Komodo dragon. The close-in agonistic display of an adult Komodo dragon is similar to that of an appeasement display of a juvenile shown here. The animal walks slowly in a stiff-legged, stilted manner. The angle of the right forelimb in this picture is reminiscent of the goose step. Note three static modifiers seen in other lizards—namely, elevated roach (nuchal and dorsal crests), extension of gular fold, and sagittal expansion. (From W. Auffenberg, "Social and Feeding Behavior in *Varanus komodoensis*," in *The Behavior and Neurology of Lizards*, edited by N. Greenberg and P. D. MacLean, Department of Health, Education and Welfare, Publication No. (ADM) 77–491, U.S. Government Printing Office, 1978, pp. 301–331.)

der to avoid being cannibalized, while the hatchlings of rainbow lizards must hide in the deep underbrush (Auffenberg, 1978; Harris, 1964). For the latter to utter an isolation call would invite disaster.

We have learned that in animals as diverse as lizards and primates, the R-complex plays a basic role in the expression of displays used in communication. The close-in challenge display of lizards compares to the broadside display of many mammals, particularly with respect to the sideways presentation and walking with awkward, stilted steps. The grizzly bear, for example, will present itself sideways to a challenger and, like lizards, walk in a wobbly, stilted manner (Stonorov, 1972).

The stilted, staccato steps of the challenge display seems to carry the message of a series of exclamation marks, calling to mind the goose step of a military parade and the similarity in profile to the challenge display of the Komodo dragon as shown in Figure 3–1. In view of these persisting similarities, it almost would seem as though the challenge display has been packaged generically and passed up the phylogenetic tree of mammals.

Among lizards, the spoils usually go to the animal of largest size. But L. T. Evans (1936) and others have shown that size is not the only factor in winning a contest. The territorial lizard on its home ground appears to hold advantage over an intruder. Recalling what takes place in a political arena, it also may be the number of displays rather than size per se, that decides the winner in a combat.

THE PALEOMAMMALIAN BRAIN (LIMBIC SYSTEM)

With the evolution of mammals, there appears to have come into being the primal commandment: "Thou shalt not eat thy young or other flesh of thine own kind." (MacLean, 1982). The later commandment, "thou shalt not kill," is inherent in the primal commandment. If, however, one were to select three outwardly expressed forms of behavior that most clearly distinguish reptiles from mammals, the triad would consist of *nursing,* the *isolation call,* and *play.* Play might be interpreted as promoting cohesiveness and harmony in the nest and social affiliation later on. Experiments, to be mentioned later, indicate these three forms of behavior depended on evolutionary developments in the paleomammalian formation of the brain.

Most of the "old" cortex identified with early mammals is found in the great limbic lobe, which constitutes a common denominator in the brains of all mammals. This cortex, together with the structures of the brainstem with which it is connected, comprises the so-called limbic system, a term that I suggested in 1952. Clinical and experimental findings of the past 40 years indicate that the limbic system derives information in terms of emotional feelings that guide behavior required for self-preservation and preservation of the species (MacLean, 1970).

Upon stimulation of the amygdala region in monkeys, one may elicit first, oral manifestations such as licking and chewing, followed many seconds later by the appearance of penile erection (MacLean, 1962). The reverse sequence may be obtained by stimulating in the septal region or related structures, accounting for penile erection. Electrical stimulation elicits oral responses and his sword for genital responses, and, thus, one finds a reconstitution of the warrior at a locus in the hypothalamus that is crucial for the expression of angry behavior (MacLean, 1964). The intimate relationship between oral and sexual functions in these parts of the brain is apparently due to connections with the olfactory apparatus which, dating far back in evolution, plays a primary role in both feeding and mating, as well as in the fighting that may precede. In this close overlapping of structures involved in oral and sexual functions, we gain insights into brain mechanisms that account for sadistic and masochistic behavior. The close tie-in of these same circuits with brain mechanisms involved in the expression of fear also may help account for vicarious sexual arousal in pyromania, reckless driving, fear-inducing sports, and the like (MacLean, 1962, 1973b).

Animals with large olfactory apparatus mark their territories with urine. The message, so to speak, is "stay away." On the other hand, as already mentioned, a number of primates use the visual display of the genital as part of their aggressive displays. In mythology, the erect genital is often associated with protective powers, but the opposite situation applies to the god, Pan, who enjoyed scaring strangers—a circumstance to which we owe our word "panic" (MacLean, 1973). Amulets showing an erect phallus have long served as a protection against the "evil eye." From time immemorial, house guards showing an erect phallus have been used as territorial markers. People continue to draw phallic representations in public toilets and to leave their names or initials as a kind of marker. Periodically, adolescents go on a rampage displaying their nakedness in public. Eibl-Eibesfeldt (1971) has described a genital display among bushman children that compares to the genital display of squirrel monkeys. Vandalism at schools and elsewhere represents another form of visual marking that is perhaps of a sadistic nature (MacLean, 1978b).

We turn next to the third subdivision of the limbic system for which there appears to be no rudimentary counterpart in reptiles and which reaches its greatest development in the human brain. It is perhaps this subdivision of the limbic, which, more than any other, accounts for the differences between reptiles and mammals—particularly in connection with maternal behavior, play, and emotional forms of vocalization, including the isolation call. It will be noted that the main pathway of this subdivision bypasses the olfactory apparatus. Data are now accumulating that the visual system may have an important influence on this subdivision. Several workers have found that damage to the cingulate cortex interferes with maternal behavior.

D. Ploog and others (1970) have shown that the anterior cingulate cortex is involved in the production of vocalizations, including the isolation call. My colleagues and I have conducted other relevant experiments. By a ma-

nipulation at the time of birth we can prevent the entire neocortex from developing in hamsters. Despite that loss, the animals engage in all forms of
hamster-typical behavior, including mating, breeding, and rearing of the
young (Murphy, MacLean, & Hamilton, 1981). If in addition the cortex of
this division is destroyed, however, young animals do not play and there are
deficits in maternal behavior. It was as though these animals had regressed
toward a reptilian condition.

To give emphasis to the role of the R-complex and limbic system in
expression of the basic animality is not to downplay the importance of the
neocortex. The neocortex mushrooms progressively in higher mammals,
reaching its greatest development in human beings. Nothing is more neu-
rologically certain than that the neocortex is necessary for language and
speech and that we owe to it the infinite variety of ways in which we can express ourselves (MacLean, 1978a).

Before some final remarks regarding the neocortex, let me make two
points about, first, the function of the cortex in general and, second, the ex-
acting condition of being a mammal. First, it usually is believed that the cerebral cortex accounts for learning and memory. Animals such as reptiles with
a rudimentary cortex are regarded as stupid learners. But let it not be forgotten that they are able to learn their territories inside out, to recognize
strangers at first sight, and so on. In addition to learning, the invention of
the cortex made it possible to accomplish what is often a prerequisite, namely,
the ability to *unlearn* what the species has learned to do over millions of years.
Under many circumstances, it is essential to unlearn an old, ingrained response before learning something new. Withholding the tendency to panic
that occurs in a burning building is a case in point. With the evolution of the
limbic system and neocortex, there appears to have been little built-in machinery to deal with "run-of-the-mill" activities and emergencies that have
been under the management of the reptilian formation for millions of years.

The second point is that, except for matters concerning family and language, it would seem that the limbic and neocortex have few wired-in pro-
grams and none in particular for dealing with situations involving large
numbers of individuals. The adoption of a family way of life appears to have
put the mammals in a bind with respect to crowds. Even herd animals tend
to group as families. When people do meet in large numbers, they seem to
do best in situations in which they are feeding together, as at feasts and music festivals or, taking advantage of the mammalian trait of play, as in local,
national, and international games, including the Olympic Games. Here again,
however, there is a primitive, child-like, fine line between having fun at play
and becoming angry and fighting. Just within the last few years we have seen
the Olympic Games become a leverage for terrorists as well as a political
means of displaying national will in showdown situations.

The mention of politics raises the important question concerning the
prevalence of violence. It needs to be emphasized that often the worst kind
of violence hinges on the choice of national leaders who, more than anyone,

have the will-to-power and the position of power to foment worldwide violence to satisfy their own needs as paranoid supermen. We often worry in this country about individual violence, but as Koestler (1968) reminds us, "The damages wrought by individual violence for selfish motives are insignificant compared to the holocausts resulting from self-transcending devotion to collectively shared belief systems" (p. 266). Franklin Roosevelt once said, "We have nothing to fear but fear itself." Living in his time, he could just as well have said, "People have nothing to fear but their choice of leaders."

In Nietzsche's superman, we hear the echoes of Aristotle's "Great Souled Man," who being so far superior to other human beings "is justified in despising other people." Similarly, Nietzsche's superman had the draconian right of riding rough-shod over other people (Kaufmann, 1968). As his sister helped to explain, "All that proceeds from power is good, all that springs from weakness is bad" (Forster-Nietzsche, 1954). Such assertions, however, must be evaluated in the light of the realization that it was we who were driven out of Eden by the great apes, and it is we, the meek, who have inherited the earth.

THE NEOCORTEX

The psychopathic ring of Nietzsche's superman reverts our attention to the neocortex—a neomammalian development that mushroomed late in evolution and achieved its greatest proportions in human beings. The neocortex is oriented primarily to the external world and seems to serve as a kind of problem-solving and memorizing device to aid the two older formations of the brain in the struggle for survival. With its focus on material things, the neocortex develops somewhat like a coldly reasoning, heartless computer. It is a type of computer that has the capacity to devise the most violent ways of destroying our own kind as well as other forms of life. As though foreseeing that a terrible genie was in the making, nature enlarged that part of the neocortex which for the first time in the world brings a sense of concern for the welfare of all living things. In the rapid progress from the Neanderthal to Cro-Magnon people, the human forehead develops from a low brow to a high brow. Significantly, the expanding prefrontal cortex underneath establishes connections with the third great subdivision of the limbic system—that concerned with parental care. The prefrontal cortex is the only neocortex that has strong connections for sensing the inside world. There is clinical evidence that the prefrontal cortex, by looking inward, obtains the "gut feeling" required for empathic identification with another individual. It is this new development that makes possible the insight required for the foresight to plan for the needs of others as well as the self, and to use our knowledge to alleviate suffering everywhere. In creating for the first time a creature with a concern for all living things, nature accomplished a 180-degree turnabout from what had previously been a reptile-eat-reptile and dog-eat-dog world.

It is presumed that we humans had our big brains for thousands of years before we developed a language of words, and it is only 2,000 years ago that we first saw the empty space—the zero—between our fingers that gave us a workable language of numbers (Hogben, 1937). In addition to this, we have acquired the transcendental language of the "golden rule" that gives us the power to bend and shape our inherent, selfish will-to-power. Keeping all these things in mind, we may well afford to strive—not to become just supermen and superwomen—but, rather, to achieve our great potential as human beings.

REFERENCES

Auffenberg, W. (1978). Social and feeding behavior in *Varanus komodoensis*. In N. Greenberg & P. D. MacLean (Eds.), *The behavior and neurology of lizards.* DHEW publication (ADM) 77–491. Washington, D.C.: U.S. Government Printing Office.

Colbert, E. H. (1969). *Evolution of the vertebrates.* New York: John Wiley & Sons.

Colbert, E. H. (1972). Antarctic fossils and the reconstruction of Gondwanaland, *Natural History, 81,* 66–73.

Eibl-Eibesfeldt, I. (1971). !Ko-buschleute (Kalahari)—Schamweisen und spotten. *Homo, 22,* 261–266.

Evans, L. T. (1936). A study of a social hierarchy in the lizard, *Analis carolinensis. Journal of Genetic Psychology, 48,* 88–111.

Forster-Nietzsche, E. (1954). Introduction: How Zarathustra came into being. In *The philosophy of Nietzsche.* New York: Modern Library.

Fossey, D. (1976). *The behavior of a mountain gorilla.* Ph.D. dissertation, University of Cambridge.

Greenberg, N. B., MacLean, P. D., & Ferguson, J. L. (1979). Role of the paleostriatum in species-typical display behavior of the lizard (*Anolis carolinensis*). *Brain Research, 172,* 229–241.

Harris, V. A. (1964). *The life of the rainbow lizard.* London: W. I. Hutchison.

Hogben, L. (1937). *Mathematics for the millions.* New York: W. W. Norton.

Kaufmann, W. (1968). *Nietzsche: Philosopher, psychologist, antichrist* (3rd ed. rev.). New York: Random House.

Koestler, A. (1968). *The ghost in the machine.* New York: Macmillan.

MacLean, P. D. (1952). Some psychiatric implications of physiological studies on frontotemporal portion of limbic system (visceral brain). *Electroencephalography and Clinical Neurophysiology, 4,* 407–418.

MacLean, P. D. (1962). New findings relevant to the evolution of psychosexual functions of the brain. *Journal of Nervous and Mental Diseases, 135,* 289–301.

MacLean, P. D. (1964). Man and his animal brain. *Modern Medicine, 32,* 95–106.

MacLean, P. D. (1970). The triune brain, emotion, and scientific bias. In F. O. Schmitt (Ed.), *The neurosciences second study program.* New York: Rockefeller University Press.

MacLean, P. D. (1973a). The brain's generation gap: Some human implications. *Zygon, 8,* June, 113–127.

MacLean, P. D. (1973b). New findings on brain function and sociosexual behavior. In J. Zuben & J. Money (Eds.), *Contemporary sexual behavior: Critical issues in the 1970s.* Baltimore: Johns Hopkins University Press.

MacLean, P. D. (1978a). Why brain research on lizards. In N. Greenberg & P. D. MacLean (Eds.). *The behavior and neurology of lizards.* DHEW publication (ADM) 77–491, pp. 1–10. Washington, D.C.: U.S. Government Printing Office.

MacLean, P. D. (1978b). Effects of lesions of globus pallidus on species-typical display behavior of squirrel monkeys. *Brain Research, 149,* 175–196.

MacLean, P. D. (1979). On the evolution of three mentalities. *Man-Environment Systems, 5,* 313–314.

MacLean, P. D. (1980). Role of transhypothalamic pathways in social communication. In P. Morgane & J. Panksepp (Eds.), *Handbook of the hypothalamus.* New York: Marcel Dekker.

MacLean, P. D. (1982). On the origin and progressive evolution of the triune brain. In E. Armstrong & D. Falk (Eds.), *Primate brain evolution.* New York: Plenum Press.

Murphy, M. R., MacLean, P. D., & Hamilton, S. C. (1981). Species-typical behavior of hamsters deprived from birth of the neocortex. *Science, 213,* 459–461.

Ploog, D. & Jürgens, U. (1970). Cerebral representations of vocalization in the squirrel monkey. *Experimental Brain Research, 10,* 532–554.

Romer, A. S. (1966). *Vertebrate paleontology.* Chicago: University of Chicago Press.

Stonorov, D. (1972). Protocol at the annual brown bear fish feast. *Natural History, 81,* 66–94.

Chapter 4

HUMAN PALEOPSYCHOLOGY

Roots of Pathological Aggression

Kent G. Bailey

An understanding of human aggression and violence continues to elude experts on human behavior. Despite great cultural and technological advances in recent times, human beings continue to be far more violent and destructive than any specific theory or philosophic frame of reference would predict. Theories premised on reinforcement and modeling principles, frustration, social stress, social anomie, violent subcultures, etc., fall short in addressing the sheer magnitude and scope of violence in modern societies. Such theories contribute part-causes to the hypothetical matrix of interlocking causes of violence, but usually fail to grapple with the following fundamental questions:

- Why is extreme violence a virtually exclusive *male* preserve?;
- Why is so much male violence *gratuitous,* that is, beyond what is needed to accomplish instrumental objectives?;
- Why does male destructiveness appear to be *enjoyable* in many instances?; and
- What are the intrapsychic dynamics involved in momentary shifts from "normal," civilized behavior to violent outbursts?

In an attempt to answer these questions, I have developed a paleopsychological approach to behavior based on the concepts of phylogenetic regression and progression. I have defined paleopsychology as the phylogenetically old psychology of the individual, those structures, tendencies, and predispositions carried over from both our nonhuman and early hominid ancestors. A full assessment of human violence requires an understanding of our basic animality and continuity with nature along with the more distinctively human problems of learning, development, and situational causality.

The Phylogentic Regression-Progression Model

Phylogenetic regression-progression theory postulates that all behavior may be viewed as falling somewhere on a hypothetical continuum (or hierarchy) proceeding from the most phylogentically primitive to the most phylogentically advanced patterns of response. "Behavior" here refers to all forms of intercoordinated response output within a given unit of time and not just motor output. It further is postulated that dynamic, ongoing behavior is a product of momentary "regressions" and "progressions" on the continuum, which reflect within-person fluctuations over time. Thus, a person might be more "animalistic" one moment (regression) and more distinctively human (progression) another, depending on the internal milieu or situational factors.

In a matter of seconds, a culturally refined, cortically controlled individual can regress to the emotionality characteristic of his evolutionary forebears, and at that moment he is little different from them. We are normally far different from *Homo erectus* or *Australopithecus,* or a baboon or chimpanzee for that matter, but under severe stress, threat, provocation, or loss of "control" through alcohol ingestion, drugs, and so forth, we temporarily lose our humanity, our culture, and rationality.

In man, the neocortical mantle is thought to be the seat of logical and mathematical reasoning, knowledge and understanding, analytical and synthetic processes, invention and fantasy, philosophy and religion, meditation and intuition. However, in man, too, some behaviors and aspects of mental disease suggest a *regression* (emphasis added) of brain functioning to a predominantly paleomammalian (limbic) or reptilian level. In this last instance, as has been observed in animal experiments, the breakdown of social, familial, parental behavior, and personal care is often accompanied by the emergence of asocial, hostile, and aggressive behaviors, and "reptilian" man emerges (Valzelli, 1981, p. 38).

In actuality, such "phylogenetic regression" reflects a general process of primitivization, dissolution, and hierarchic disintegration, which involves both ontogenetic and phylogenetic components (Bailey, in Press; Meerlo, 1962). The proportionate loading of each is the crucial issue in primitive behavior, e. g. pathological aggression, determining whether primarily atavistic or merely repressed material is called up. For example, the vicious "biting" attacks of Ted Bundy on his victims appear nothing less than regressively recovered predatory patterns of orality mixed with other forms of sexual violence (Bailey, 1985), although his general animosity toward women was no doubt ontogenetically acquired. The phylogenetic component in deep regression is often subtly interblended with other regressive material and is only evident on close analysis. Nevertheless, the phylogenetic component often is one of the most important factors in the causal array subserving pathological forms of aggression (Bailey, 1985).

Whereas the worst of Ted Bundy's attacks plumb the depths of regression, the thoughts of Stephen Hawking, the brilliant physicist and nearly perfect "cerebral being" (Boslough, 1984), serve to define the upper pole of progression. Hawking suffers from the crippling and deadly disease amyotrophic lateral sclerosis (ALS) and is now confined to a wheelchair and suffers total paralysis of the body. Nevertheless, his mind, now freed from the lower body needs and processes, seems even more capable of generating brilliant thoughts about the universe than before the disease (Boslough, 1984).

SOME PRINCIPLES OF PHYLOGENETIC REGRESSION

Theoretical principles and supporting argument are extensively outlined in Bailey (1985), but a few major points may be summarized below.

1. Regression may occur in any functional system (e.g., motivational, emotional, hedonic, imagistic, fantasy, behavioral), but is *least likely* to be observed at the overt behavioral level. A corollary point is that most phylogenetic regression is covert and internal, but such regression may exert significant, although subtle, effects on observable behavioral processes. For example, an insult might elicit a major motivational-emotional regression, but, by virtue of neocortical filtering (morals, values, prohibitions, etc.), little outward effect might be obvious.

2. It is easier and usually more pleasurable to phylogenetically regress than progress (Meerlo, 1962). We regress into pre-established motivation-emotion-reward-behavior linkages which are thoroughly interwoven into the evolved neurohumoral hardware and software of body, while progression seemingly has much less to build on. Furthermore, following Herrnstein's (1977) argument that acting in accordance with one's species imperatives is inherently rewarding, we would expect that "acting naturally" would be more pleasurable than acceding to the arbitrary demands of social morality and culture. It is noteworthy in this regard that "lower activities" such as eating, sexuality, and sensuality are rated by college students as far more pleasurable than "higher" activities such as studying, going to class, or working mathematical problems (Bailey, Burns, & Bazan, 1982).

3. Intelligence is a major mediator of regression-progression, but not in direct 1-to-1 fashion. High intelligence, however, provides the potential for progressing beyond animal needs into the world of ideas and reflection. Low intelligence, on the other hand, limits the possibilities for phylogenetic progression although reasonably high levels may be achieved through accelerated educational and socialization practices. Extremely low intelligence is associated with impaired capacity for enculturalization (MacAndrew & Ed-

gerton, 1964), a greater reliance on subcortical mechanisms such as territoriality and dominance (Hereford, Cleland, & Fellner, 1973; Paluck & Esser, 1971), and heightened sensitivity to phylogenetically conditioned releasing stimuli such as the threatening stare (Bailey, Tipton, & Taylor, 1977). Whereas the retarded person is typically not characterized by social mischief, the male of low-to-moderate intelligence is at risk for regressive acting-out in the form of juvenile delinquency (Sagarin, 1980), physical violence, and murder (Heilbrun, 1982; Holcomb & Adams, 1982; Holland, Beckett, & Levi, 1981). The dull, normal sociopath is especially prone to impulsive violence (Heilbrun, 1979), and many (although not all) sex offenses and rapes are committed by those of lesser intelligence (Rada, 1978), education, and socioeconomic level (Dietz, 1978).

4. Given that regression to natural patterns is easy and pleasurable, it follows that a great amount of *inhibition* is necessary to keep regressive processes in check. Human beings are creatures of inhibition, both internally in terms of natural excitation/inhibition systems and externally in terms of social and cultural controls. Given what human beings *can* do, we actually do very little, and given the magnitude of our wants, we actually satisfy few of our needs. Frustration is the price we pay for social order and civilization, and the highly socialized individual must exhibit reliable forms of self-denial. In many areas, such as murder, rape, or child molestation, inhibitions must act in failsafe manner if one is to maintain good standing in society.

5. Phylogenetic regression may be viewed as a form of hierarchic disintegration where neocortically mediated sociocultural functions give way to lower, more urgent and powerful functions in the paleomammalian and reptilian brain structures. Paul MacLean's (1954, 1978, 1982) theory of the triune brain hierarchy implies momentary phylogenetic regressions and progressions as the focus of brain activity fluctuates between lower and higher functions in ongoing behavior. As I see it, the brain works as a dynamic cerebral system of regression-progression processes and MacLean's three-brains-in-one gives meaning to the sheer complexity of it all. Brown's (1977) four-fold elaboration of MacLean's system is summarized below:

Species Level	Functional level	Genetic level
human	symbolic (asymmetric, neocortical)	onto-phylogenetic
neomammalian	representational (cortical)	phylogenetic
paleomammalian	presentational (limbic)	phylogenetic
reptilian	sensori-motor (subcortical)	phylogenetic

6. Phylogenetic regression is premised on the idea that considerable phylogenetic continuity exists for many human morphological and behavioral traits. There is a remarkable degree of genetic overlap, for example, between chimpanzees and humans, suggesting the likelihood of many homologous structures. Given that humans and chimpanzees share about 99

percent of their genes (King & Wilson, 1975; Yunis & Prakash, 1982), and further that the resemblance between the DNA of humans and chimpanzees is greater than that of the mouse and rat (Luckett & Szalay, 1975), it follows that relatively little "phylogenetic regression" is required to reach the chimpanzee level of functioning! I refer to the shared chimpanzee-human genes as the *phylogenotype,* while the remaining distinctly human genetic material (one percent or so) is called the *transgenotype.* The phylogenotype (P) and transgenotype (T), when added together, comprise the overall genotype (G) of the person (see Bailey, 1985 for an expanded version of the $P+T=G$ formula). The theoretical importance of the phylogenotype is obvious vis-à-vis the issues of phylogenetic continuity and regression.

7. Along with the 99 percent chimpanzee-human overlap, it is noteworthy that approximately 99 percent of hominoid evolution occurred during the hunting and gathering mode of adaptation (Campbell, 1979), meaning that approximately 90 percent of all the people who ever lived were hunter-gatherers (Lee & DeVore, 1968). Only 10,000 years ago 100 percent of the world's population were hunter-gatherers, while at present, a mere .003 percent fall in this category (Coon, 1971). Lee and DeVore (1968) conclude from this that the origin of all common characteristics in humans must be sought in preagricultural times. The implications for phylogenetic regression are obvious:

That we moderns are hunter-gatherers at heart has direct implications for the phylogenetic regression-progression model. The reasoning goes thusly: if virtually all of human evolution occurred in the hunting and gathering modality, and if that evolution defines the essential nature of the human species, then two conclusions follow: a. the biological nature of man was designed for hunting and gathering (and not for modern civilized life), and b., post-agricultural cultural evolution, involving an extremely short time period within which the neuropsychological systems of the body remained essentially unchanged, has contributed little to the fundamental nature of man and represents "a thin veneer" over the quintessential hunter-gatherer lying underneath. It furthermore follows that when we phylogenetically regress under provocation or threat *we are most likely to regress to some aspect of our essential hunting and gathering nature.*

PASSIVE AND ACTIVE REGRESSION

Passive phylogenetic regression occurs when neocortical inhibitory controls are relaxed and primitive motives, feelings, thoughts, or behaviors "slip through," usually unconsciously. By contrast, the active form occurs when the neocortex not only fails to inhibit lower processes, but actually sides with them and provides *a priori* and *ex post facto* rationalizations for asocial or antisocial actions. Raping under the influence of alcohol or drugs would exemplify the passive form, while the use of Nazi propaganda to incite violence and persecution against Jews or ideologically based terrorism illustrate active phylogenetic regression. As MacLean has stated "the human capacity for such active regression makes our species, at one and the same time, the most resourceful and destructive on earth, for our great intelligence allows us to manufacture lofty rationalizations and justifications for every sort of inhumanity imaginable." Passive regressions in the form of tantrums, fighting, and even infanticide have occurred since time immemorial, with little threat to the species as a whole, but the world now stands poised for its own destruction through intellectually and culturally supported prejudice and violence.

THE PRIMERS AND ELICITORS OF PHYLOGENETIC REGRESSION

Postulated causes of phylogenetic regression may be classified into two polar areas: priming conditions and proximal elicitors. *Primers,* or priming conditions, are stimuli that contribute to states of readiness, but are, themselves, incapable of immediate response elicitation. *Proximal elicitors* are stimuli that are sufficient to "set off" or release a response or response pattern; they often serve to release previously primed readinesses or tendencies of the organism. A primer or elicitor is defined entirely by its consequences; a primer contributes to readinesses short of overt response while the elicitor actually releases readinesses into behavior. Usually, primers operate internally and elicitors externally, but this is not a hard and fast distinction. The major primers and elicitors I have listed are shown in Table 4–1. As is evident, some elicitors (or primers) are part of evolved elicitor-response relationships which go far back in phylogeny (for example, many of the social releasers), although others have little or no innate evolutionary history (alcohol, drugs, overpopulation, etc.).

CORRELATES AND CONSEQUENCES OF PHYLOGENETIC REGRESSION

Listed below is a sampling of theoretically derived consequences of phylogenetic regression. Not all consequences are likely to occur at once, and it is not clear always which are causes and which effects (for example, reduced inhibition), but most seem to be on the effect side.

1. Phylogenetic regression is accompanied by differing degrees of *primitivization of consciousness.* At the upper pole of progression, we might imagine a brilliant astronomer at his/her desk deriving mathematical equations to predict the presence of a black hole in the Milky Way. At the height of concentration, his/her consciousness and intellect are at asymtote and are focused on the task like an electron microscope. This refined consciousness is under the direction of the neocortex and is controlled largely by "will." In contrast, in the throes of orgasm, consciousness of objective surroundings is severely diminished and freed from mental control and essentially runs its

Table 4-1

Primers and Elicitors of Phylogenetic Regression

Internal Conditions

The genotype
    The phylogenotype
    The transgenotype
Hormones and neurotransmitters
Biorhythmic and biometerological factors
Brain damage and dysfunction
Cognitive factors
    Dreams
    Images
    Fantasies
    Emotional thoughts
    Unemotional thoughts

External Elicitors

Pain, injury, and fear
Chemical and drug effects
    Various classes of psychoactive drugs
    Ethyl alcohol as a special case
Special releasing stimuli in animals and humans
    Chemical releasers
    Visual and auditory releasers
    Alarm and distress calls
    Social releasers
    Ritualized and display behavior
    Human social releasers
Day-to-day stresses and strains
Overpopulation and crowding
Deprivation and frustration
Groups and crowds
Anonymity and deindividuation
Differences between people
    Physical differences
    Behavioral and mental differences
    Differences in beliefs
Power, riches, and money

Notes:
1. Primers and elicitors in Table 4-1 are discussed in detail in Bailey, 1985.
2. Phylogenotypes, the hypothetical genotype of the species nearest to humans (viz., the chimpanzee); transgenotype distinctively human genetic material. Both of these comprise the human genotype.
3. Internal conditions usually serve as "primers" and external conditions as "elicitors," but the distinction is not a fast one.

own course. Awareness of pleasurable feeling may be acute, but directed consciousness is virtually nonexistent.

2. *Reduced inhibition* is another consequence of the regressive process. Modern society is premised on massive inhibition of instinctive processes in the forms of moral proscriptions, rules of law, and fads and fashions, but in regression many of these controls are lost. In deep regression, there is a decided shift from reliable external controls to weak and unreliable paleopsychological or natural inhibitions which are often insufficient to the task. For example, one may suffer one humiliation after another in silence, but once the breaking point is reached, primitive material floods forth virtually unchecked in extreme, all-or-none form. Such primitive material may come from any of the major functional systems (fear, sex, aggression) singly or in combination, depending on the internal milieu and external eliciting circumstances.

3. Segments and part-segments of *evolved behaviorial patterns* often are released in phylogenetic regression, which intermix with other systems (motivational, emotional, imagistic, etc.) called into play. Whether vestiges of older "fixed-action patterns" or weaker behaviorial tendencies, they rarely emerge in pure form, but are, in piecemeal fashion, subtly interwoven into the ongoing stream of behavior. The sucking reflex in infants closely approximates the fixed-action pattern described by ethologists (Eibl-Eibesfeldt, 1970), as does the infant smile (Gray, 1958), and sexual foreplay and copulatory response in adults (Schur, 1960). To these, we also might add the distinctive grimaces, postures, and offensive and defensive maneuvers that accompany play fights (Aldis, 1975) and actual hand-to-hand combat. Based on *in vivo* film sequences of naturally occurring behavior across a variety of cultures, Eibl-Eibesfeldt (1970) and Hass (1970) described many other presumably phylogenetically conditioned action patterns: protecting oneself from behind, intermittent scanning of the environment while eating, flirting pattern in females, the universal raised eyebrow greeting, "arrogance and disdain" pattern, exhibiting the tongue to show disdain and rejection, offering food to appease another, and dominance and submission displays.

4. A proportionate increase of *nonverbal-to-verbal* forms of communication is expected in phylogenetic regression. Even in our most progressive moments, the nonverbal-verbal ratio is large, but the verbal mode may drop out entirely in deep regression and be replaced by nonvocal patterns and primitive vocalization (screams, grunts, groans, etc.). At those times, animal-human differences in communication patterns are minimized:

> The behaviorial intercourse established by innate bodily signal codes held in common by man and beast forms part and parcel of archaic communication. Everyone understands and reacts to distress calls of animals. Certain emotional expressions are immediately understood. Crying, laughing, rhythmic tapping, fright reactions, shouting, fainting, itching, dancing movements, sneezing, convulsions, erotic gestures—they all evoke immediate understanding and response (Meerlo, 1967, p. 8).

5. Theoretically, accentuated *sex differences* are expected in phylogenetic regression. The reasoning goes thusly: given large gender differences phylogenotypically (viz., between chimpanzee males and females) and large differences during most of hominid phylogeny (e.g., the hunting and gathering phase), it follows that "natural" gender differences, or parts thereof, may be recovered in the regressive process. So viewed, extreme androgyny or high gender similarity would be primarily socioculturally derived and part of the "thin veneer" of culture which may be lost in threat- or stress-induced regression. Evidence is circumstantial on this point, but androgynous patterns are extremely rare in pre-technological societies and rather tenuously held in even liberal modernist societies (see Tiger & Shepher's 1975 discussion of reversion to "natural patterns" of women in the kibbutz). Bokun (1977) writes that modern human beings under the stress of revolutions or catastrophes may behave comparably to "our human ancestors in the savannah" (p. 28), and McLeod's (1984) observations of people in catastrophe suggested reversion to natural patterns with men playing tough, protective roles and women exhibiting "selfless concern for others," helplessness, and despair.

7. Last, but not least, *primitive social approach behavior* may be released in phylogenetic regression. For a variety of reasons, negative, rather than positive, behavior may be expected in regression (see Bailey, 1985), but there are, nevertheless, many possible prosocial correlates and consequences. Imprinting and attachmental processes, primitive love and kinship, playfulness, and group togetherness all have deep roots in phylogeny, and through mild and benign regressions we have access to them. Such access allows us to be healthy, interesting, and creative people, and failure to draw on ancient prosocial reserves is at the root of many forms of psychopathology (for example, depression, neurosis and rigidity, sociopathology and violent criminality, social alienation, and family pathology, etc.; see especially Bolton, 1983).

THE PRP MODEL AND PATHOLOGY

Several principles of pathology may be derived from the phylogenetic regression model.

Once-adaptive and never-adaptive releases often occur in the context of brain damage or dysfunction. If damage or dysfunction is mild and primarily disinhibitory, then release of once-adaptive patterns is likely: with severe damage, however, motivation-emotion-reward-behavior patterns are not only released, but released in disjointed and maladaptive fashion. Whereas well-integrated dominance aggression might be released under the influence of alcohol (disinhibited once-adaptive pattern), situation-inappropriate rage and violence may occur with direct damage to the aggression centers of the brain (never-adaptive dysrelease—see Bailey, 1985, Chapter 10; Moyer, 1976; Valzelli, 1981). In addition to aggressive dysrelease, many other pathological reactions are caused by, or exacerbated by, brain dysfunction or atypical brain function: delinquency and sociopathy, schizophrenia, sexual anomalies, obsessive-compulsive neurosis, depression and mania, and disturbed cortico-limbic psychic functioning (see Bailey, 1985, for referencing). Also, of particular interest is the disinhibitory model of psychopathology developed by Gorenstein and Newman (1980), which focuses on the relation between septal dysfunction and a number of psychopathological syndromes, e.g., psychopathy, hysteria, hyperactivity, impulsive personality, and alcoholism.

The PRP model implies that *fixations* on the regression-progression continuum are possible. If behavior reflects ongoing, momentary regressions down and progressions up the continuum as proposed, then it follows that some individuals have wider response continua than others (for example, from deeply primitive to highly advanced, as with Ted Bundy, the infamous mass murderer (Bailey, in press). Other people may have truncated continua congenitally or otherwise (for example, the mentally retarded, brain-damaged, severely psychotic); although others may be paleopsychologically fixated and never progress to neopsychological levels of functioning (for example, the feral children of fact and fancy, (MacLean, 1979). In modern society, severe phylogenetic fixations are rarely encountered, for almost all people have the capacity and experiential background to sample culture in some degree.

Much more common are deep regressions, which may occur in essentially normal individuals who possess sufficient ego-strength to progress back at will, and sufficient cultural sensitivity to avoid being labeled deviant for their activities (for example, individuals who engage in private, perverse sexual activities, or who use hard-core pornography with no apparent ill effects). Given the Pandora's box or release implications of the PRP model, however, it is hypothesized that few people are able to deeply regress to primitive levels of sexuality or violence without residual effects, sometimes more-or-less permanent ones.

The common belief that once one kills it is much easier to kill again (Kagan, 1984) is consistent with a regression-release explanation, as is the paradox of sexual hyperactivity (rather than sexual avoidance) that sometimes occurs in individuals raped or sexually molested (Yates, 1982). Equally paradoxical is the finding that abused children are at extreme risk for being abusing parents themselves. Having been helpless victims of violence, one might expect abused children to learn passive, avoidant, and phobic responses, making them *less* likely than average to abuse. To argue that the abused abuser has simply modeled violent responses is to beg the question: the *behaviors* may be modeled, but what of the *motivation* to harm and hurt? It seems that recourse to a release explanation of some kind is needed to deal with the motivational issue here.

Frequent, dyscontrolled, and labile regressions usually are associated with severe psychopathology such as psychosis, brain damage, and primitive psychopathy. In these instances, movement on the phylogenetic continuum is under little or no conscious control, and is symptomatic of underlying pathological processes typically at the structural level of analysis (genetics, hormones, neurotransmitters, neurophysiology, etc.). Such passive regressions are both effects and causes, and they act to severely disrupt the normal human nature-culture coupling which defines normality for Technological Man. The peculiar disinhibitory characteristics of the schizophrenic, for example, produces frequent, deep, and labile regressions, which represent a pathological kaleidoscope of presently adaptive, once adaptive, and never adaptive responses.

In the schizophrenic, we see high-total failure of neoadaptive processes and a resurgence of pathologically mixed and situation-inappropriate paleological processes (Arieti, 1970). The caricatures of dominance and territoriality (Esser, Chamberlain, Chappel, & Kline, 1965; Horowitz, Duff, & Stratton, 1964), obsessive concern with oral-predatory themes, fantasies of mutilation and destruction, hypertrophied xenophobia of the paranoiac, confused sex role behavior and sexuality, and the tonic immobility of the catatonic (Gallup & Maser, 1977), seem to reflect processes which were once-adaptive sometime in phylogeny, but are inadequately recovered and integrated in the schizophrenic. In them, we see pathological depth, frequency, and lability of regression in bold relief.

At the other extreme is inflexibility of movement on the regression-progression continuum. The rigidity and tension of the neurotic, the character armor and ingrained habit patterns of the personality disorder, and certain other symptoms of schizophrenia (e.g., concreteness, stereotypy, rigidity, perseveration) would fall in this category. The normal individual can laugh, play, love, express sexuality, express anger and hostility, and otherwise regress in controlled and situation-appropriate fashion. Some individuals develop controlled or adaptive regression to a fine art (actors and other showpeople, prize fighters, professional wrestlers, police and military personnel, charismatic public speakers, etc.), while most of us are consigned to a dreary sameness of habit and behavior. Most of us spend more time performing old habits than in learning new ones, and only a few enviable people develop artistry in benign regression. Such artistry is notably absent in virtually all forms of psychopathology, save for the sociopath who employs regressive charisma for personally adaptive, but socially offensive purposes. For most disturbed and nonnormal individuals, motivation-emotion-reward-behavior patterns are compulsively repetitive, self-defeating, and illogical on the face of it. Only when we approach the problem paleopsychologically do we see older patterns of logic and adaptation operating.

SUMMARY OVERVIEW

Paleopsychology is defined as the phylogenetically old psychology of the individual, those structures, tendencies, and predispositions carried over from both our nonhuman and early hominid ancestors. The phylogenetic regression-progression model assumes that both normal and abnormal behavior in humans is, in large measure, erected on these paleopsychological foundations. Of central importance is how the paleopsychological foundation structures interact, synergistically and antagonistically, with the higher neopsychological functions.

The phylogenetic regression model was described in some detail, with emphasis on chimpanzee-human genetic overlap and the central theoretical importance of the hunting and gathering phase of human evolution. Also, some of the primers and elicitors, and correlates and consequences of phylogenetic regression were reviewed.

REFERENCES

Aldis, O. (1975). *Play fighting*. New York: Academic Press.
Arieti, S. (1970). The structural and psychodynamic role of cognition in the human psyche. In S. Arieti (Ed.), *The world biennial of psychiatry and psychotherapy*. Vol. I. New York: Basic Books.
Bailey, K. G. (1985). *Human paleopsychology: Applications to aggression and pathological processes*. Hillsdale, N.J.: Lawrence Erlbaum.
Bailey, K. G. (in press). Ted Bundy: A paleopsychological analysis of a mass murderer. *New trends in clinical and experimental psychiatry*.
Bailey, K. G., Burns, D. S., & Bazan, L. C. (1982). A method for measuring "primitive" and "advanced" elements in pleasures and aversions. *Journal of Personality Assessment, 46,* 639–646.
Bailey, K. G., Tipton, R. M., & Taylor, P. F. (1977). The threatening stare: Differential response latencies in mild and profoundly retarded adults. *American Journal of Mental Deficiency, 31,* 599–602.
Bokun, B. (1977). *Man: The fallen ape*. Garden City, N.Y.: Doubleday.
Bolton, G., Jr. (1983). *When bonding fails: Clinical assessment of high-risk families*. Beverly Hills, CA.: Sage.
Boslough, J. (February 1984). Inside the mind of a genius. *Reader's Digest,* 118–124.
Brown, J. (1977). *Mind, brain and consciousness*. New York: Academic Press.
Campbell, B. G. (Ed.). (1979). *Humankind emerging*. New York: Academic Press.
Coon, C. S. (1971). *The hunting peoples*. Boston: Little, Brown.
Dietz, P. E. (1978). Social factors in rapist behavior. In R. T. Rada (Ed.), *Clinical aspects of the rapist*. New York: Grune & Stratton.
Eibl-Eibesfeldt, I. (1970). *Ethology: The biology of behavior*. New York: Holt, Rinehart & Winston.

Esser, A. H., Chamberlain, A. S., Chappel, E. D., & Kline, N. S. (1965). Territoriality of patients on a research ward. In A. H. Esser (Ed.), *Recent advances in biological psychiatry.* New York: Plenum.

Gallup, G. G., Jr. & Maser, J. D. (1977). Tonic immobility: Evolutionary underpinnings of human catalepsy and catatonia. In J. D. Maser & E. P. Seligman (Eds.), *Psychopathology: Experimental models.* San Francisco: W. H. Freeman.

Gorenstein, E. E. & Newman, J. P. (1980). Disinhibitory psychopathology: A new perspective and model for research. *Psychological Review, 87,* 301–303.

Gray, P. H. (1958). Theory and evidence of imprinting in human infants. *Journal of Psychology, 46,* 155–166.

Hass, H. (1970). *The human animal.* New York: Putnam.

Heilbrun, A. B. (1979). Psychopathy and violent crime. *Journal of Consulting and Clinical Psychology, 47,* 509–516.

Heilbrun, A. B. (1982). Cognitive models of criminal violence based upon intelligence and psychopathy levels. *Journal of Consulting and Clinical Psychology, 50,* 546–557.

Hereford, S., Cleland, C. C., & Fellner, M. (1973). Territoriality and scent-marking: A study of profoundly retarded enuretics and encopretics. *American Journal of Mental Deficiency. 77,* 426–430.

Herrnstein, R. S. (1977). The evolution of behaviorism. *American Psychologist, 32,* 593–603.

Holcomb, W. R. & Adams, N. (1982). Racial influences on intelligence and personality measures of people who commit murder. *Journal of Clinical Psychology, 38,* 793–796.

Holland, T. R., Beckett, G. E., & Levi, M. (1981). Intelligence, personality, and criminal violence: A multivariate analysis. *Journal of Consulting and Clinical Psychology, 49,* 106–111.

Horowitz, M. J., Duff, D. F., & Stratton, L. O. (1964). Body buffer zone. *Archives of General Psychiatry, 11,* 651–656.

Kagan, D. (June 1984). Serial murderers. *Omni,* p. 200.

King, M. C. & Wilson, A. C. (1975). Evolution at two levels in humans and chimpanzees. *Science, 118,* 107–116.

Lee, R. R. & Devore, I. (1968). *Man the hunter.* Chicago: Aldine.

Luckett, W. F. & Szalay, F. S. (Eds.) (1975). *Phylogeny of the primates.* New York: Plenum.

MacAndrew, C. & Edgerton, R. (1964). The everyday life of institutionalized idiots. *Human Organization, 23,* 312–318.

MacLean, C. (1979). *Wolf children: Fact or fantasy?* New York: Penguin.

McLeod, B. (1984). In the wake of disaster. *Psychology Today, 18,* 54–57.

Meerlo, J. A. M. (1962). The dual meaning of human regression. *Psychoanalytic Review, 49,* 77–86.

Meerlo, J. A. M. (1967). *Communication: Concepts and perspectives.* Washington, D.C.: Spartan Books.

Moyer, K. E. (1976). *The psychobiology of aggression.* New York: Harper & Row.

Paluck, R. J. & Esser, A. H. (1971). Territorial behavior as an indicator of changes in clinical behavioral condition of severely retarded boys. *American Journal of Mental Deficiency, 76,* 284–290.

Rada, R. T. (Ed.). (1978). *Clinical aspects of the rapist.* New York: Grune & Stratton.

Sagarin, E. (Ed.). (1980). *Taboos in criminology.* Beverly Hills, CA: Sage.

Schur, M. (1960). Phylogenesis and ontogenesis of affect- and structure-formation and the phenomenon of repetition compulsion. *International Journal of Psychoanalysis, 41,* 275–287.

Tiger, L. & Shepher, J. (1975). *Women in the kibbutz.* New York: Harcourt Brace Jovanovich.

Valzelli, L. (1981). *Psychobiology of aggression and violence.* New York: Raven Press.

Yates, A. (1982). Children eroticized by incest. *American Journal of Psychiatry, 139,* 482–485.

Yunis, J. J. & Prakash, O. (1982). The origin of man: A chromosomal legacy. *Science, 215,* 1525–1530.

Chapter 5

THE FETAL ORIGINS OF LOVE AND HATE

Lloyd deMause

We are accustomed to thinking of our lives as individuals as starting at the moment of birth. In fact, virtually all contemporary psychoanalytic theory denies the possibility of mental life before or during birth. The newborn is believed to be without memory, ego, objects or mental structure. As one psychoanalyst puts it, "Psychoanalysis does not really ask 'Where did it begin?' Instead, it asks a rather different question, 'When after birth did it begin?' " (Peterfreund, 1971).

Most of us have seen a newborn baby, although what we may have seen was a newborn baby that was drugged. If it is not drugged, you look at a newborn baby and you find that it is a rather sophisticated human being. The baby is alert, it looks around, smiles, is interested in things. It acutely listens to sounds. It can tell its mother's voice from other people's voices—if there is one person on one side of the room and the mother on the other side, it will turn toward the mother because it has been listening to the mother's voice while in the womb. In fact, one experimenter proved babies can remember and choose to hear *The Cat in the Hat* if the mother had read this story to them while they were in the womb (Lewis, 1984).

When you stick your tongue out, the baby can stick its tongue out. It is, therefore, able to identify you as being similar to itself. If you blink, it will blink a certain percentage of the time, if you do it in just the right way. The newborn baby's focal length is only 10 inches (which is to say, the normal distance from the baby at the breast and mommy's face). In the past, they used to give tests to determine an infant's vision, but the tests were given at a distance that was beyond the focal length, so they said, "Look, it can't see." Experimenters are now proving that the newborn baby can learn, store memories, use them later on, etc.

Now, this is true of a newborn baby at birth, nine months after conception. This is also true of a baby two weeks prior to birth. There is no crucial difference between a baby outside the womb and a baby at 8 1/2 months' term inside the womb, in terms of ability to taste, feel, smell, remember, learn, etc. Every new discovery about the fetus challenges the notion that it is a "tabula rasa," that it has no object relations, has no memory or feelings, as is stated in most of the psychological studies. If a premature newborn baby is capable of having emotions and remembering them, then, the fetus inside the womb which is the same gestational age can surely do the same.

Advances in fetal knowledge have, in the past two years, been so rapid that "a student could compare the literature of today with that of 20 years ago and conclude that two different species were under study." (Emde & Robinson, 1979).

The results of recent studies have been all in one direction: to push, earlier, the onset of all developmental stages and sensory abilities of the fetus (Rugh & Shettles, 1971; Ingelmann-Sundberg & Wirsin, 1965; Annes, 1978).

When we look into the literature that has come out in the last 10 years describing what the inside of the womb looks like, what the baby can do in the womb, precisely what affects the baby, and what its life is like, we begin to get a very startling picture.

Pioneer psychoanalysts and psychotherapists who assumed that mental life is begun at birth all described the womb as a nice, safe place, and assumed that we would all want to crawl back in again. Not so at all!

The fetus inside the womb is in a place of great risk and stress. Liley (1972) captures the difference between the old and the new views of the environment of the womb when he writes:

> Perhaps nowhere does the notion of foetal life as a time of quiescence, of patient and blind development of structures in anticipation of a life and function to begin at birth, die harder than in the concept of the pregnant uterus as a dark and silent world. . . . . A pregnant abdomen is not silent, and the uterus and amniotic cavity . . . . may be readily transilluminated with a torch in a darkened room (p. 103).

The womb is, in fact, a very noisy, changing, very active place in which to live, full of events and emotions both pleasant and painful.

Take a look at a picture of a fetus from any book on birth. The picture, you should remember, is one of an aborted fetus, since we cannot take clear photos of a fetus inside the womb. Therefore, you should modify the picture a bit. In the aborted fetus, the blood is not pumping, so imagine that the umbilicus that you see is about triple in size. That is to say, imagine the umbilicus as your fifth limb. It is really a big thing coming out of the middle of you, pumping blood all the time, back and forth.

If we could take a picture of a placenta with a little camera inside the womb, one could see it looks like a disc with veins popping out, full of blood. The veins and the umbilicus very much resemble tree branches, and the fetus touches and strokes the branches regularly.

The fetus inside the womb is facing this tree for much of the time. It doesn't know what a mother's body is or what a mother's face is. All it knows is amniotic fluid, the umbilicus and a tree—the placental disc. The placental disc is its heart. It cleanses the blood of carbon dioxide and other waste matter and pumps oxygen and nutrients into the fetus. It is its first object.

The question arises: can the fetus actually see that tree? No, it primarily feels it. It can't see very well. It feels what is in front of it. I watched my own daughter via ultrasound and could see her touching her placenta and holding her umbilicus.

Whatever happens to the mother happens to this fetus. If the mother smokes a cigarette, the baby smokes a cigarette. If the mother takes an alcoholic drink, the baby takes an alcoholic drink. Fetuses who are exposed to alcohol grow slower, aborting more, are often premature, and have more physical abnormalities, mental retardation and hyperactivity—not to mention the extremely painful withdrawal symptoms associated with the fetal alcoholic syndrome (Stevenson, 1977). The same principle holds, of course, for thousands of other drugs, including aspirin and caffeine, all of which go directly to the fetus across what used to be wishfully termed the *placental barrier* and produce many harmful and painful effects, including hypoxia (low oxygen) (Harbison, 1975; Scott, 1971).

Equally important are various nutritional factors, with malnutrition among the poor (or among the well-to-do with poor eating habits), causing a wide range of harmful physical and behavioral defects (*Child at Risk,* 1980; Sontag, 1944; Lloyd-Still, 1976). Far from being a safe, cozy haven to which we all want to return, the womb is, in fact, a dangerous and often painful abode, where even today "more lives are lost during the nine gestational months than in the ensuing 50 years of postnatal life." (Stevenson, 1977, p. 3.)

But the fetus is not only in distress when the mother smokes, drinks, or takes drugs. It also is affected both biologically and psychologically by the mother's fear, anger and depression. The biological mechanisms for transmitting these maternal emotions to the fetus are many. When the mother feels anxiety, her tachycardia is followed within seconds by the fetus' tachycardia, and when she feels fear, within 50 seconds the fetus can be made hypoxic through altered uterine blood conditions. If the blood count gets too low, the baby becomes hypoxic and it feels that the waste is building up in its system, doesn't have enough oxygen, and often can black out.

That these effects are painful to the fetus is no longer in doubt—ultrasound and other modern techniques often show the fetus in terrible distress, writhing and kicking in pain during hypoxia. One mother whose husband had just threatened her verbally with violence came into the prenatal study center with her fetus thrashing about and kicking so violently as to be painful to her, and with an elevated fetal heart rate, which continued for many hours (Sontag, 1965).

Of course, during labor, the baby is regularly hypoxic, and this is extremely painful to it. But even before birth, the fetus experiences regular "normal hypoxia." One reason is that the baby before birth outgrows the placenta in man far more than in any other mammal. That is to say, we are really not meant to have that size placenta. The placenta stops growing at about seven months, and, in fact, regresses in efficiency. It becomes tough and fibrous rather than spongy, its cells and blood vessels degenerate and it becomes full of blood clots and calcified areas. The placenta is essentially failing you at term and that failure triggers the mechanism that enables the baby to be born.

As we have seen thus far, the womb is a place full of pain from which the baby, at times, wants to escape. But that is not to say that the fetus also does not feel enormous amounts of joy. It gets food from the placenta through the constant exchange of blood, and that blood is its life supply. It depends on the placenta for the nutrition and constant cleansing of the blood, and it responds to every decrease in placental functioning with visible anger, as shown by its thrashing movements and elevated heart rate.

The placenta-umbilicus *gestalt* is the fetus' first emotional object. As early as the second trimester, the fetus has actually been filmed in endoscopic motion pictures grabbing and holding its own umbilicus in a seeming effort to comfort itself when it is startled by the bright lights of the intrauterine camera (CBS-TV, 1977).

Over and over again during its early life in the womb, the fetus experiences cycles of painful activity painful hypoxia, periods of thrashing about and then restored quiet periods as the placenta begins to pump newly oxygenated bright red blood again.

Facing something on which you totally depend, that you have experienced differently at different times, I speculate that you split it into two objects. You feel happy when the *nurturant placenta* supplies you with bright, red blood full of nutrients and oxygen, and you are in pain when the *poisonous placenta* pumps you full of blood which is dark and polluted with carbon dioxide and wastes. You need not have very complicated mental mechanisms at that early stage to have an imprint or mind set or memory, or whatever you want to call it, of a *poisonous placenta* and a *nurturant placenta*. The ability to integrate these good and bad objects into one will be the main task of your early infancy.

In the final months before birth, as the fetus outgrows the placenta, the womb gets more crowded and the blood more polluted, and the fetal drama steps up in intensity. The fetal drama is experienced long before the birth trauma, as the fetus learns that its good feelings are often interrupted by painful feelings, which it is helpless to avert and its once-peaceful womb slowly grows more crowded, less nurturant and more polluted, until it is finally liberated only by the battle which is the upheaval of birth itself.

The fetal distress results in a true "trauma" as the fetus has as yet none of the psychological defense mechanisms to handle massive anxiety and rage. Therefore, as psychoanalysts long ago found true of all traumatizations, the psyche then needs, for the rest of its life, to endlessly re-experience the trauma in a specific "repetition compulsion" which, as Greenacre first pointed out, is similar to "imprinting" in lower animals (Greenacre,1967; Krystal, 1968; Cohen, 1980).

Beyond the medical evidence of the fetus' experience in the womb, the question arises about whether any of this is remembered. Psychoanalysis and early childhood observations provide a great deal of material showing that we do remember the placenta, the umbilicus, and the womb.

One can begin by looking at Hall's book on dreams (Hall, 1967). He counts the number of times in which there is fetal material in 596 unselected dreams—rooms full of water, warm puddles, etc., and finds that they occur almost one-third of the time one is dreaming.

One can look at the work of Grof (1975), who used LSD for psychotherapeutic regression. In more than 3,000 LSD therapy sessions in both Europe and the United States, he found that patients regularly relived their birth experiences. He posited four "Basic Perinatal Matrices" which he believed his patients regularly relived under LSD. In the first matrix, "The Primal Union With Mother," the patient feels as if he were in the womb, experiencing a paradise, a oneness with God or Nature, a sense of sacredness, "oceanic" ecstasy, and so on. They re-experience swimming around and getting whatever they need, a feeling of joyful happiness in a cozy, roomy womb.

Matrix two he calls "Antagonism with Mother." The experiences are derived from the beginning of labor when the cervix is still closed and you have a feeling of entrapment, of everything being futile, of trying to get out of places, of crushing head pressures and cardiac distress as the placenta is being squeezed by the contractions, thus cutting off the blood supply. You feel that you are being sucked into a whirlpool, being swallowed by a terrifying monster, dragon, octopus, python, etc.

It seems to me that one reason enemies are almost always pictured in cartoons as dragons, octupi, and spiders is because the placenta is an octopus-looking thing, with a tangle of veins and arteries coming out of a body.

Sometimes, the placenta is pictured as a tree because of its tree-like branching, with the umbilicus as trunk. It may appear as the cosmic tree, as a sacred tree or pole, the tree of life, etc. in primitive and archaic religions, in historical religions, and in past and contemporary political symbols.

The feelings of matrix two can regularly be seen in cartoons of America in distress, as during the hostage crisis in Iran. *Time* magazine showed flags being put right up against the faces of the hostages. They are being strangled by the flag. That is what you feel like at the beginning of labor, when the placenta is smashed up against your face, the umbilicus is pressed by the contractions, and you are not getting oxygen. You are in distress and you are going to have to fight your way out. You are going to fight the enemy: the poisonous placenta, the strangler.

The flag is essentially the symbol of the placenta and the flagpole is the umbilicus. The most-used colors of the flag, red and blue, represent the colors of the blood going in and out of the placenta. The flag looks most "lifelike" when it is waving, reminding us of the watery amniotic fluid. When we say the pledge of allegiance, we place our hand over our hearts and then point it toward the flag, tracing the flow of the arterial blood. A Nazi would stand before the red flag, called the blood flag, and salute (pour the bad blood into) a swastika. Swastikas are found as far back as 500 B.C., in the public triangle of the Earthmother votive. The swastika in early states is unmistakably the symbol for the womb and the vagina. The Nazi stands before the flag and says, "Sieg Heil," which means "Heal me." With his extended arm he is throwing his emotional "poison" into the swastika for cleansing, just as he once pumped real poisonous blood into a placenta to be cleansed.

The notion of the flag as the symbol for the placenta seemed outrageous at first, but as I looked at the history of flags, the further back I went, the more flags I found with placental trees on them—cosmic trees, trees of life, etc. Finally, I discovered one of the earliest flags—actually a battle standard—from pre-dynastic Egypt. It looked like a lump with a long, dangling thing. It turned out that it was the *actual preserved placenta and umbilical cord* of the king. When a king was born, they would save the placenta, stuff it, and then place it on a flagpole and call it his double, (*ka*), his helper, his twin (Seligman & Murray, 1911). So the first flag was, indeed, a real placenta, not just a symbolic one.

Continuing to Grof's third matrix, which he calls "Synergism with Mother," the cervix opens and you experience going down long tunnels, the birth canal. There are fantasies of titanic fights, sadomasochistic orgies, explosive discharge of atom bombs and volcanoes, brutal rapes, and suicidal self-destruction, all part of an overwhelmingly violent death-rebirth struggle accompanying the birth contractions.

Matrix four is the "Separation from Mother," where you experience the end of the birth struggle, the first breath, feelings of liberation, salvation, love and forgiveness, along with fantasies of having been cleansed, unburdened, and purged.

You don't have to depend on Grof's LSD work alone for these stages. You can go to people like Kelsey (1953) and others (Ferguson, 1977; Verny, 1982) who have actually taken people through age regression by hypnosis and recovered details from birth which are quite fascinating in terms of their ability to replicate what it was like.

One colleague, Al Lawson, gives a very interesting example of the kind of memory which is rather startling (1984). He was interested in UFOs and had already recognized the fetal symbols they represented. For example, there is the large central disc (the placenta), the ladder that comes down (the umbilicus), and the appearance of the creatures in the UFO who, of course, look very much like fetuses, with big heads and other fetal resemblances.

If you've ever watched films about UFOs, you've seen that when they open up, they usually do not have normal doors. There is usually something round that splits open, rather like the way the cervix opens. Feeling that this was still only theory, Lawson decided to test out whether it made any real sense.

He hypnotized volunteers who knew little or nothing about UFOs and said, "Make up a story about a UFO abduction." All but eight made up stories about long dark tunnels, cervical-type openings, going through a hole, breathing problems, and other typical birth experiences.

The eight stories that did not match the others described people just sitting there when a great big thing hovered over them and a great big claw came down and grabbed them up, or otherwise imagined instantaneous transportation into the UFO.

Following the telling of the stories, Lawson asked many other questions, including the one that asked, "How were you born?" Everyone but one of the eight said that they had been born by Caesarian section. The eighth one was asked to check with his mother about his birth, and only then learned that it had, in fact, been Caesarian, not vaginal, as he had been told. Thus, there was 100 percent correlation between the way people imagined UFOs and their own birth experience, even to the extent of correcting the conscious knowledge of one birth experience.

Evidence for the existence in memory of the birth experience has also come from the work of various "rebirthers," who believe that re-experiencing one's birth is therapeutic. Beginning with the "natal therapy" of Elizabeth Feher and including the "birth primaling" of Janov (1973) and others (Feher, 1980; Rowan, 1978), a vast body of psychological material on birth feelings has accumulated during the past decade. Janov (1973) describes startling reenactments of exact details of the birth process, a spontaneous production of the patients themselves, acted out before Janov had published his books on the fetal experience. Our difficulty in accepting these as memories comes from the partial amnesia we develop toward our own painful fetal and birth experiences.

It is my contention that when you are born and cut off from the umbilicus you lose your first object, and from then on you are searching for the *nurturant placenta* and fighting the *poisonous placenta* for the rest of your life. The umbilicus-placenta was once yours, the umbilicus a vital, pulsing "fifth limb" which you had even before you had arms or legs, and which you feel still exists, and a "phantom placenta" that feels as though it is still attached, rather like the "phantom limb" feeling that is often experienced by people who have had a limb amputated. Just as people who have limbs cut off have an itch in the toes that are no longer there, you keep going around all the time having an itch in your phantom placenta. Thus, you can experience the aura of the placental origin of every God "from whom all blessings flow" and every Leader "from whom all power flows." This is the origin of feelings of "the sacred," "the numinous," or "the charismatic." As Rudolph Otto (1923) first discovered and Mircea Eliade (1959) has since thoroughly documented, one knows one is in the presence of the sacred by the feeling of awe and terror before an object which has the presence of mystery and overwhelming power, something "wholly other," which is not really human but is intimately connected to one's essential self—a perfect description of the placenta. This is the feeling of awe before the original sacred object that the fetus feels before the placenta, and it is the feeling of awe and terror evoked in us now by the "phantom placenta."

The idea that gods and kings should be placentas may seem even more bizarre than it once seemed that they should be parents. Yet, if you examine the traits of sacredness and charisma dispassionately, you will see that divinity carries far more placental than parental qualities: self-sufficient, arbitrary, hidden, mysterious, omnipotent, unapproachable, asexual—all these are not qualities of any living parent but rather of a living, all-powerful "thing" on which one depended entirely but whose arbitrary actions one cannot affect and with which one has constant, silent exchanges.

The drama of the suffering fetus is the deepest level of meaning of all ritual, whether it be religious or political, in all primitive, archaic, or historical groups. What we find are a few ritual group-fantasies, which are repeated over and over on different evolutionary levels, according to the childbearing modes reached by the group.

The fetal drama has five elements: the poisonous placenta, the suffering fetus, the growing pollution, the nurturant umbilicus, and the cosmic battle that punctuates our rebirth. I suggest that every god and every leader is ultimately the poisonous placenta, the displaced container for the poison. Even those leaders and gods, who appeared to be beneficial, showed their dreadful aspect in the fear and awe with which they were regarded. This is easier to see in primitive and archaic gods, where either monstrous gods are directly worshipped or else the good gods easily turn into monsters. The basic form of the poisonous placenta in group-fantasy is the serpent or dragon, seen as Gorgons, Pythons, all types of snake-like gods, all based on the placenta-umbilicus *gestalt*.

The suffering fetus is the hero of the drama. The hero of all group-fantasy, all myth, all ritual, is, of course, ourselves—the suffering fetus. We deify and identify with all those who are fated to face suffering and death from Morduk to Tammuz, from Osiris to Christ—who is essentially an innocent baby made to suffer on the cross. In the cross, we recognize the placental tree, the tree of life and death and rebirth once again.

The growing pollution is the buildup of the wastes and the group feeling that the world is forever in danger of being swamped by blood pollution, coming from the fetal experience.

If you want to see the best picture of the drama of the dying of the nurturant placenta and the horrors of the poisonous placenta in the cosmic battle, see the two movies, *E.T.* (Spielberg, 1982a) and *Poltergeist* (Spielberg, 1982b). Spielberg made both at the same time, splitting the fetal drama off into separate movies. *E.T.* is the nurturant placenta, attached to the boy. *E.T.* takes a drink and the boy gets drunk. He is the one you love in the movie, quite inexplicably, and he's the one whose death you fear.

Look at the movie *The Red Balloon* (Lamorisse, 1956). It is the same story. Why a balloon? Why red? You grow to love it in the movie, and when it dies, it loses its air with a loud sigh, and everybody in the theater cries—adults, children, everyone. Why should millions of people cry when a red membrane deflates? It is just a balloon that follows you around on a little string (the umbilicus) and then it goes flat. Of course, it is a powerful memory we re-experience.

That's the same thing that happens in *E.T.* It's first loved, but then, for no apparent reason, it starts calcifying, turning whitish. It is the calcifying, "dying" placenta. Doctors are brought in. The audience re-experiences being separated from their placentas, but then, at the end, E.T.'s heart starts beating again! This is what happened when your own heart started beating to replace the placental pumping.

If you want to see the negative aspects of birth, see *Poltergeist.* Note the monstrous power of the monster coming out of the TV set to grab the child, and the startlingly real birth canal, complete with rope (umbilicus).

The fourth element, the nurturant umbilicus, is symbolized by standards, flag poles, trees of life. This explains why flags are so important. Most battles take place around a flag. The battle is to capture the flag, whether territory was taken or not. During the protests of the 1960s and 1970s, the full power of the police was evoked whenever a flag was at stake. The flag is the symbol of the placenta and you could demand anything, even stopping the war, but you could not desecrate the flag. When we put the flag up on the moon, we put wires on to make it stand straight out, because if the flag were to hang down lifeless, that would be a forecast of doom.

The cosmic battle is the fifth element of the universal myth. It essentially is the final end of the world, the apocalypse, the deluge, the breaking of the waters, the feelings of being torn from limb-to-limb. Into this basic experience is poured all the sadistic and masochistic fantasies added from later childhood.

The basic cleansing ritual of every primitive and archaic group is the sacrifice of the beast, and this beast ultimately symbolizes the poisonous placenta killed in the fetal drama.

The prototypical sacrificial ritual is described by Hubert and Mauss (1964) in their classic book, *Sacrifice,* as follows: The sacrificer is first shaved and purified of pollution, then dressed in an animal's skin. "This is the solemn moment when the new creature stirs within him. He has become a foetus . . . . he is made to clench his fists, for the embryo in its bag has its fists clenched. He is made to walk around the hearth just as the foetus moves within the womb." Then he kills the sacrificial beast, which is dressed in all sorts of placental symbols, either actually or symbolically eats its body and drinks its blood, and pours it on the altar or smears it on himself.

In our own lives, we relive the cosmic battle over and over. As feelings of guilt, depression, and rage slowly build up in all of us due to our failed search for love, we regress to that fetal level to relive our fetal experience from the moment when we were once whole, because we get so far divorced from ourselves during our daily life. "Rebirthing" is one technique for some people. Ecstatic religious states, no matter how induced, are all similar in repeating the fetal drama. From shaman to priest to political leader, we look for someone to put us into a fetal trance and connect us with our earliest traumas.

Every time man does something which stirs his punitive archaic superego—at bottom, the poisonous placenta—every time he goes on a hunt, builds a house, plants a crop or gets married, he must sacrifice through various rituals, repeating the original birth of the fetus and the killing of the placental beast. The same pattern can be seen in wars. We never go to war during the first year of a new leader because we see him as strong. As the group itself becomes full of pollution, however, it imagines that the leader has become the hated placental beast, and it must either kill him in a regicidal or revolutionary act or find a sacrificial beast, an enemy, as substitute.

What distinguishes civilization from the primitive cultures is that states are able to perform cleansing ceremonies in wider than face-to-face groups. Until you get to the point of having your cleansing ceremony at a distance, which requires much sublimation, you can't have unified groups acting together.

It long has been accepted that people get together to form groups in order to do work, to be more efficient. Utilitarianism is our central dogma today. I have found that people really get together to deal with their common anxieties, to do therapy, to cleanse themselves of the accumulated products of guilt, desire for revenge, feelings of frustration, hate, and pain. That this sometimes has utilitarian results is secondary. But the cleansing rituals come first. States which, like the Aztec, invent cleansing rituals which rebirth their emotional world effectively but which are engaged in continuous wars and human sacrifices, which are hardly utilitarian, prevail nonetheless.

In looking at social problems, it is customary to blame society for the effects it has on the individual. I believe it is the other way around. I believe it starts with the evolution of childhood. The more loving and empathic the childrearing, the more the stark elements of the fetal drama are modified. Every act of good childrearing contributes to containing the child's fears and mitigates the severity of the split between the idealized and poisonous primary object. Every failure of parenting reinforces the archaic fears and rages of the fetal drama. The so-called "death wish" and "basic fault" exist at birth because of the very real, frightening experiences of fetal life.

Only when mothers are able to give children a little better childhood than they received, will we then, a generation later, initiate progress and things going in a new direction. There is no way to get a psychosocially better human being other than through better mothering. I say "mothering" because for most of history it was the mother who cared for the child. There is no way, other than through good care-taking, that you can get a more mature human being. Then, you inevitably see progress at a later stage.

In cultures where, for some reason, the childrearing is frozen, the society freezes. The Chinese society became frozen in the second century B.C. when they started foot-binding and started crippling little girls. This was done because they chose to get revenge against the next generation rather than move in a new direction. Similar patterns may be found in societies which practice clitoridectomy. Wherever you see a society that persecutes children, you'll find a frozen culture.

Likewise, where a society seems to have dramatically moved forward, childrearing was found to have improved thirty, forty, fifty years earlier. For example, in 1710–1715 we first began to see manuals on childrearing that said, "You don't have to beat your child, no matter what the Bible may say about sparing the rod and spoiling the child. You have to punish your child, but I'll tell you what to do—you tie them to the bedposts in the bedroom and leave them alone; or you pray for six hours and let them think about how bad they were and how they hurt God." This may seem terrible to us, but it's psychological, not physical, punishment, and whatever psychological pressure does, it's still better than fearing for your life, because many children prior to this time were beaten so badly they feared for their lives. So the advice was, isolate your kid, have him think on his sinfulness, and that will cure him, and you won't have to beat him.

Almost 30 years later, a new school of penology arose which said, "It's strange that people are not punished by psychological means." Until that time, jails were not used to punish people. Jails were where you held people until trial, and after the trial, if a man were judged guilty, he would have his arm or ear cut off or be sent to Australia. Now, they began to design prisons where prisoners were isolated in cells around the jailer, who would exert moral pressure, like a parent, and give them the opportunity to change. This occurred precisely 30 years after the childrearing manuals started talking against physical punishment.

It is precisely because of these periods of change that the cycles of history are so lawful. War, for instance, occurs every 21 or 22 years for most nations. Now, war is our major cleansing ritual in modern society; we no longer purge ourselves and re-experience the fetal drama in shamanistic trances or Aztec-like human sacrifices. Once a generation, we sacrifice our youth to the bestial enemy, in order to cleanse ourselves of the guilt produced by too much prosperity and change. Like primitive tribes, we call ourselves by the name of the rite of passage we shared with our age-group; the Vietnam generation, the Korean generation, the World War II generation. After the blood of those sacrificed is spilled on the battlefield, the nation is reborn, and has "the best years of our lives," as the movie termed the post-World War II period.

The evidence for the four-stage fetal cycle in modern national politics is contained in my previous work on group-fantasy (deMause, 1975, 1976, 1977b, 1979). The nationalist group-fantasy within which we enact the fetal drama today consists of the worship of a "national will" as interpreted by elected leaders, inevitable growing pollution of the "national life-blood," a collapse of national will, and a sacrificial battle against a bestial enemy, often another nation, to cleanse the national bloodstream and accomplish the re-birth of national vitality. Americans today, like Paleolithic men 15,000 years ago, still worship a Poisonous Placenta in the form of a dangerous Great Bear, filling our political cartoons with its pictures and devoting much of our energies to its killing—only now, it is a Russian bear who we are hunting. We elect leaders and hope they have the power to hold off the dangerous beast— which is why America has never gone to war in the first year of any president's term.[1] But the growing pollution of national life-blood is irresistible, the collapse of group defenses inevitable, and national sacrifice and rebirth painful. As Hitler said to an aide on the eve of his invasion of Poland, as they both, in a trance-like state, watched the red glow of the northern lights, "This looks like lots of blood. This time things won't go without force."[2]

Since all our "greatest" leaders—from Caesar and Napoleon to Church-ill and Roosevelt—were sacrificial priests with the blood of millions on their hands, we must take very seriously this central ritual, as seriously as, say, the Aztecs took *their* periodic ritual sacrifice of youth to their god. When our magazines show an America bristling with atomic missiles pointed at a Rus-sian bear, a psychohistorian must learn to take the image as an accurate ren-dering of what current American group-fantasy *feels* like.

Recognizing that unconscious group-fantasies build the groundwork for wars, I have proposed a Nuclear Tensions Monitoring Center as a means of better understanding and preventing a future nuclear holocaust (deMause, in press).

The purpose of a Monitoring Center would be to describe, measure, and publicize the increases in violent group-fantasies in each of the nuclear na-tions and give continuous psychological help in decreasing nuclear tensions. This, I believe, could begin to apply our knowledge of the unconscious sources of human aggression by making the unconscious conscious. Perhaps then we might escape the trap of periodic ritual sacrifice, avoid future ca-tastrophes and allow better understanding to break the recurring cycle of war.

---

[1]This is true of all of America's major wars. The two that started soonest after the be-ginning of the new presidency were minor wars: the Mexican and the Spanish-Amer-ican: both started 14 months after the elections, of Polk and McKinley, respectively. Note that even though the Civil War officially began immediately *after* the election of Lincoln, in fact, it was his election (as war leader) that *confirmed* the war, which was the solution to the unresolved "collapse" phase of the previous administration.

[2]Cited in John Lukacs, *The Last European War: September 1939—December 1941*. Garden City, NY: Anchor Press, 1976, p. 45. My thanks to David Beisel for this reference.

REFERENCES

Annes, L. F. (1978). *The child before birth.* Ithaca: Cornell University Press.

CBS-TV (1977). *The miracle months.* March 16, 8:00 p.m. EST.

Child at risk: A report of the Standing Senate Committee on Health, Welfare and Science (1980). Quebec: Canadian Government Publishing Center.

Cohen, J. (1980). Structural consequences of psychic-trauma: A new look at 'Beyond the Pleasure Principle.' *International Journal of Psycho-Analysis, 61,* 421–432.

deMause, L. (1975). *The new psychohistory.* New York: Psychohistory Press.

deMause, L. (1976). The formation of the American personality through psychospeciation. *Journal of Psychohistory, 4,* 1–30.

deMause, L. (1977a). The psychogenic theory of history. *Journal of Psychohistory, 4,* 253–267.

deMause, L. (1977b). Jimmy Carter and American fantasy. In L. deMause & H. Ebel (Eds.), *Jimmy Carter and American fantasy.* New York: Psychohistory Press.

deMause, L. (1979). Historical group-fantasies. *Journal of Psychohistory, 7,* 1–70.

deMause, L. (1982). *Foundations of psychohistory.* New York: Creative Roots.

deMause, L. (1984). *Reagan's America.* New York: Creative Roots.

deMause, L. (in press). A proposal for a nuclear tensions monitoring center. *Journal of Psychohistory.*

Eliade, M. (1959). *The sacred and the profane: The nature of religions.* New York: Harcourt, Brace, Jovanovich.

Emde, R. H. & Robinson, R. (1979). The first two months: Recent research in developmental psychobiology and the changing view of the newborn. In J. Noshpitz (Ed.), *Basic handbook of child psychiatry,* Vol. 1. New York: Basic Books, p. 72.

Feher, E. (1980). *The psychology of birth.* London: Souvenir Press.

Ferguson, M. (1977). Using altered states of conscious to improve recall. *Quest, 1,* 123.

Greenacre, P. (1967). The influence of infantile trauma on genetic patterns. Ins. Furst (Ed.), *Psychic trauma.* New York: Basic Books.

Grof, S. (1975). *Realms of the human unconscious: Observations from LSD research.* New York: Viking Press. There is a good summary in his Perinatal roots of wars, totalitarianism and revolutions: Observations from LSD research. *Journal of Psychohistory, 4,* 269–308.

Hall, C. S. (1967). Prenatal and birth experiences in dreams. *Psychoanalytic Review, 54,* 157–174.

Harbison, R. D. (Ed.). (1975). *Perinatal addiction.* New York: Spectrum Publications.

Hubert, H. & Maress, M. (1964). *Sacrifice: Its nature and function.* Chicago:

University of Chicago Press, p. 21.

Ingelman-Sundberg, A. & Wirsen, C. (1965). *A child is Born*. New York: Dell.

Janov, A. (1973). *The feeling child*. New York: Simon and Schuster.

Kelsey, D. (1953). Fantasies of birth and prenatal experiences recovered from patients undergoing hypmoanalysis. *Journal of Mental Science, 99,* 216–223.

Krystal, H. (Ed.). (1968). *Massive psychic trauma*. New York; Internationl Universities Press.

Lamorisse, A. (1956). *The red balloon,* a film. Paris: Films Montsouris.

Lawson, A. (1984). Perinatal imagery in UFO abduction reports. *Journal of Psychohistory, 12,* 211–239.

Lewis, Peter H. (August 26, 1984). What's on babies' minds when they come into the world? *New York Times,* p. 8E.

Liley, A. W. (1972). The foetus as a personality. *Australian and New Zealand Journal of Psychiatry, 6,* 103.

Lloyd-Still, J. D. (Ed.). (1976). *Malnutrition and intellectual development*. Littleton, Mass.: Publishing Sciences Group.

Norwood, C. (1980). *At highest risk: Environmental hazards to young and unborn children*. New York: McGraw-Hill.

Otto, R. (1923). *The idea of the holy* (J. W. Harvey, trans.). London: Oxford University Press.

Peterfreund, E. (1971). *Information, systems, and psychoanalysis*. New York: International Universities Press, p. 74.

Rowan, J. (Ed.) (1978). *The undivided self: An introduction to primal integration*. London: Center for the Whole Person.

Rugh, R. & Shettles, L. B. (1971). *From conception to birth: The drama of life's beginnings*. New York: Harper & Row.

Scott, D. H. (1971). The child's hazards *in-utero*. In J. G. Howells (Ed.) *Modern perspectives in international child psychiatry*. New York: Brunner/Mazel, pp. 19–60.

Seligman, C. G. & Murray, M. A. (1911). Notes upon an early Egyptian standard. *Man, 11,* 165–171.

Sotag, L. (1944). Difference in modifiability of fetal behavior and physiology, *Psychosomatic Medicine, 6,* 151–154.

Sontag, L. (1965). Implications of fetal behavior and environment for adult personalities. *Annals of the New York Academy of Sciences, 134,* 782–786.

Spielberg, S. (1982a). *E.T. The Extra-Terrestrial,* a film.

Spielberg, S. (1982b). *Poltergeist,* a film.

Stevenson, R. E. (1977). *The fetus and newly born infant: Influences of the prenatal environment* (2nd ed.). St. Louis: C. V. Mosby.

Verny, T. R. (1982. *The psychic life of the unborn*. Paper given at the Fifth World Congress of Psycho-Somatic Obstetrics and Gynecology, Rome.

Chapter 6

HOW WE BECAME (IN) HUMAN

Gerard G. Neuman

This chapter deals with the origin and development toward the new species "human," not "Homo sapiens." It is an interpretive internal, rather than applicative, external account. It is not still another account of how we became an Ape Man from a Man Ape, then moved to *Homo habilis,* to *Homo erectus,* to Neanderthal Man, to Cro-Magnon Man, and then into history, mostly seen in terms of our physical properties and surviving implements. Finding the missing links through integrating archeological artifacts with the increasing knowledge of physical anthropology has already been done many times. After all, bones and stones survive, evidence for feeling, thinking and behavior in general have to be inferred.

We will attempt something that has not been systematically done thus far, something the more orthodox archeologist may consider even hazier and softer than the conclusions now possible from the limited physical history of man. We will try to use the background of the personality sciences to throw light on the inner man and woman.

What is the evidence for the validity of the assertions we will be making? First, we will draw on the interpretation of behavior as it can be deduced from the artifacts and from the continuing residues as still observed in present behavior and thought, as well as thoughts, feelings, and behaviors as expressed in the altered states of consciousness—dreams, illusions, delusions, and many forms of fantasy life. Second, the evidence as it exists in the content of rituals, myths, fairy tales, etc., which bear witness to times seemingly left behind by the advance of overt culture and civilization. Our method will be based on skills developed from the analysis of observation of behavior, psychological depth analysis, and skills developed in the clinical performance of dynamic depth psychology.

Australopithecus (circa 5 to 2 1/2 million B.C.)

There are many places to localize the origins of the human species. Some scientists believe that the change in dental formation toward the human dentition, as evidenced by the jaw of *Ramapithecus,* who lived more than 15 million years ago, and the possibility of erect bipedality, is a good beginning. I believe that all we learn from that fact is that nature prepared the hominoid to survive the shift from tree to savannah by giving him the ability to chew more grain and hard vegetarian items as he lost the good supply of plants and fruit from the trees. The climate was becoming colder and the trees could not support as many apes. Possibly, additional finds may make other conclusions possible.

There are a number of theories as to how and why we split from the simian adjustment. A number of researchers believe we came off the trees because the opportunities on the land were seductive to this group of the population. I do not find this likely, as we were awkward on two feet, had no tools as yet for our freed arms, and did not have a larger brain than any other apes (approx. 450 to 550 cc). It is my belief that it was the weakest of the apes who had to become the strongest to survive the natural disaster of the defoliation of the trees. Even the baboon, who wanders far away from the tree by day, comes back at night to a fallen tree, the "sleeping tree," which gives no real, but seemingly nostalgic, protection at night. (Is this instinctually repetitive "nostalgia" a forerunner for the later symbolic constructions when a further development of the upper cortex makes this possible?)

Giving up the tree when we committed ourselves to try our luck in the savannah may have been a necessary, but certainly a very courageous, decision on our part. We are the only simian species which made this definitive commitment, and I, as a descendant, am proud that my forebears decided to stand on their own two feet, look the uncertain world horizontally in the eye, and change our whole physique to obtain this primeval sense of self-confidence. We became our own walking tree, as it were, by providing our own food and protection. It is what some people would call courage, and other more fearful types, sheer madness.

Why did we choose to become bipedal, possibly 10 to 15 million years ago? So far, there are many guesses. The most often mentioned are:

1. That we could look over the tall grass of the savannah and have a better visual field; and
2. That we wanted to have free hands to carry tools and bring food back to our families.

None of these answers really satisfies me. How tall is tall for the grass of the savannah? Did the grass stop growing when it reached our eye level, which at that time was not much more than one meter? As far as tools go, there is no evidence of our carrying tools any earlier than about 2 million years ago, when we had walked on two feet for a very long time. Neither is there any evidence that we carried food to our families at that early date. (We have to wait for *Homo habilis* or *Homo erectus* a few million years down the line before we can reasonably assume this.)

To return again to the question: Why the upright stance? A few years ago, when I had dinner with a group of rather eminent archeologists, we came to talk about Lucy, recently discovered by Johanson (1981). I ventured the opinion that Lucy walked erect in order to keep things in perspective. Most everybody laughed, thinking this was a nice dinner joke. They still don't think that I really meant it. It is my opinion that the various early bipedal forms of *Australopithecus* discovered a new principle of hunting, gathering food and defending themselves against predators, in other words, to have a new look at the world as it existed for them at that time. Focused vision had been specialized earlier; smell, the major element of land-living mammals, had been largely lost as not too useful away from the ground; sensitive hearing, and color, and focused vision had been retained. Most of the ground animals use moment-to-moment scent in hunting and stalking animals. We introduced the principle of flexible visual holding in the distance, an element that made all later conjectural thought, preopositional language, and higher mathematics possible. Even the most advanced chimps and gorillas to whom we have taught language have not been able to develop conjectural or prepositional speech or thought processes. They are tied to the immediate object. We, as humans, will continue to improve the manipulation and handling of distant objects, either directly or, later on, more abstractly and symbolically.

What happened to us emotionally at that time? We probably became very angry at having lost the security of the tree, the security of a more stable environment as we had known it, as well as the even more basic fact, namely, that to nurse we had to be specially held by mother, and as sitting or walking erect made the distance between lap and breast longer, nursing became more strenuous. Mother had to walk to keep up with the group, which is fine for the group, but not always kind to the infant. What did we do with the anger? At first, starting as vegetarians, we began catching and eating small animals. Here, we needed the anger to help us keep moving, and to help us in killing the other moving things which did not wait for us as roots and small insects did. We began to almost harness this, as yet, poorly integrated rage. The rage had to be newly developed or, through a generational process of neoteny, redeveloped (Gould 1977). The monkeys in the trees largely had lost the predatory sense of rage.

We had to go back into our philogenetic history to reach the time of the hunting animals within us to be able to learn from the predators, who were also our threat in the open. There were the hyenas, leopards, lions, and wild dogs. We rather quickly learned that if we wanted to survive, we had to learn especially from the hyenas and dogs, as they hunted in groups. The lions and leopards had little to teach us outside of constant alertness and awareness of the far horizons around us. As our eyes and somewhat inferior ears gave us no real protection at night, we learned to avoid the preferred hunting time of the larger canines.

There developed a balance between the experienced rage and the necessary availability of it for handling the ecological situation with so little protection. Later on, as we developed weapons and tools, this oversupply of adrenaline for fight and flight would either be externalized into homicide, wars, and lesser forms of brutality, or internalized into all our psychosomatic illnesses and our various forms of psychological deviations. It is this precipitously acquired modality of over-aggression, which, since the days of *Australopithecus*, we have never been able to control. In the prehistory of ontology, we also find the origin of the new personality formation pre-natally, and at birth or in early childhood we experience the trauma more consciously, but it does not originate there, as past personality theories try to make us believe. We recently have begun to extend the understanding of human experience into the womb (Grof, 1975; Verny, 1982; deMause, 1982). There is no question that initial traces of love and rage exist there. Our therapeutic skills need to creatively develop means of reaching these early pre-object phenomena, of moving the traces into sensate, perceptual channels, almost custom-made for each individual, if we want to transform the over-aggression into helpful energy. It is this restitutional transformation which occupies each of us all our lifetime and becomes the central problem of the activities of the educator and the treating therapist.

But back to our ape-man *Australopithecus*, whom we still do not have to claim as one of us, if the killing aggression frightens us. If so, we are in good company. The most creative of archeologists studying early man, Raymond Dart (1959), ran into this problem from 1925 on, when, after finding the skull of the Taungs baby, he developed increasing evidence that *Australopithecus* (as he named that humanoid creature of better than two million years ago) was an adept killer of other animals, baboons, and, later, fellow-humanoids, as well, relying on aggressive skills which allowed us to survive. Even though he was endorsed by the two grandfathers of prehistorical research, Breuil (1952) and Washburn (1960), many scientists still preferred to place this aggression on hyenas and leopards, to keep our forebears and, by extension, ourselves, a "moral" species.

From various locations in South Africa, Taungs, Sterkfontein, and Makapansgat, Dart exhibited 42 skulls of baboons, 64 percent of which had been fractured by blows from the front. All but two had received blows from the left side, indicating that *Australopithecus* was lateralized in the human direction. As we developed more courage and strength, attacks usually were made face to face. More important, the deadly hits were all highly accurate. The bones used as weapons were generally the thigh and arm bones of the antelope, one of the preferred weapons derived from previously killed animals for their developing meat-eating diets. The favorite dessert later on became the brains of infant baboons, later humanoids, "as the fragile, porcelain-thin skulls of the infant were emptied of the brains and then crushed in the hand and thrown aside as a human child might throw away a breakfast eggshell." (Dart, 1959). Adult skulls were crushed impatiently with hammer blows to get to the brain as quickly as possible. There were not just a few, but many finds of such crushed skulls in Africa and, as history went on, all over the then populated world, including Asia and then into the South Sea Islands. One example can be seen in Figure 6–1.

The skulls were crushed quickly and impulsively. At that time, defense against our aggression was not only not needed, but conversely, we needed the availability of that aggression to hold our own. We could not afford to wait to analyze our possible sense of paranoia before attacking to kill since, as the saying goes, "Even the paranoid sometimes has enemies," and many a predator that we had possibly deprived of his carrion might have been just that. Our earliest social groups may not have been too different from the hyenas as we observed their successful survival. Here, we are completely guessing, as there is no way of knowing what the human group was like, not having any even semi-permanent living and butchering areas. Later (400,000 B.C.), as we get to *Homo erectus*, we seem to resemble more the group arrangement of the wild dogs in our hunting groups.

There is one important observation we can make looking at the baboons, the one simian group that dared to leave the immediate environment of the tree. The groups that dare to go further build more of a male-female-children grouping, as the female needs more direct protection (Campbell, 1979, p. 480). Mary Leakey (1979) at Laetoli in Tanzania found footprints of adults and children who followed in the adult footsteps dated about 3 1/2 million years ago. We will be more certain when we reach *Homo habilis* at about 2 million years ago. We know that the male did not share food out of sheer altruism. Most of the gathering was done by the female and their patient finds provided the staple for the times of unsuccessful hunting for meat. So, if you wanted to survive as a male, it was a more than even exchange.

Dart (1959) shows us that before we had stone tools, there was a bone culture where we produced the necessary tools of double-ended clubs, daggers, scrapers, and other split bones to kill and cut the tendons of the prey. In Makapansgat, he found 369 lower jaws (mandibles) of antelopes used as scrapers, and 336 double ridged lower ends of upper arm bones. He found an uncountable number of prepared little knife-like blades. The similarity of form definitely suggests some preplanning of a higher form than now practiced by chimpanzees and higher apes. It took present day researchers eight hours to make bone tools needed by *Australopithecus,* so it must have taken our forebears days, showing more patience than we would assume. It suggests a precision grip of the right hand and the ability to manipulate objects at a distance, expanding on the brain power achieved through bipedal "perspective." Remember, we had committed ourselves to ground living and to

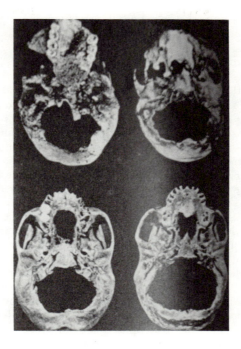

Figure 6–1. Skulls which have been broken at the base in order to extract and eat the brains. (From J. Jellinek, *The Pictorial Encyclopedia of the Evolution of Man*, Hamlyn Publishing Group, Ltd., 1975.)

finding other ways of frightening away enemies than by showing our canines. Those had to be sacrificed to horizontally chewing grains and pulp. We did not give up using our screaming vocal cords while showing clubs instead and remaining in a group.

It was probably at that time that we became addicted to flesh eating, especially in times of drought. At that time, there were at least two groups of *Australopithecus*. One remained near the trees and remained vegetarian. Interestingly, they were more robust and were, therefore, later named *Australopithecus robustus*. This group died out. Possibly he was too specialized and when the drought finally caught up with him, he could not survive, or possibly we, more accomplished and more intelligent meat eaters, ate him, as we progressed beyond him. The existence of *robustus* in sites with many animal bones raises this suspicion, since they were not meat eaters. We were later named *Australopithicus gracile* (more lightly built), preferred meat, and flexibly moved on (Gowlett, 1984, pp. 41–42). It is worth repeating that in those days, we had to become convinced killers without the slightest doubts if we were to survive. Without a more permanent homesite, the injured or the doubtful fell by the wayside.

Homo habilis (circa 2½ to 1½ million B.C.)

We meet a different man at Olduvai, the archeological site explored by Louis and Mary Leakey (1971). A time span from 1.8 million to 700,000 B.C. has elapsed. *Homo habilis,* as they named their find, had changed physically from *Australopithecus,* moving in all respects into a more human form. A circle of stones was found about four meters across, suggesting fundaments of a shelter. An increased selection of tools, including choppers, spheroids, discoids, polyhedrons, and various forms of scrapers made from stone, was carried to the site from a distance of up to 10 to 15 kilometers (Gowlett, 1984, pp. 42–43). The cranial capacity of *Homo habilis* had advanced from 500 cc of the higher ape, gorilla or *Australopithecus* to under 700 cc. We had grown in size, though the increase is not that spectacular and can possibly be accounted for by sheer learning from increased hunting techniques and tool manufacture and use. At least, this is what the "boy scout" prehistorian in us would like to believe—a nice, orderly increase based on academic-like learning.

This, however, was not to be. Between *Homo habilis* and *Homo erectus* in a matter of less than a million years, we find a rise from 650 cc to 950 cc, and from *erectus* to Neanderthal man, in less than half a million years, a rise from 950 cc to 1350 cc. This increase in brain mass is greater than any change in biology observed for any evolving species and has not found any good explanation by anyone.

In addition, there are also other changes that have not found any convincing explanation.

1. The loss of our fur. Many explanations have been put forward, based on the idea of providing better ventilation or better personal hygiene. Think for a moment: is our own man-made clothing really superior to the fur that nature gives animals as a matter of course?

2. The loss of *estrus,* the natural control of population in every animal group. This has created serious problems for the human species, as the overhanging threat of the population explosion is almost as great as the threat of the atom bomb.

3. The high degree of mental disorder, unmatched by any animal species, as well as our inability to gain control of our aggression.

Although it cannot be proven easily by human experimentation, it is my assumption that our change to meat eating and our increased addiction to eating brains, from early man through the Neanderthal era, when it began to diminish, was the basic cause of all these changes. A major gland in the structure of the brain is the pituitary gland, often called the master gland. It is related to the growth of body hair, sexuality (especially female menstrual cycles), and overall growth and strength. In addition to the raw warm brain tasting good to early man, he also felt that it increased his sex drive and his strength. His experience showed him that eating the brains of wise, older men could increase his intelligence, courage, and other virtues ascribed to the experienced leaders. He also learned that his memory was strengthened, giving him greater efficiency in the necessary tool making and hunting techniques. In his emotional development, he had reached what we now call the cannibalistic stage of the infant, where everything important is taken in orally and evaluated orally. After that evaluation, objects begin to develop some constancy for us.

Most students of these cannibalistic procedures, now completely unacceptable to us even if admitted at all, retreat into describing it as ritual cannibalism, a *pro forma* procedure arising from early wishes. Addictions do not begin on a symbolic basis, however. Just as meat eating became more addictive during periods of drought, so brains became more desirable as more individuals became head hunters. The earliest hunters may have fallen into the habit when the carrion left over for them as scavengers only contained the skull, too difficult for an already satiated predatory animal to open. We had bones to smash skulls and limber fingers to scoop out the contents.

We now associate addiction with orality. We humans are the only species with innumerable addictions, be they to the widely known alcohol, food, nicotine and drugs, or to the derivatives, such as workaholism, pornography, or other deviate habits. In fact, there are very few individuals who do not have some addiction.

Experiments with worms and other lower forms have shown that intelligence and memory can be transferred from one individual to another by the feeding of brains. One very cynical individual recently thought he was making a joke when he said that the problems in our educational system could be solved by feeding the brains of the teachers to the students, rather than exposing them to all those years of misery.

To summarize, the progress of our species, which was already moving at too fast a rate, was further accelerated to a point where we fell all over ourselves and began to reap the harmful effects. We cannot evaluate all the internal chemical changes produced by the increase of pituitary activity, but we do know of two observable changes related to the increased size of the head. First, as the brain size increased faster than the skull, all the convolutions of the brain still did not solve the problem for many, and either the top of the head did not find closure or, in other instances, holes were drilled to create space.

Second, for the whole species, birth became much more difficult as the birth canal could not be enlarged if we wanted to continue on a bipedal basis. Birth had to occur within nine months, which is actually too early for our species. The infants who are lucky to be born late usually gain from the extra time in the womb. As it is, 40 percent of what we would normally experience inside the womb is being externalized at a time when we are most dependent and can least afford it. As the birth experience is made more difficult for both mother and infant, rage increases for both, to be carried from generation to generation. Theorists who observe wars breaking out almost every 20 years, and who connect outbreaks of war with birth, might find this increased rage as part of the fuel of the cycle. Although we joke today about "head shrinkers" in our culture, tribes in the South Pacific and the Guineas, often still practicing cannibalism, take this procedure very seriously.

Homo Erectus (circa 1½ million to 100,000 B.C.)

Let us now look at *Homo erectus* with a brain size of between 775 cc and 1325 cc. For many of us, his stage represents the beginning stages of human being. We find beginning defense systems and most of all, the control of fire, which for the first time allowed us to control some basic elements in nature. We improved hunting considerably, as we had learned to trap animals, but we also began to cook certain grains, which had previously been poisonous and now became edible. Other foods became chewable.

Fire helped us to hunt animals of any size, though it took a long time to learn to make fire. Patience was required to keep a fire going as long as possible, until we learned to make fire any time we wanted to, and patience did not come easily to us at that time.

Having learned to control the flame (usually considered an oral object as it consumes things), we learned to control other aspects of oral rage and moved slowly into an early anal defense system.

After organizing and executing a big hunt, the danger existed that we would be so hungry that we would attack our fellow hunters before dividing the game. Therefore, controls were set up by creating seven or eight parallel sites, where we would evenly divide the largest chunks of the elephant, the deer, or whatever else we had hunted (Freeman, 1980). The equal space between the sites was the first artificial concrete control in history. (This ritual of balance was also found in the symmetry of the Acheulean hand axe which had begun to come into use at that time.)

We would then take the large chunks of meat to smaller sites, again equally spaced. Thus, the butchering was done in concrete step changes, making the use of the game more rational for all concerned, while satisfying our hunger.

The last large site had a fireplace and seemed to be used as the first planned community gathering, where, around the fire, we would communicate something that had just recently occurred, possibly at the hunt. It had to be recent, as our memory power was probably only equal to that of a one-, or at best, two-year-old. Our communication, still not eloquent enough to deal with things not immediate, might have taken the form of demonstrating the activity in actual motion, which would, in later times, be ritualized into more stable dance forms. At that community site were found tools and flakes of tool making, indicating that after the stomach was full and the need for human companionship satisfied, possible planning for the next hunt could begin. Again, this would be a long step forward toward the development of rational thinking. This new, beginning development of planful thinking served both the purpose of acting defensively to mitigate the overactive anxious limbic system, as well as fulfilling fragmentary functions of planning for the future with the help of the newly enlarged frontal lobes of the brain.

It was at this time that we developed, for the first time, a symbolic expression of the number three, as the immediate present shrank to an instant and made room for the perception of a past and a future, small as these new time zones had to be. The past allowed for the earliest beginnings of a culture and the future, for the creation of a primitive spiritual world. The smoke from the fire, for example, would go to a heaven. Later, as we would be able to "give" a formed object, we would make a "burnt sacrificial offering" at a more spiritual stone, now called altar, and, as anal defenses took hold, the "awful" would take both the split meanings of the "terrible" and the "sacred." Most languages still have the two roots for the same adjective/noun. The uncontrolled cannibalistic act with the new helpful defense maneuver of a reaction formation could then be acted out in a more ritualistic fashion. Not only did this maneuver make it more acceptable, it also offered the basis for the development of the "most holy" in many future religions.

For *Homo erectus,* many aspects of human behavior began to sprout almost simultaneously. He established partially permanent caves, where he returned for his stay of three to six months of the year. He left for hunting seasons, probably also coinciding with the annoyance of the flies, which became bigger, more numerous, and more bothersome. The very large species of flies were attracted to the camp by the, as yet, minimal sanitary conditions. With the capability of establishing anal defenses, however, mothers began to teach the young to find separate places for elimination, and thus some beginning hygienic principles were established. The monkey or ape in the trees never had to worry about excreting, and the wandering bipedal Man-Ape also had an easier time with it. Freud explained that the major frustration for the young child is to be forced to adjust to adult human civilization. As a species, we had the same problem, beginning with the time of *Homo erectus.* The frustration had to be released into aggressive outbursts, and this may be one of the reasons why the camps remained only semi-permanent, although the peripatetic hunter probably gave realistic hunting reasons to his spouse, as many a hunting or fishing husband does today.

There were other changes in the family as well. As mothers were gathering at the environs of some general area, they could bed down their infants for very short spans of time, which, to the infant, must have seemed like an eternity. It moved them to keep calling on mother, out of which call early vocal mother-child communication developed, leading to lullabies and early speech. Finer motor controls, as developed in concert with other areas of behavior, made the beginning of a more structured speech possible. It is very unlikely that the linguistic structure described by Chomsky (1964) existed before *Homo erectus*.

Early speech and early toilet-training established the earliest forms of structure. As provided by mother, they helped secure more firm boundaries around objects, replacing the earlier part objects with the apprehension of the whole object. Bipolar concepts of the anal level became more firmly established. A division into concepts of "we" and "they" allowed for a more ordered energy flow and better definition of love and hate, pleasant and unpleasant, male and female, life and death, etc. *Homo habilis* had been able to think in classes of objects, but only on a momentary, concrete basis. Beginning abstractions now became possible.

The *we and they*, probably arising out of and defending against the fear of maternal incorporation, may have allowed exogomous spouse choices, (initially through the hunting and stealing of the prospective spouse), thereby establishing an initial defense against incest. Communication on a higher than instinct level set more defined distances between them, but by increased empathy capacity also brought people closer. Mankind had started to establish its first internal emotional defense structure. As the forces of instinct and aggression still had to be overly strong for a still precarious existence, however, the defenses also still had to match them. The superego forces fighting off the instinct became so overpowering that the cure became worse than the disease. At the end of Neanderthal time, approximately 300,000–400,000 years later, that group became extinct without any reasonable explanation, except perhaps the one just given. At this level of *Homo erectus*, we are still at the early anal level, where problems are solved, such as they are, on a realistic, generally uncreative, and largely unempathic level. The earliest form of empathy appeared in the form of the maternal response to the infant's cry for attention.

This may be a good time to sketch a bit of the developing brain structure as estimated by Kochetkova (1978), a Russian paleoneurologist, based on the knowledge gained from endocasts made in Russia and in this country, primarily by Ralph Holloway (1979). (Brains as such are not preserved in archeological sites, while skulls are.) *Australopithecus*, during his long existence, had changed his brain only slightly, moving into the *homonid* direction by showing a slight enlargement of the frontal lobe, which is man's proudest part of the thinking apparatus. As mentioned earlier, clearly defined differences not only in brain mass but also in organization can be seen between *Homo habilis* and *Homo erectus*, and especially were obvious between early and late forms of *Homo erectus*. Reasons for this abnormal growth were discussed earlier. The areas of growth cover the inferoparietal and temperoparieto-occipital subregions of the modern human, which, thereby, become the philogenetically newest areas of the brain. The inferoparietal subregion (being uniquely human) integrates the auditory, visual, and tactile receptors. This allows for the implementation of stereognosis, of cause and effect relationships, comprehension of one's own speech as well as that of others, and later of graphics, writing, and calculations.

The inferoparietal lobe comprises no more than 4 percent of the cortex in the ape, but it takes 8 percent in the human (Kochetkova, 1978). Chimpanzees, for instance, cannot associate thoughts with events or have an independent conception of the shape of an object. This is why the abstract idea of the shape of a future tool was such an achievement for early man. *Homo erectus* with his Acheulean hand axe had achieved this. It is unfortunate that we do not have a complete enough skull between *Australopithecus* and *erectus* to more clearly define the origin of Area 45 ("Broca's area"), an area necessary for speech. We are quite certain, however, that although limited in making certain vowel sounds, Neanderthal man had some form of human speech beyond the earlier only emotionally based exclamations and sign-language. As the "integrative" areas of the brain develop, so the occipital region of the brain (controlling vision) decreases throughout anthropogenesis, and increasingly so at the end of the Paleolithic era. Even the Babylonians were able to see better than we do. (When I count the number of people wearing glasses now, I wonder whether present man was created below what we call the normal 20-20 vision, or whether the shrinkage of the occipital lobe is going on before or behind our very eyes.)

The frontal lobe, which connects into all parts of the brain, makes past, present and future, planning, abstracting, and understanding of the inner man possible.

On the whole, then, in the developing human brain there is a decrease of growth rate in areas related to the mere sensory perception of the world, but an increase in areas related to certain motor functions such as the hand, and an intensified development of regions that implement highly organized forms of "rational" behavior. (Unfortunately, due to the necessary self-protection caused by the speeded up evolutionary demands, they seem to be either preponderately blocked or overstimulated by activities of the lower brain center, rather than easily integrated with them.)

The complex form of cognitive integration that takes place is primarily a function of the prefrontal area of the brain with the simultaneous participation of the posterior parieto-temporal and the occipital regions. Analysis and synthesis of signals (primarily done by the left hemisphere) represent the most advanced, the tertiary areas of the cortex, Luria's areas of integration (Luria, 1973); signals that have already undergone multiple processing in the primary and secondary zones.

In summary, we can say that *Australopithecus* had mental processes and a sense of awareness not much above an ape. He was not capable of reflecting on causal relationships between objects or their origins. He did have the ability to form general ideas.

Homo erectus had developed an understanding of the final ideal shape of his tool and of the plan for its realization. A constant flexible comparison between the planned and the actual had been achieved. He had also developed an emotional defense system, which, to a large degree, controlled outburst of overwhelming oral rage, allowing for more balanced human functioning in all areas and serving as an emotional plateau from which progress to the next stage, the Mousterian or Neanderthal man became possible.

Neanderthal (circa 150,000 to 40,000 B.C.)

Neanderthal man has been underestimated ever since he was named and identified. It is likely that we sensed he had come too close to being us, for us to accept him as a relative. He was for a long time seen as a bent-over brute who could fill the part of the awkward unfeeling animal-like hybrid of a late Saturday night B movie. Part of this characterization is correct, but much of it is not. The part that is correct is related to a man whose emotions are not as yet refined, who, in his increased sensation of anxiety, was, in today's perception, highly paranoid, and who, at even slight provocation, would just as soon attack and kill as say "Good morning." This very fact, that his compulsive and fantasy defenses became insufficient as his general sense of awareness grew, is likely to have finally contributed to his mysterious demise.

On the positive side, generally not that well understood, are assets that place him at the beginning of "homo sapiens." He was in control of his expected life experience as a family man, hunter and gatherer, a beginning social structuralist of his group, and a beginning culture bearer in creating the first recognizable religious or at least spiritual rituals. In his secular life, he sewed clothing, well fitting and warm enough to allow him to live in areas covered by ice and snow during much of the year, and to build dwellings which could withstand most of the storms and adversities in, at times, very inclement climate. His assortment of arms was effective enough to hunt any type of animal he desired. He relied heavily on spears, which he was able to use in close combat as well as a projectile.

In his emotional development, we know that he was a heavy dreamer, a fearful dreamer. In his burial rituals he cut off the feet of his dead, or at least bound them, so that they could not leave their graves and haunt him at night. On the top of the burial sites, Neanderthalers would put a large grave stone, often interpreted as a marker, but in reality more as a safeguard against the grave opening at night and allowing the dead to haunt the killer or self-accused killer. Markers were not needed by a man who could tell from every footprint and other natural signs the total identity of the hunted originator and its detailed relationship to the overall territory, with which he, the hunter, was intuitively familiar.

Living in a spirit world, however, his dreams became the origin of his magic world, where his fearfully interpreted thunder and storm became bad omens; where his language, still largely based on the spontaneous emotional expression of his limbic system, produced exclamations of curses and, later possibly, prayers. It produced a world of magic connections now associated with the analogical level of thinking, related to the unconscious pre-conscious. The poorly defined internal boundaries would put him in the class in today's diagnosis of personality, as borderline at best. His less-than-successful attempts to gain control over his fears are seen, for instance, in his division of work and living areas, which he kept in separateness with phobic intensity (Freeman, 1980). The children's game of jumping on one foot from square to square while avoiding stepping on even one crack, and the jingles sung while jumping, are remindful of those days.

Let us go through some of the evidence for these observations. They come from the analysis of general archeological artifacts assigned by dating to these times, of burial rituals, of the bear cult, and of the finds in a number of special sites such as La Ferrassie and Shanider. Neanderthal man, to his detriment, did not produce any art or other more complex creative expression of his inner world as a means of externalizing his inner tension. On a beginning level of externalization, it is likely that he painted his face and body for magical purposes and or to magically frighten the hunted or, at times, feared animal. As the paint is a forerunner of the mask, it can conceivably be considered a forerunner of art. Another transitional forerunner: some baton-like sticks were found, which probably represented more of a conversion of fecal or penile forms, rather than serving any practical purpose. There is the likelihood of reverence being paid to elders who had special skills. We have some guesses as to the use of medicine men or shamans, which we will discuss later in relation to the finds at Shanidar.

Evidence of cannibalism appeared in numerous sites. The mutilated remains of 20 Neanderthals—men, women and children—were found at the site of Krapina in Yugoslavia, skulls smashed into fragments, limb bones split sideways for the marrow (Freeman, 1980). Another 20 similarly mutilated individuals were found in the cave of Hortus in France. These remains were found among other animal bones and food refuse, indicating that no distinction was made between human meat and that of bison and reindeer (Garn, 1971). Within the Neanderthal culture, we find both compulsive cannibalism and ritual cannibalism, showing the beginning institutionalization of a reaction formation. There is a hint of this ritualistic beginning on the banks of the Solo river in Java where 11 skulls were dug up and no other skeletal parts found except for two legs. In that site, thought to be more than 100,000 years old, the facial bones had been smashed off every skull and not a single jaw or tooth was left. The bodiless isolation of the skull and the opening at the *foramen magnum* is enough to hint at some ritual (Freeman, 1980).

Other bodiless skulls of Neanderthalers with the opening of the *foramen magnum* widened by hacking at bony edges with stone tools have been found in Europe as well as Asia.

The skull of a six-year-old child was found in a cave on the Rock of Gibraltar, brought there without any other human bones (Campbell, 1979). A similar find was made at Ehringsdorf, Germany (Campbell, 1979). Here, the jaw of an adult and the remains of a 10-year-old child were unearthed. The woman had been repeatedly clubbed on the forehead; her head was severed from the body to get at the brain.

A definite ritual setting of cannibalistic origins was unearthed at Monte Circeo (Gowlett, 1984), a limestone hill 55 miles south of Rome. Within a cave, a corridor opened into a chamber, where nobody had set foot for possibly more than 60,000 years. This chamber turned out to be a weird sanctuary. The explorers could see that a shallow trench had been scooped out of the ground leading to a space where a single skull with *foramen magnum* opening enlarged was surrounded by an oval ring of stones. This site is reminiscent of sites of present-day rituals of head hunting tribes in New Guinea, where, often when a child is born, a man from another tribe is killed. The father or male relative of the infant beheads the victim, extracts the brain, bakes it with sago, a starch made from the pith of a palm, before eating it. This is done in the belief that the newborn child cannot be given a name without the ritual treatment of the brain of a man whose name is known. The Neanderthal site at La Ferrassie of about 60,000 B.C. has some aspects of a similar ritual (Heim, 1976).

The dead body, as in most graves, is put into a fetal position, indicating some cyclic awareness of life (womb) and possible return after death. This grave site, however, as seen in Figure 6–2, has a very special significance in terms of emotional development. It gives evidence of the highest level Neanderthal man reached, bringing him almost to the brink of moving from the polarized diadic to the more triadic integrative level of thinking and feeling.

The rock shelter appears to have served as a family cemetery. Six members were buried there. These were a man, woman, two children about five years old, and two infants. The presumed parents (1 and 2 in the picture) had their heads almost contiguous, possibly indicating some beginning awareness of cognitive values. Graves 3 and 4 contained the children. The most important finding though is grave 5, where an infant, or possibly, a fe-

Figure 6–2. La Ferrassie, France. (From B. G. Campbell, *Humankind Emerging*, Little, Brown & Co., 1979.)

tus is buried. This grave is the top of a structure of triad grave formations, horizontally and vertically. This could not have been constructed accidentally because of the precision of the placement of each grave. It, therefore, must have had ritual meaning. It is likely that the whole family grave formation is related to the burial of the infant, which is most remarkable as only strong ritualistic needs, a strong denial of death and aggression, could have motivated this early man to erect such an elaborate construction for a mere infant, at a time when even adult human life was not held that dear. The repeated triangular arrangement symbolized the beginning of family awareness. It is not certain at what point fathers were connected with childbirth in man's understanding, but here, connections are made. The formation added up to nine graves in relation to the fetus or newborn. With their great awareness of the phases of the moon, there is little doubt that there was not only a recognition of three present members making a family, but also, the awareness of a nine-month gestation period connecting father's siring of the infant with mother's continued birth process. The infant grave also contained three beautiful flint tools and is covered by a stone representing an inverted breast formation.

Before we consider the Neanderthal who constructed these graves too far advanced in civilization, we must take at look at grave 6, where a six-year-old headless child is buried. The body and head are buried separately. This grave represents the whole range of their culture, from cannibalism to spiritual defenses.

What Neanderthal man has given us was the move from being controlled by forces outside of ourselves, to attempts at gaining control not only physically, but spiritually or by magic. To achieve this, sufficient intelligence was required to translate physical distances into cognitive abstractions and an awareness that emotional rewards could be achieved through rituals and prayer.

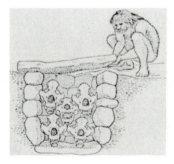

Figure 6–3. Bear skulls stacked in a pit. (From B. G. Campbell, *Humankind Emerging*, Little, Brown & Co., 1979.)

At the "Cave of the Witches" west of Genoa, Italy, deep in the cave, the hunters would throw clay pellets at a stalagmite which had as much of an animal shape as the Neanderthal's ability in art execution allowed. His aim was accurate; he did not need the exercise; what he needed was the good will of the "forces" that controlled the universe. We see here a ritual magical exercise to enhance his hunting success (Time-Life, 1973).

An even better example of his striving for power relates to his "bear cult." Here, we can see the origins of procedures which, in more recent time, developed into religious rituals we can more easily recognize. Emil Bächler, a German archeologist, excavated the cave of "Drachenloch," located 8,000 feet up in the Swiss Alps. Although the front section of the cave seemed to be a dwelling place, deep inside, it contained a cubical chest made of stones and holding seven bear skulls, all arranged with their muzzles facing the cave entrance (see Figure 6–3).

Still deeper in the cave were six bear skulls placed in niches in the wall (Maringer, 1960). Drachenloch is not unique. Other finds are extant from Regourdou in Southern France or Wildkirhli in another Alpine area. The now extinct *Ursus speleaus,* a larger form of a cave bear, was usually the owner of the cave that Neanderthal man wanted for his habitat. He would fill the cave with smoke just before the first rays of the sun would hit the entrance of the cave. When the bewildered bear, half-blinded by the smoke, would exit the cave, a few men with spears would attack him while others, waiting on top of the cave, would drop rocks on his head.

The erect bear (Figure 6–4) must have reminded him of a superhuman, possibly godlike, creature. He also made some connection between mascu-

Figure 6–4. Cave bear. (From B. G. Campbell, *Humankind Emerging,* Little, Brown & Co., 1979.)

linity and power as we often find the pubis bone of the penis preserved next to the bear skull. The more orderly stacking of skulls, as seen in Figure 6–3, was a forerunner for urns of human bones and skulls now found on some altars in churches in Spain and other countries.

Although we do not know what the actual rites were in Neanderthal days, we have some related material from some Lapp tribes in Siberia and the Ainus of Northern Japan. In some communities, bear cubs designated as holy are nursed by designated women in the community. When the bear reaches adolescence, he is killed, and after the fantasized transformation by the masters of the universe, is then worshiped as a god-like creature. The bear is chosen by certain Siberian tribes, as he is considered the mythical first human being, and they make profound apologies before killing him. Are we reminded of the ritual of the last meal offered to our criminals before execution?

Similarly, the Ainus treated the captured cub as an honored guest, later sacrificed in winter at the conclusion of a long ceremony, where Ainu men drank its blood and the presiding shaman prayed to the creator. The more primitive the mental organization of a tribe, the more overt and contiguous the killing, eating and restitutional ritual.

Conversely, the more advanced the mental structures, the more creative form can be attached to the restitutional ritual, leading to the later forms of art, education, and religion. The more anal part of organization, as represented by the organized stacking of the skulls, leads in its creative forms to better arms and machinery, technology, and science. Just as in forms of art, so in machinery and science, the underlying elements of aggression and control can be discerned. Technological advancement, thus, results in more differentiated and, alternately, more abstractly integrated transformation of basic aggression and its restitutional elements.

One other excavation of Neanderthal man needs to be mentioned, which is the work of Ralph Solecki (1971) at Shanidar in Northern Iraq, done in the 1950s. After nine years of excavation, he discovered the largest collection of Neanderthal skeletons ever found in one place, dating back to circa 60,000 B.C. The highlights of the findings are a controversial pollen analysis of soil from the grave, possibly that of a leader, which suggests the symbolic use of flowers. This is controversial, however, because some prehistorians doubt the purity of the pollen sample. Solecki inferred the capacity for mourning at the loss of a loved one. To me, the relation of the herbal pollen to the remains of an elder may point to the activity of a medicine man or his forerunner. Another skeleton of an old man, who had been injured from birth and could not have taken care of himself, suggested to Solecki that he had been cared for by the group. He was killed by a blow to the head, either accidentally by a rockfall, as Solecki suggests, or murdered by the group.

In summary, it appears that Neanderthal man has given us all the defensive prototypes based on the imaginary displacement of emotion from threatening objects learned first in his excessive dream activity, mainly produced by the right hemisphere of his brain. We find projection and beginning awareness of introjection, displacement, beginning reaction-formation, and the beginning of sublimatory or other restitutional activities. But, here is the rub. The fear of being aggressed against and, possibly even more, the guilt of his own aggression, became so overwhelming that his own obsessive defenses or paranoid symbolic or actual acts could not protect him from the overpowering anxiety. The lack of expressive art, the lack of a more differentiated religious system, and the, as yet, somewhat restricted language capabilities, left him inferior to the succeeding Cro-Magnon man, who, in all probability, helped him to become extinct, although there is no real evidence of that fact.

Cro-Magnon Man (circa 40,000 to 10,000 B.C.)

About 40,000 B.C., Cro-Magnon man (Homo sapiens) entered the scene, first discovered in Europe. No one is quite sure how, but reconstructions truly make him appear to be a real brother. In other words, if he sat next to us on the subway, he might look a little wilder than a very refined type of our species, but he would not evoke undue attention. He had lost the heavy ridges around his eyebrows and the protruding bump at the rear. He had exchanged his outthrust face, broad nose, and almost chinless jaw for the looks of modern man. He had developed into a hunter par excellence, had possibly added the bow and arrow to his already rich armamentarium, and, what surprises us most, lived in settlements which contained a well-designed special building for use as a work area. In that area, he produced, for example, rather sophisticated ceramics—clay objects such as Venuses (goddesses) and little animals, which he had the capacity to glaze in his kiln, a skill not found again until almost 2000 B.C. in Japan. He was not only able to make and keep fire going at will, but was able to control the necessary degree of heat by widening or narrowing the channel for the flame inside the kiln.

He seemed to have lived a freer and happier life, as compared to compulsive, or even paranoid, Neanderthal man. He freely intermingled pleasure, work, and family life in an almost playful, child-like manner. What made this higher culture and more mature mental health possible?

It is my opinion that the change came when he discovered the cycle of life, the seasons, the possibility of rebirth. Being much more stationary, he observed that the death of winter was followed by the rebirth of spring. His world became a more caring and benign mother substitute, which, reintrojected, made for a greater degree of empathy, creativity, and hope for the future. Evidence for this is almost endless in terms of his art as found in his sculpture, cave paintings, and the evidence of his music. A detailed description of all this would require a few books. An analysis of one painting, the "Dead Man," in an an IPOM Paper (I, no. 4) as well as the work done by

Robert McCully and Les Freeman, give samples of the kind of analysis possible.

The main point to be made here is the demonstration of a restitutional process through opened channels of feeling, thinking, and doing, which has made progress and survival of mankind possible for at least another 40,000 to 50,000 years. Aggression and cannibalism seemed to have greatly decreased by the time of Cro-Magnon, although was still existent.

Figure 6–5 is the first piece of art found in the world, the so-called "Venus of Willendorf," which gives us a good idea of early Cro-Magnon man's emotional life. She was found near the fireplace at a settlement located between present day Vienna, Austria and Brno, Czechoslovakia. She was created by a "shaman artist" (Figure 6–6). He can hold her in his left hand while working on the figure with his right. Cro-Magnon man could hold the Venus as he would have wanted to be held by a good, protective mother. She is faceless and only the hair and the generative aspects of her body are highlighted. Although highly abstracted, the fertility aspects are evident on many planes. The entire sculpture has the form of an egg, intuitively suggesting the biological beginnings of life, later symbolized in the world-egg origin of life. As in many early sculptures, a number of visualized forms become possible. It can be the figure of a maternal woman, or if we squint, we can see the whole figure as a face with the breasts becoming the eyes and the pubic area becoming the mouth area of the face. The emphasized features are the maternal stomach and breast areas, while the limbs of locomotion such as arms and legs are greatly diminished by comparison. Normally, the physically stronger arms would support the weaker breast, but here, the emotionally invested stronger breasts support the weaker arms. Man was able to sense creation in his mind and body 38,000 years ago as we no longer can, making his creations—the sculptures and paintings—truly eidetic. (Only some of our children have retained that ability.)

Why do we find sculpture 10,000 to 15,000 years before paintings done with similar skill? Our first identification is with a three-dimensional body ego: the two-dimensional painting becomes an abstraction from it with the help of the gradually increasing capacities of the left hemisphere.

This progress can be seen in the artifact of the Venus of Lespugue in France (Figure 6–7) almost 10,000 years later, where the upward elongation of the position of the head suggests a more cognitive view of the world.

The period of the Venuses is followed by a 10,000 to 20,000 year period of indescribable beauty in artistic creation, reaching a zenith in the caves of Altamira and Lascaux. Visitors describe their impression after entering these caves today as being comparable to the feeling of finding onself in a place like the Sistine Chapel of Rome. In 15,000 B.C., we reach mankind's first high peak of artistically creative self-actualization, possibly reached again about 400 B.C. in Greece and about 1500 A.D. in the Italian Renaissance.

However since the highest achievements in art are restitutional for the

Figure 6–5. Venus of Willendorf (Austria). (From J. Augusta, *Prehistoric Man*, Hamlyn Publishing Group, Ltd., 1960.)

Figure 6–6. Cro-Magnon ceramic artist at work. (From J. Augusta, *Prehistoric Man*, Hamlyn Publishing Group, Ltd., 1960.)

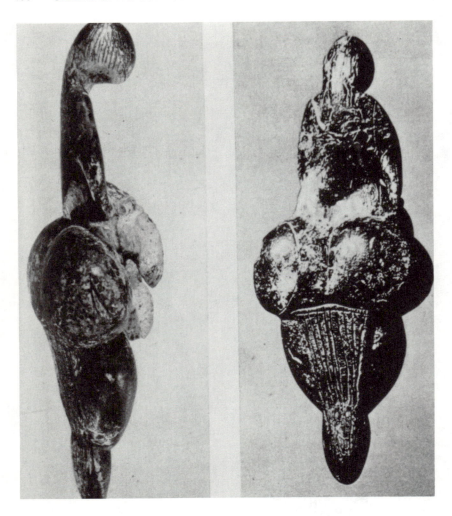

Figure 6–7. Venus figurine from Lespugue, France. (From J. Jellinek, *The Pictorial Encyclopedia of the Evolution of Man,* Hamlyn Publishing Group, Ltd., 1975.)

underlying tensions produced by the non-integrated, underlying aggression, because at times additional methods of discharge have to be found. They can be external; wars, conflicts, crimes, etc., or turned inward to be expressed symptomatically as illnesses. Symbolic internalization is a more sophisticated form of restitution than acting out. We have one instance in the Upper-Paleolithic where there is evidence of art being a symptomatic rather than symbolic expression.

The cave of Gargas, near Toulouse in Southern France, appears to have been devoted to the glorification of hands. One hand near the center of the cave takes a position similar to a central crucifix in many churches and probably served the same purpose. Just as the crucifix allows the parishioner, among other restitutional purposes, to find a symbolic expression for his sense of guilt, so the glorification of the hand has to be seen in a similar light, when we study the purpose of the whole cave, often called the "Cave of Hands."

The walls of the cave contain paintings of 154 hands painted in black, red, or, less frequently, in ochre, providing a spectacular sight, sometimes a horrible sight, when it becomes clear on close inspection that many of them are amputated and severely deformed. On analysis, we find 22 right hands and 36 left hands (explained by the left hand usually serving as the model for the executing right hand) but more important, only 10 hands are intact compared to 144 hands which are mutilated. Interestingly, the thumbs are always intact while fingers are either partially or totally amputated. We will never know the exact meaning of the ritual symbolized by the services in this cave, and interpretations usually reflect the theories of those making them. There can be little doubt, however, that we are looking at a spectacle of guilt being expiated, which must basically be related to having used the hands for aggressive activities which the normal social order or the individual makeup could not comfortably integrate.

We know that the cave was not just a fad or temporary fluke by the animals represented in the other paintings in the cave. They represent a long stretch of time, going through rich and poor periods in climate and availability of prizes for the hunter. The style of the paintings similarly expresses the long stretch of cave use. The latest and most mature style shows the development of "eidetic" to "embedded" imagery. A discussion of these perceptual features would take us too afield for this discussion and will be developed in other publications related to the development of more specific paleolithic art forms.

This magnificent paleolithic artistic cycle ends about 10,000 B.C. in the caves of Buxu, as seen in Figure 6–8.

The cognitive integrative form has fallen apart and we are left with the most minimal remnants of skeletal bones such as the spine.

Mesolithic Man (circa 10,000 to 6,000 B.C.)

Another cycle starts about 10,000 B.C. in eastern Spain and Northern Africa. This period, called the Mesolithic, shows in the paintings a move from the frozen eidetic to the dynamic mobile presentation of live scenes. People fight, play, hunt, and the artist and viewer can identify directly with the de-

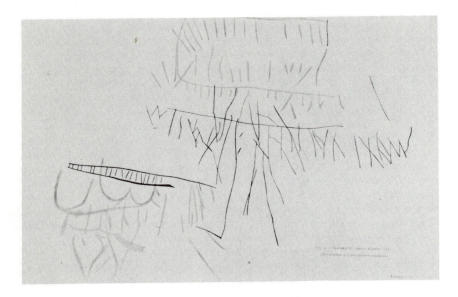

Figure 6–8. La Cueva del Buxu (Astorias). (From Hugo Obermaier, Memoire 20 of the Commission de la Vestigationus Paleolithecos de Prehistoricos, 1918.)

picted figures, their behavior, clothing, etc. A great step of progress had been achieved in making much of the ego-alien external world, ego-syntonic (as most of the pictures depict aggression). Art greatly helps self-expression. If I want to be stronger, I make myself bigger in the picture or give myself arms or legs with much stronger muscles. This flexibility allowed for great social progress in all spheres.

One painting even suggests the depth of time in addition to movement. The man climbing the tree to gather the honey remembers the "good old times" when he was only threatened by the bison, rather than face the present nuisance of the bees. This is quite a sense of humor and sophistication for 6000 to 7000 B.C.

We begin to see the rise of early cities in Jarmo and Jericho in Mesopotamia and the details of housing projects and religious activities in Anatolia (present-day Turkey). Here we are on the threshold of "history," the written transmission of man's affairs, usually highlighted by his wars, peace treaties, rulers and power plays. We have remained fascinated by the aggressive aspects of our historical development.

Figure 6–9. Honey gathering in prehistoric Spain. (From *Nature*, 268 (5617).)

I hope this chapter has given some flavor of man's desperate attempt to first survive under terribly untoward conditions, and being trapped and defeated by the need for aggressive capacities, which, through their seductive and addictive elements, have taken control of us, rather than allowing us to reverse the process.

Our mind has continued to alternately differentiate and integrate its apperceptive potential, only to find that the more science and technology seem to advance, the more terrible the aggressive elements that keep breaking through. Armaments usually have led the technical progress from the club to the spear, the bow and arrow, the gun, and now the atom bomb. We have achieved some form of technical or even scientific progress, but control of the internal monster still eludes us. The last chapter will try to show the possibility of moving toward an integrative approach that may possibly allow us to become truly human.

REFERENCES

Barriere, C. *The prehistoric cave Gargas.* Toulouse: Institute of Prehistoric Art.

Breuil, H. (1952). *Four hundred centuries of cave art.* Montignac: F. Windels.

Campbell, B. G. (1979). *Humankind emerging.* Boston: Little, Brown.

Chomsky, N. (1964). *Current issues in linguistic theory.* Mouton: The Hague.

Dart, R. (1959). *Adventures with the missing link.* New York: Harper and Brothers.

deMause, L. (1982). *Foundations of psychohistory.* New York: Creative Roots.

Freeman, L. G. (1980). Personal communication.

Garn, S. M. (1971). *Human races.* Springfield: Charles C. Thomas.

Gould, S. J. (1977). *Ever since Darwin: Reflections in natural history.* New York: W. W. Norton, pp. 63–66.

Gowlett, J. (1984). *Ascent to civilization: The archeology of early man.* New York: Alfred A. Knopf.

Grof, S. (1975). *Realms of the human unconscious: Observations from LSD research.* New York: Viking Press.

Heim, J. (1976). Les hommes fossiles de Ferrassie [The human fossils of Ferrassie]. In *Archives de l'Institute de Paleontologe Humane* (*Archives of the Institute of Human Paleontology*), *35.* Paris: Masson.

Holloway, R. I. (1979). The casts of fossil homonid brains. In Isaac & Leakey (Eds.), *Human ancestors.* Readings from *Scientific American.* San Francisco: Freeman, pp. 74–83.

Johanson, D. (1981). *Lucy: The beginnings of humankind.* New York: Warner Books.

Kochetkova, V. E. (1978). *Paleoneurology.* New York: John Wiley & Sons.

Leakey, M. D. (1971). *Olduvai Gorge III.* Cambridge: Cambridge University Press.

Leakey, M. D. (1979). *Olduvai Gorge, my search for early man.* London: Collins.

Luria, A. R. (1973). *The working brain.* New York: Basic Books.

Maringer, J. (1960). *Gods of prehistoric man.* New York: Alfred A. Knopf.

Solecki, R. S. (1971). *Shanidar: The first flower people.* New York: Alfred A. Knopf.

Time-Life Books (1973). *The emergence of man: The Neanderthals.* New York: Time, Inc.

Verny, T. R. (1982). *The psychic life of the unborn.* Paper given at the Fifth World Congress of Psycho-Somatic Obstetrics and Gynecology, Rome.

Washburn, S. L. & Howell, F. C. (1960). Human evolution and culture. In S. Tax (Ed.), *The evolution of man.* Chicago: University of Chicago Press.

Chapter 7

THE TWO PHASES OF
THE "GREAT MOTHER"

Robert S. McCully

Few westerners, apart from specialized scholars, are aware that mankind's beginnings began under the rule of matriarchal-mother authority and that this form of absolute rule dominated the beginnings of cultures over a period of approximately 20,000 years. For this entire period, the authority of males was inconsequential even after the documentation of recorded history. The deities of earliest mankind were entirely and dominantly moon-fertility, mother-goddesses. Even today, one sees traces of female-dominated theology much more clearly in the Orient than in our Occidental cultures. For example, the cult of the goddess Kali survives potently in India and related cultures in the eastern world today. She is viewed as holding "all-power."

Students of prehistory such as Leroi-Gourhan (1965), Giedion (1962), Neumann (1955), and Marshack (1972), to name a few pioneers, are of the opinion that a consciousness capable of establishing symbolic equivalents of subjective ideas arose first in the upper Paleolithic period. This kind of conclusion emerges from the earliest dating of oldest known and still extant artifacts. These included cave paintings and engravings, bone carvings, grave arrangements, hieroglyphs, symbolic use of red and yellow ochre in grave objects, and low relief sculpture and carvings, some affixed to rock shelters, and others in the form of mobile and portable objects, usually fertile female forms, carved in various kinds of durable stone.

The Paleolithic or Old Stone Age lasted approximately one million years, with upper Paleolithic times, those when Cro-Magnon men fashioned mankind's earliest known symbolic artifacts, extending 150,000 to 200,000 years, ending in the Neolithic period, around 9000 B.C.

In order to comprehend something of the psychology of ancient mankind, it is important to introduce a concept difficult to elucidate, one we will call "the reality of subjective or inward psychic experience." The concept is alien to western tenets of science. We are asking the reader to accept inner psychic reality as quite as real as the more tangible and more familiar parameters of outer reality.

As early as 1695, Wilhelm Leibniz (1646–1716) noted that it would be absurd to suppose that the reality behind all natural phenomena is the con-realities) to the "ancients" and enormously facilitated a personal exchange Freud, which in turn contains what we are calling contents equivalent to subjective or psychological realities. This concept, somewhat alien to the Occident, has long been known and attended to in the Orient. That is, Oriental/Buddhist art forms most often aim to recapture experiences originating from trances, reveries, and foci in inner psychological experiences considered as real and meaningful as, say, walking to the market to buy food. This Oriental tradition is so ancient that its methods and tenets were set down as long ago as 200 B.C. as noted by Patanjali, founder of Yoga philosophy, and precisely followed as techniques today (Dvivedi, 1934). This, then, makes their art forms not haphazard but conforming to a precise method, while allowing individual ways and means of expressing whatever artifact is at hand.

Now, the Occidental world recognizes that a source exists within us that gives rise to symbol formation, myths, fantasies, and those features we discern in our dreams. Yet, our tendency is not to think of these phenomena as "real," whereas the ancient world and also the Orient for long periods of time reacted to these experiences as being quite as "real" as outer experiences. This is difficult for our scientific-saturated consciousness to comprehend, but we must do so, if we would grasp the ambience of ancient psychology.

A marked turn toward understanding the psychological world of the ancients in our cultural past emerged when Jane Ellen Harrison (1962), one of the great minds penetrating the Greek consciousness, made the signal point that a major factor behind the Greek genius most likely lay in the manner in which their religion was as real to them as was outer reality. This is the point we are endeavoring to emphasize. The Greeks did not behave toward their Gods "as if" they were real, they *were* real to them. We believe this same approach was characteristic of early man and his theo-mythologies. Failing to grasp this relationship results in a relative failure to grasp the psychology of the Ancients.

Both Freud (1946) and Jung (1979), in the early part of this century, hypothesized that the gods to the ancients were actually equivalent to projections of unrealized forces within the unconscious. It was *this kind of quality* that caused the ancient deities to feel *real* (since they were, indeed, subjective realities) to the "ancients" and enormously facilitated a personal exchange between early man, their deities, and the incarnations of those deities, who presided over a given deity's precise rituals. There were then no consciously imposed barriers between deity-representative and an ancient cult member's relationship to that particular surrogate. In this way, the impact and movements of the fantasy image of the deity-goddess reverberated or resonated within movements *inside* psychic forces within the unconscious itself. Sensing this experience enables one to grasp what we have called "psychological or subjective reality," a phenomenon unrelated to the contents of outer reality. When we are free to attend to it, we recognize that these inner events go on in us today and are probably a part of the human condition.

The prime point for my thesis is that the inner resonance between intrapsychic experiences and outer representations of a deity was essential for the primal deity-cults that linked or glued members of the most ancient societies together.

There are, to be sure, parallels between religion and devotees in the Middle Ages and our thesis here, but this chapter is not focused on later eras, only the earliest ones. Thus, we have suggested that the power held by the Great-Mother-Goddess was twofold in essence. First, her cult members believed her (as vehicle of childbirth) responsible, as insurer of fertility, and essential for the continuity of the species. This was particularly important in the upper Paleolithic times because of the sparseness of the human population and the short life-span, an average of 26 years. Second, the being and presence of the mother goddess had a reality based on her image as a projection of real but unconscious content inside the human psyche. Her rituals and image set moving the psychic connection between her and cult members' subjective counterparts, which were projected onto her. Hence, artifacts associated with her theomythology were "numinous," that is, carried significance beyond the ordinary, inspiring awe and powerful respect.

Figures 7–1 to 7–4 show the actual image of the Great-Mother-Goddess, aspects of her milieu, and her descendents rooted in the origins of our own culture.

From the Laussel goddess to the Aegean-Cretan goddess, we cover a sweep of at least 20,000 years, finding her rule and power virtually unchanged, with males in her service and her powers *necessitating* placation and obedience.

I should like to piece together and trace the origins of qualities associated with this primal goddess, based on artifacts and practices known to have continued within the ways and means of her worship down into recorded history. I will show how she came to have, even from the beginning, two sides—one positive, the other negative. I will strive to present the salient features known to have been associated with her. The information here is based on several central works I should like to note: Andre Leroi-Gourhan (1965), whose compendia on prehistoric art is perhaps the major achievement on the subject in this century; M. Esther Harding (1935), an early disciple of Jung, whose careful study of antique feminine mysteries has provided us with a widely rich source; Erich Neumann (1955), whose compendia on varieties of mother goddesses offered countless items of interest; R. Briffault (1931), an important source of behaviors in matrilineal cultures; C. Herberger (1979), whose work on the significance of calendric symbols in the ancient world offered new and stimulating insights; and finally, the works of Carl Gustav Jung himself, sources too numerous to list, coming from the sweep of 20 volumes of his *Collected Works* (1957–1979).

First, it is essential to link all of the early goddesses, and in particular, the Great-Mother-Goddess we have just viewed, with the moon. The vast majority of these goddesses were moon goddesses who held power over fertility cults. Moon goddesses were primary and vastly dispersed in various forms within the prehistoric era, down into the Neolithic period, overlapping with biblical times and our own Judeo-Christian origins.

I will attempt to delineate qualities of the primal moon-mother-goddess of prehistoric times as prototypal for more complex forms of her being that arose later. Within the Paleolithic world, she held *supreme power,* referred to by British author, Rider Haggard (1966) as "Sho-who-must-be-obeyed."

The initial rituals associated with the celebrants and worship of the Great Mother were either well known to all members of the cult or were known only to initiates, hence, in either instance, would not be recorded as such. It ap-

Figure 7–1. Limestone rock shelters, Dordorgne, France.

Figure 7–2. Goddess of Laussel. Low relief in limestone, 22,000 B.C. Figure heightened with red ochre. No facial features carved, symbolizing her impersonal nature. Her right hand holds a bison or goat horn, displaying 13 notches. Drawing on a source that provided me with a clue (Marshack, 1972, p. 29), this may mark the time, 13 days, between the waning moon and emergence of the new moon. Thus, she becomes symbolic of the nurturant Goddess, and holds the horn as a life-furthering crescent. In Cretan cults this symbolized the highest fertility. Her left hand sinks into the fecund zone of her fertile capacity. (From Time-Life Books, *Cro-Magnon Man*) "The Emergence of Man" series by Tom Prideaux and the Editors of Time-Life Books), Time, Inc., 1973.)

Figure 7–3. Male acolyte, Laussel. This figure attends the goddess, beautifully carved much below her in low relief in limestone. He wears a short girdle since males must be covered in her presence. (From J. Jellinek, *The Pictorial Encyclopedia of the Evolution of Man*, Hamlyn Publishing Group, Ltd., 1975.)

Figure 7–4. Aegean-Creto goddess, Knossos, 2000 B.C. The Mother-Goddess is shown in the moment of her manifestation. She is attended by male acolytes in girdles, whose raised arms show reverence to her epiphany. Her goddess character as mother nature is revealed by exposed breasts. She holds the labrys or double axes in both hands. These sacrificial axes were touched *only* by females, originating from the flint knife, used to perform ritual, sacred castration of chosen males. (From Sir Arthur Evans, *The Palace at Minos*, Vol. II, pt. 2, Suppl. Plate XXVI.)

pears that the primary outlook or philosophy of Cro-Magnon hunting cultures were not rooted in life as an expected, unchecked progress onward and upward to ever-self-renewing goal-heights, as ours today tends to be, but quite contrarily, life was viewed as a struggle, or conflict, between growth and decay.

The mood-tone of this view (which Esther Harding, 1935, found as an ever-recurring theme in her researches) probably connects directly with the qualities of growth and decay vividly reflected in the regular phases of the moon ever waxing and waning. Changes in the moon itself served as an equivalent within the character of the moon-mother-goddess. Cult members made this connection, projecting moon-qualities on their goddess herself. The ancients were impressed with what I might call "that which grows also recedes and disappears." This could be counted on as an eternal consistency. Thus, for the ancients, life was a circular recurrence: What is built up will be bound to decay. Apparently, this itself was not disquieting for them but merely expected.

Hence, we note that the precise qualities of the moon from which similar qualities were attributed to the goddess were a *light phase* or the waxing moon. This light phase was considered generative, and, thus, a growing phase starting with the new moon. A parallel to this, still found in remote corners, is planting agricultural seeds in accordance with moon phases. After waxing, at a predictable point in time, the moon's waning phase began, and was considered the beginnings of a *dark phase,* and to be an opposite to generative, becoming destructive for mankind. Fear and awe increased as the moon became darker, finally disappearing altogether. During the dark phase, the ancients felt abandoned by the goddess and prey to a variety of destructive forces. The good offices of the nurturing Great Mother had ceased, and nothing checked ghosts, floods, and disasters. These two opposites define the character of the Great Mother, whose qualities were seen as identical to visually observable characteristics of the moon.

Thus, the moon-mother-goddess ruled according to either principle, a generative-nurturing-guardianship mood or attitude, versus a destructive, violently aggressive stance; this side of her was known as the terrible-devouring-mother. Whatever the mood of the goddess, her being and presence existed not to be loved but to be *placated.* Her dark side was viewed as a total abandonment of her rule over and furthering the energies of *good* for mankind, and her dark side engendered a belief of rampant evil forces wielding themselves up against mankind. Harding, Jung, and Neumann, have surmised that probably all of the rituals of the earliest religion associated with the Great Mother were connected with the means of furthering or placating the opposite moods of the powerful goddess. Figure 7–4 from Knossos, precisely shows placation at her epiphany. Male acolytes either raise their arms to her in reverence or bring her sundry gifts.

Herberger (1979) makes an especially important point when he considers how time for the ancients, fixed by them even as we ourselves have done on heavenly bodies and the precision of their movements, was a constantly revolving rhythm. Time was a *divine mystery* for ancient measurers and observers. Passage of time, as well as ritual calendric rites, precisely marked rhythms of life and death in the world of prehistory. Note should be made that time was *circular* in the ancient world, and not *linear* as we envision time today. Ancient monuments like Stonehenge in Britain were set with absolute precision for marking all important mileposts of circular time, which, for them, was played back on itself. This divine view of time was directly linked with religious beliefs which, we imagine, highlighted well-being versus disaster.

The linking of the passage of time and the phases of the moon with woman in general, and the great goddess in particular, has been associated with womens' menstrual cycle since recorded history. The menstrual cycle defined women's role and connection with the goddess in fertility cults. Contrarily, men had no obvious cycle connecting them with the goddess, making self-definition for men more difficult. However, men continued to try to define themselves and experience a theological separation from the feminine power of the goddess. The nature of men did not correspond to cyclic qualities that linked every woman with moon and moon-goddess.

One can see, in Figure 7–5, how circular time was the obvious basis for the Hindu concept of transmigration, a concept born of moontime, representing the Great Round of growth and decay, ever-returning, and set in a context of Hindu religion as a function of matriarchal power.

Some elaboration about the aggressive side of the Great Mother may be in order, since the view of aggression in females has often been sidestepped in Occidentals, and its expression has been stereotyped as primarily a feature in the domain of males. Actually, this is an odd state of affairs, since there has never been a dearth of feminine aggression, and men tend to be quite fearful of it and rather helpless when it rises and boils over. We have shown how the waning moon leads us directly to the aggressive side of the externalized prototype of the mother, indicating that the Great Mother's characteristics had a counterpart or connectedness with psychic sources extant in all women, since she was the prominent representative of the feminine side of life. Here, we mean destructive aggression and not simply assertive tenacity. Briffault's (1931) research illuminates what we have referred to as the terrible-devouring-mother (p. 165):

> Primitive women were not only as courageous as men but even more cruel and ferocious. American Indians handed prisoners to women to be tortured, and squaws excelled in the ingenuity of cruelty . . . . Fiji women, during battle, would rush upon a fallen foe, tear his body open with their teeth and drink his blood, then lead their children over the battlefield to kick and tread on bodies of enemies.

The venom of these acts is tantamount to how fearful the ancients were of what they referred to as the Terrible Mother. We will show later how sub-

Figure 7–5. Tibetan Wheel of Life, 18th century. Its whole represents the Sansara, or world or ego existence; the demon holding the wheel represents the negative force of clinging to life. The cock, pig, and snake in the hub are the equivalents of lust, greed, and ignorance. There is a dark, downward moon-path; then a light, upward one. The circle around the center has six partitions or conditions of existence (deities, man, demigods, hell beasts, tortured souls). The outer circle represents the causal nexus or sequence of events leading to death and rebirth amongst life forms. The moon appears on the left.

tle aggression in mothers toward their children can be enormously destructive, later emerging in a profound psychological fashion.

In order to emphasize the pervasive impact of the moon on the ancient world, we mention some remnant connections between moon and the consciousness of much earlier men, handed down in folktale and what some would call superstition or nonscientific attitudes. The moon infused almost every part of early cultures. Agriculture, itself, was controlled by how the moon was regarded. Only recently, I saw slides on Tibetan herbaceous medicines, some of which were being grown in large containers put outside only in the moonlight for growing. Markings on the moon were interpreted in the Orient as a hare on the moon. The moon is linked with the belief of the "lucky rabbit foot," which was thought to be most powerful if caught in a graveyard at the time of the full moon. The full moon "brought out human links with animal predation" in the werewolf myth. Even the Easter bunny can be traced to the moon-rabbit.

In the middle ages, witch sabbaths, themselves incarnations of the aggressive side of the moon-mother-goddess, were timed to the phases of the moon. Witches of the middle ages mixed beneficial, magic brews, or formulas during the light of the moon, and evil, violent potions when the moon was dark.

Menstruation was a "moon-change" and primitives linked it to infection, thus, rendering females taboo when menstruating. Both primitive men and animals, in early times, lived by the regulation of sexual congress by females rather than the males of the species. Taboos were developed to combat what they believed was a real psychological danger, that is, at certain times primitives knew that aggressive, feminine instincts, when loose, could be destructive and the undoing of others, men and women alike. Not infrequently, mood swings occur in females during the premenstrual stage, sometimes temporarily affecting relationships. In his research, Briffault (1931) concludes, primarily because of matrilineal customs, that a brother-sister incest taboo was probably the most powerful of the early incest taboos. By contrast, priestesses of the Great Mother were expected to conceive via their son-lovers; hence, the mother-son incest must have become a more powerful taboo in later times. These qualities grew out of the widespread manner in which females controlled society and customs, underscored by the example set by the mother goddess, through rituals controlled by her priestesses, who in ritual took a son for procreation, then sacrificed him immediately afterward.

In the 13th century, the infamously cruel Ghengis Khan traced his ancestry to a king whose *mother* was "impregnated by a moon-ray." Paradoxically, Mt. Sinai was the mountain of the moon, prior to its becoming the site on which monotheism acquired patriarchal laws. A moon-tree played a significant role in Assyrian and Minoan rites, said to have occurred in sacred groves of trees first, then later in palaces, and then even later in temples. In

India, the "tree on the moon" had an earthly counterpart whose sap, allowed to ferment, became *soma* in India. Intoxicating drinks were connected with religious ecstasies, and drinking fermented juice of the moon tree gave immortality. Here again, immortality connects with circular time and the promise of the stages of the moon in the sense that what began, decays, but returns again, making the ever-returning round an equivalent of immortality.

In Egypt, a moon-barge took the dead to the underworld. In Mexico, Indian mothers held newborns up to the moon to acquire ever-renewed life as suggested by the moon cycle. Monday is moon-day; menstruation is "moon-time" (*mens* is Latin for moon). The Celts regulated time by the moon, not the sun. China uses a moon calendar, and "honeymoon" was Aphrodite's month. Easter still falls on a first Sunday following a particular full moon. The Jewish calendar is entirely lunar.

Tracing the moon-mother-goddess into the Neolithic age reveals that her power continues as a widespread and potent force. However new forms, insects and animals tend to become associated with her, and while most certainly the connection was always symbolic, the precise symbolism becomes difficult and hazardous to identify. Sometime between 4500 and 2500 B.C. the mother goddess began to be competitive and juxtapositioned to patriarchal deities. Marija Gimbutas (1982) has devoted meticulous research to the gods and goddesses of the Neolithic era and down into recorded history. She notes that after 2500 B.C., there was a melange of the two mythic systems. Prior to this, the moon-mother-goddess ruled alone for approximately 20,000 years, a theology most contemporaries, apart from scholars, are unfamiliar with. In searching within the contents of the dual theologies of matriarchal and patriarchal systems, modern archeologists, historians, and sociologists tended to accept Neolithic kingship as being as equivalent to the power of kings in the Middle Ages. This often was not true, and behind the kings, female deities, descendants of the mother goddess, held power over him. For reasons like this, historians of the era of transition from Neolithic times and those of early recorded history have, at times, innocently misread where the power of authority lay and precisely who wielded it.

For instance, Ishtar, the Assyrian moon goddess, held the power of life and death over her widespread followers. The first born child of a female was demanded by Ishtar in human sacrifice (thousands of infant bones have been uncovered at her shrines) and particularly designated males were required to castrate themselves and leave their testicle on her altars. The zodiac of the ancient world was known as Ishtar's girdle, and this moon-mother-goddess wore a necklace of testicles in depictions and descriptions of her. A study of the iconography of Tibetan deities enables a student of theology to study ancient and modern scroll paintings, which, themselves, are a virtual melange of two systems, one matriarchal and the other patriarchal, since Tibetan theology was actually a combination of Buddhism and an earlier, dominant religion in Tibet called Pon, a daemonic system linked closely with moon-goddess-power.

Ishtar's power was felt by the enslaved Hebrews (722 B.C.) whose apparent yearning for a feminine deity was expressed or illustrated when they fell to worshiping the Golden Calf (as the Bible recounts), a chief symbol of the moon goddess, Ishtar. Raphael Patai (1967) records that Astarte (Ishtar) was mentioned nine times in the Bible and Baal was her "brother-consort." He goes on to inform us that three Hebrew-connected goddesses were named in the Bible, the Queen of Heaven, Asherah, and Astarte. Therefore, in the precisely patriarchal theology of the Hebrews, mother goddesses faded in and out, being, at times, prominent, even inside Yahwist monotheism. Asherah was the chief goddess of the Canaanite pantheon, dating back to the 14th century B.C. Baal was her child, and her sons were kings. Patai indicates that Asherah held power because of the psychological need for a mother goddess felt by the Hebrew people. She was popular for at least three centuries, and, for the 370 years that Solomon's temple remained standing in Jerusalem, her statue was part of the legitimate worship within that temple for at least two-thirds of that time. She was also the goddess of Tyre and Sidon.

One especially well-documented example of the confusing mixture of kingships and dominant goddess control behind the king's power-source is illustrated by King Minos. The Minoan culture was named for him, while it was not he, but a queen-female-goddess who actually ruled the scope, sequence, and outcome of Cretan culture directly from ancient female goddess traditions. She and her priestesses wore their breasts bare representing their nurturing phase and the "light moon" and "mother nature."

Views of several of the goddesses from the Aegean-Minoan traditions are shown in Figures 7–6—7–9.

In the full panel of Figure 7–9, only partly shown here, the priestesses are drawn by two griffins, and they are startled by a dark-crested bird, an epiphany of the Great Goddess herself in her death aspect. The bird is probably a hen-partridge, and its crest represents the last crescent phase of the darkening moon, giving her similar characteristics as Hecate, the devouring and destructive phase of the moon with its parallel associated to the mood of the Great Mother. The Minoan kings, who ruled at the pleasure of the Goddess, were ritually sacrificed at the seventh lunation following the end of an eight-year cycle, thus, in the ninth year of their reign. The king knew his fate from the start. The two priestesses in their chariot (Figure 7–9) bear the dead Minoan king, taking him to the underworld. The panel is taken from the end of a sarcophagus, dated 1400 B.C.

According to Herberger (1979), the Sphinx has a female head representing the moon-mother-goddess. Her famous riddle was taught by females, the Muses, and the answers to the riddle were moon-answers such as "Who are the two sisters that gave birth to one another?" The answer to which is, "The new moon and old *crescents.*"

Figure 7–6. Mother-goddess of the animals. Fresco, Tiryns, Greece, 1400 B.C. This shows all animals as her children; here, goats, or ibex, pull her chariot. She wears a diadem, long bell skirt, open bodice exposing breasts, elaborately dressed hair, and holds a pyx or casket showing processions of animals going toward, then away from her, an eternal cycle.

Figure 7–7. Goddess on Gem Stone. An especially interesting symbolic scene of the Great Goddess as mother to all living things including plants. Both she and her attendants have plants in their hair; The adults are bare-breasted, the left one swings systrums in one hand and holds the figure eight shield in her other; the one beside her has the labrys, or double ritual castrative axe, next to her while she reaches out to touch one of the plants being held by the Great Goddess, the bunch is of center petals of the pomegranate, a symbol of fertility in the Orient. In a palace at Nimrud in Assyria (885 B.C.), there is a carving of Gilgamesh, the first hero, who proudly holds high an identical pomegranate bunch, symbolizing his triumph over the advances of Ishtar, whose seductions he resisted entirely. This comparison gives almost a living mood to the power of the symbols of these matters to the ancients. The goddess sits under the moontree being harvested by a girl, gathering soma fruit; above her is the crescent moon on its dark, destructive side, clouds are on the left, and a star disk above. Another girl holds plants or flowers and ritualizes herself before the Great Goddess. (From E. Neumann, *The Great Mother*, Bollingen Foundation, Inc., 1955, 1963.)

Let us stop here and connect some of the meaning of this ancient past for psychological aspects of mankind today. We draw on Harding's interpretations here, Jungian in origin. According to Jung, each gender has a contra-sexual opposite within; one is dominant, the other recessive, at least under ordinary circumstances. The moon-goddess myths were equivalent to an inner or subjective reality of feminine psychology. The moon for men is an equivalent as an image of the feminine principle. The feminine principle

Figure 7–8. Demeter with Kore and Triptolemus. Demeter as Great Mother with Kore her daughter, and Triptolemus, Demeter's son-lover, who, unlike male acolytes, *bares* his genitalia to her. The son-lover is being endowed here with fertility, illustrating how females endowed men with their virility; this is done symbolically with a cereal, probably wheat. Marble, 450 B.C. at Eleusis. It is not an agricultural rite, but represents a sexual and spiritual fecundating function *given to males* by the goddesses. (From E. Neumann, *The Great Mother*, Bollingen Foundation, 1955, 1963.)

is dominant and lived out in females, whereas for men, the feminine principle is the "ruler of the night," that is, rules his unconscious functions. The ancient initiation rites were an equivalent of education of the emotional life.

The feminine principle was the same as the essence of inner laws. Women were mysterious to men because the feminine principle evades definition through the logic of consciousness men tend to rely on and make judgments therefrom. Usually, the feminine principle and its attributes are not present within masculine consciousness, and when females act according to their feminine nature, it tends to be mysterious or not precisely intelligible to masculine logic. Something similar in reverse holds true for women, since more often, masculine logic is not their means of interpreting life. Masculine consciousness is connected symbolically with the sun-world, a precise, unchanging world, while feminine consciousness has a kinship with the moon-world, its changing phases, and links to her own cyclic moods and perceptions.

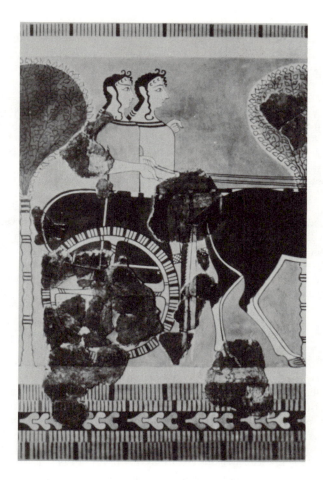

Figure 7–9. Two priestesses, Tiryns, Greece, 1400 B.C. Not shown is that they are being drawn by two griffins; they carry the body of a just-sacrificed Minoan king.

Although we consider such things as human sacrifice, the sacrifice of first born, and emasculation via castration as well as ritual death of kings, as barbaric, the mental climate of the ancient world was different. Those chosen, (probably representing only a few members of the cult) for cult rituals, even ending in death, were of the opinion, as was the goddess demanding them, that their qualities were sacrificed to cultural fertility; consequently, all would be returned to the culture in a growth-producing, positive way, just as the moon cycles and regenerates. The goddess, therefore, was the vehicle by which regenerative powers were returned to mankind.

A few final remarks and descriptions may enhance our grasp of the psychology of the first powers that ruled and constellated psychological responses in those men of prehistory who created mankind's first symbols. The priestesses of the Great Mother were "virgins" (from the Latin meaning unwed, as was Virgo in the Zodiac) for life, that is, they never wed, but were not chaste. It was their sons who usually became the kings, first under the power of mother goddesses, then later, usually through some military feat, became independent and ruled independently of the goddess. The spiritual model for this was Hebrew monotheism (itself possibly originating in Egyptian culture). The Great Mother's priestesses, sacred duties included tending sacred fires and acting as guardians of snakes kept in pits nearby. The snake was important because it disappeared into the ground, or down to the "underworld." The moon-mother-goddess was the goddess of love, but not of marriage. No male god ruled her. She became the mother of a son-lover, whom she aggressively controlled. Although he might be destined to die in ritual sacrifice, he, like the moon-cycles, would return as her son. When he became her lover, however, he must die. The Great Mother was gentler to women than to men, who had reason to greatly fear her dark side as devouring mother. She was often inimical to males per se. Yet, as Harding (1935) emphasized, it is important to recognize that the *sacrifice* in ancient rituals functioned to renew or insure the power of the deity because that power depended on service given by humans to the deity. It is important to remember, as Figure 7–8 shows, that it was the goddess, herself, who gave men their essential virility.

Drawing on observations made by Harding, some qualities of the sun-disc-god, or much later developing masculine counterpart to the moon-fertility-goddess, may be useful. Harding has noted that sun worship, a symbol of independent masculine power, tended to be instigated within recorded history by edict of a military dictator, and he was attended by male priests. The Emperor Constantine (sole emperor of the western world by 312 A.D.) decreed in 313 A.D. that Christianity would be the official religion of the western world. He was a prime example of the dominant masculine side in human nature. Symbolically speaking, he was a consciousness-sun-god, and these were usually war gods and connected with spoils of war or personal aggrandizement, wealth, and overcoming enemies. By contrast, Harding notes, the feminine principle in human nature remains symbolically in the moon-goddess as mother nature herself and guardian of her fecund powers. Laws controlling the feminine principle rose up spontaneously from within, although the laws of the masculine world emerged from experience and conscious logic. Modern science, for example, is representative of a masculine point of view. Symbolically, its sun-aspect glorifies the intellect, harbors the belief that mankind's problems can be solved by governmental decree, and that what is "good" can be taught, for example, in school. In this way, we might say the world today is ruled outwardly by the sun-symbols of masculine ascendance.

Yet, as cartoons today show, feminine rule remains powerful psychologically. Here, we have contemporary examples of how a male can become devoured and castrated on a very real, but symbolic level, by a quality in the female figure, a power that can be traced to the power of the most ancient goddess, the terrible-mother in her role as a destructive-castrating force, inimical to males and their independence of her (for example, McCully, 1971, p. 83).

We have aimed to describe, illustrate, and create a mood enabling us to recreate a picture of the power, function, and impact of the Great Mother or ruling goddess of the ancient world, primarily focusing on upper Paleolithic times. We have used known data to reconstruct the primary qualities of the nature or personal characteristics of the goddess. These qualities are twofold and opposites, one side of her character being positive, fertile, and sustaining for mankind, and the other, destructive, abandoning, and inimical to human welfare.

The nature of the goddess clearly took primary qualities from moon phases; one bright and waxing, the other dark and waning. By virtue of ancient society's relationship to the goddess, her priestesses and surrogates, and by performing prescribed rituals, ancient members of her cult projected onto the goddess unconscious contents originating in themselves. In the instance of the ruling goddess, this projection is an equivalent of the feminine principle in females of the species. Through the goddess and because of her responsibilities in furthering fertility, mankind was ruled for 40,000 years or more by feminine, not masculine, power. We have shown how man began to react to matriarchal power in the Paleolithic era. Masculine power really began to rise and mix with the power of the Great Mother within the Neolithic period.

We have shown how females still carry qualities of the two sides of the Great Mother, and may, in a usually nonconscious way, link with the negative aspect of the goddess and contribute to psychological distress in others. At the same time, it is the nurturing, sustaining side of the feminine principle that has provided and contributed much to the progress made by mankind through its constructive nature.

REFERENCES

Briffault, R. (1931). *The mothers.* New York: MacMillan.

Dvivedi, M. (1934). *The yoga-sutras of Patanjali.* Madras, India: Theosophical Publishing House.

Freud, S. (1946). *Collected Papers,* Vol. 1–5. New York: The International Psychoanalytic Press.

Giedion, S. (1962). *The eternal present: The beginnings of art.* New York: Pantheon Books.

Gimbutas, M. (1982). *The goddesses and gods of old Europe.* Berkeley: University of California Press.

Gould, S. (1984). Human equality is a contingent fact of history. *Natural History, 93,* 26–34.

Haggard, R. (1966). *She.* New York: Pyramid Books. (Original work published 1887.)

Harding, M. E. (1935). *Woman's mysteries.* New York: Longmans, Green.

Harrison, J. E. (1962). *Epilegomena to the study of Greek religions and themes.* New York: University Books. (Original work published 1921.)

Herberger, C. (1979). *The riddle of the sphinx.* New York: Vantage Press.

Jung, C. G. (1979). *Collected works.* Princeton: Princeton University Press. (Original work published 1957.)

Leibniz, W. (1974). *Encyclopaedia Britannica,* vol. 13. Chicago: William Benton, p. 915.

Leroi-Gourhan, A. (1965). *Treasures of prehistoric art.* New York: Harry N. Abrams.

Marshack, A. (1972). *The roots of civilization.* New York: McGraw-Hill.

McCully, R. (1971). *Rorschach theory and symbolism.* Baltimore: Williams & Wilkins.

Neumann, E. (1955). *The great mother.* New York: Pantheon Books.

Patai, R. (1967). *The Hebrew goddess.* Jerusalem: Ktav Publishing.

Chapter 8

INFANTICIDE AND AGGRESSION TOWARD CHILDREN AS REFLECTED IN GREEK AND EARLY CHRISTIAN FANTASY, DREAMS, MYTHS, AND REALITY[1]

Robert Rousselle

Among Freudian and neo-Freudian analysts, Freud's interpretation of the Oedipus myth usually was accepted until George Devereux (1953) introduced the Laius complex. Using data gathered from his anthropological and psychoanalytic research, Devereux, in a reexamination of the Oedipus myth, argued that Oedipus' murder of his father was a response to his father's homosexual rape of Chrysippus and exposure of Oedipus. The same psychodynamics are found in the myth of Tantalus, who included his son Pelops in a cannibalistic feast. In a series of papers over the next 15 years, Devereux used ethnopsychoanalytic data to expand and buttress his theory (1955, 1963, 1978, 1980).

Psychoanalytically inclined scholars from several disciplines have continued the investigation of parental cannibalism. Psychoanalyst Dorothy Block (1978) has shown how a child's fear of parental violence, either cannibalistic or some other kind, often results in severe personality disorders. Douglas Milburn (1982) sees cannibalism as one component of the filicidal tendency of Western Civilization. Expanding the investigation into primitive societies, Eli Sagan (1974) interprets cannibalism as the earliest expression of parent-child aggressions.

An examination of several myths and rituals from archaic and classical

[1]Revised version of paper presented at Eighth Annual Convention, International Psychohistorical Association, 1985.

Greece and, half a millennium later, from early Christianity, shows a preoccupation with parental cannibalism. Although we have no definite, undeniable examples of cannibalism of any kind from that period, the appearance of myths and rituals of this kind reveals much about the fantasies and repressed desires of these cultures, and about the cathartic means by which they were overcome.

We will use the primeval succession myth of Ouranos, Kronos, and Zeus as the paradigm of the Greek parent-child relationships. The earliest and "classic" version is found in the *Theogeny* of Hesiod, dating to the eighth century B.C. (1913).

The first pair of gods to conceive offspring were Gaia (Earth) and Ouranos (Sky), to whom were born the Titans, the youngest of whom was crafty Kronos. Hating his children, Ouranos hid them in a secret place in Earth. Gaia, distressed and physically uncomfortable, made an adamantine sickle and planned with Kronos that he would hide in ambush and castrate his father when he came to lie with Gaia. Everything succeeded according to plan, and Kronos became the ruler of the gods.

Kronos was told by his parents that he would be overthrown by one of his sons, so he swallowed each of his children as they were born. His wife Rhea then bore Zeus in hiding and gave Kronos a stone wrapped in swaddling clothes, which he swallowed. Zeus grew quickly and Rhea gave Kronos a potion, causing him to vomit up the stone and all his children. Numerous battles over the next 10 years raged among Kronos and the Titans and Zeus and his brethren and allies until Zeus was victorious. Kronos and the Titans were incarcerated in Tartarus, deep below the earth.

Zeus, himself, was destined to be overthrown by the son of his wife, Metis. When she was pregnant, Zeus swallowed her, thus preventing the birth of the child and any chance of the mother coming to the child's aid. Thus, Zeus continued to rule.

Hesiod's *Theogeny* is a rich, multifaceted poem allowing various interpretations on many different levels. Recent interpretations have focused on the entire poem as a statement of familial patterns of interaction, male-female relations, and the establishment of justice (Arthur, 1982; Humphreys, 1983). Our discussion concentrates on the three passages cited above as a paradigm of the parent-child relationship.

All three fathers fear or hate their children and try to do away with them. Kronos swallows all his children out of fear of the one destined to overthrow him, while Zeus swallows the pregnant mother whose son is fated to depose him. Ouranos' motive is said to be hatred of his children, though later in the poem he is said to have imprisoned his fifty-headed, hundred-armed sons Obriareus, Cottus, and Gyes because he hated their overwhelming manliness, shape, and size. Although Kronos and Zeus perform acts of cannibalism, Ouranos, actions are less clear. He conceals his children in a hollow, or vault, deep within Earth, and Gaia groans because she is monstrously full. Kronos ambushes and emasculates Ouranos as he has intercourse with Gaia.

Though unspecific, the children of Ouranos appear to be hidden in the womb of Gaia, and Kronos waits in ambush near the vagina (Kirk, 1970). The children in the womb represent an interminable pregnancy, which is a common motif in other cultures of a wish not to give birth, an analogue to abortion. The unborn child of an interminable pregnancy is frequently accused of trying to kill itself and the mother (Devereux, 1976).

Gaia and Rhea help their sons overthrow their father, while Metis is swallowed in order to prevent that from happening. Ouranos is punished by castration, which feminizes him. Hesiod only tells us that Kronos is imprisoned deep within womb-like Tartarus, yet lines 207–210 and 472–473 may imply that the same fate awaits Kronos in retribution for castrating his father. Indeed, later authors mention the castration of Kronos, including Timaeus (circa 356–260 B.C.) and Lycophron in the fourth century B.C. Devereux (1970) argues that, in addition to the castration of Kronos, the eventual castration and feminization of Zeus is anticipated in Greek myth and literature.

As a paradigm of Greek parent-child relationships, the myth shows that Greek men feared their children as people who eventually would supplant them, while it seems, on the surface, that Greek women treated their children in a more positive manner. We later will see that women had their own hostilities toward their children, which, out of social necessity, had to be repressed in order for society to survive. As abortions and infanticides abounded, prolonged pregnancies and cannibalistic feasts were fantasized. Castration and feminization of the father represented the fathers' fears and their sons' fantasies related to them.

Historical examples reflect the same pattern (Eyben, 1980). For example, men determined the fate of the newborn child: whether to accept or expose it. In Athens, as in most Greek states, it was father's decision, whereas in Sparta a council of elders made the determination. In some states such as Gortyn, even a divorced woman had to hand over the newborn to her ex-husband, who decided its fate (Lacey, 1968). Abortion frequently was resorted to by prostitutes and errant wives. It was also an accepted means of limiting family size. Here, too, the father was the decision-maker (a right protected by surviving legal fragments).

Abortion was common. The techniques were many, with varying degrees of success or danger. The Hippocratic Oath notwithstanding, many physicians were willing to help a woman abort a child (Preus, 1975). The frequency with which infanticide was practiced is debated, and recent studies indicate that, on demographic grounds, infanticide cannot have been very widespread (Engels, 1980). On the other hand, the father did have the right to accept or reject his child, a right the mother did not have. Whether the child was exposed depended on its health, the family's ability to feed another mouth, and the father's temperament (Lacey, 1968). On occasion, even an older child was killed. Aeschines (circa 397–322 B.C.) tells us of a daughter who was walled up and starved to death by her father for not preserving her virginity until her marriage. In this case, the father rid himself of a child he did not want, although in the case of infanticide, hostility toward one's children could easily be transferred to the newborn.

Greek society in Athens and Sparta could be defined as "father-avoidance." In Athens, the infant was raised by his mother, who spent most of her life at home. If the family was well-off, a nurse or a male slave would help take care of the child. The father's traditional place was not at home, but at work, in the agora or in the assembly. In one of his dialogues, Plato (circa 429–347 B.C.) has Laches say that those occupied with public affairs "are too apt to be negligent and careless of their own children and their private concerns," a point later echoed by the Boiotian Plutarch (circa 50–120 A.D.). After the child reached puberty, he was taught his lessons in civic and military obligations, not by his father, but by a male lover in his twenties. When the youth reached his twenties, he in turn, became the lover and teacher of a teenage boy. In an idealized passage in the *Symposium,* Plato claims that the bonds between lovers are stronger than those between parent and child. At 30, the young man was ready to marry and leave his children in the hands of his wife, while he fulfilled his civic duties (Marrou, 1964).

In Sparta, fathers spent most of their adult life in a perpetual military camp, living and sleeping in the barracks. Even after completion of training at age 30, few went home to live with their wives. Children were brought up by the women of the house, girls remaining at home until marriage, boys until they were seven years old. From ages 7 to 30, boys were trained as soldiers and supervised by older men, male lovers, and their other leaders. The Spartan father had similarly little to do with his children.

Devereux (1967) suggests that the "prolonged adolescence" encouraged by this method of childrearing was the major cause of Greek creativity. In addition, the custom was also an effective means of separating and protecting the children from the destructive, cannibalistic impulses of the father. This was in contrast to the Roman fathers, who carefully watched over their sons' education.

Men were allowed to act out their cannibalistic fantasies in several religious cults, some of which owed their legendary foundations to an act of parental cannibalism. The Arcadians were the oldest and most primitive people of Greece. Their legends tell of an early king, Lykaion, who sacrificed a child and tried to feed it to Zeus in a cannibalistic feast (Hesiod). Some versions specify the child as Nyktimos, the son of Lykaion. Zeus punished Lykaion by turning him into a wolf. Plato and Pausanias (circa 150 A.D.), 600 years later, tell of reputed human sacrifices at the shrine of Zeus Lykaios, where any man who ate human entrails became a wolf for nine years.

Scholarly interpretations of such a paucity of data vary. For example, J. G. Frazier (1921) suggests that the rite reflected the initiation of the eight-year tenure of the king or priest of the Wolf-God. Walter Burkhart (1983) interprets it as an initiation rite for young men into the secret society of the wolf-men. Certain points are clear, however. To eat of the child's body is re-

jected at that stage of development and becomes a crime punished by met-
amorphosis into a wolf. Those who managed to avoid human flesh in the feast
were allowed to return to human society. The fantasy of parental cannibalism, however, is enacted as part of the religious festival and meaningfully
participated in by those who are believed to have eaten human flesh. The cave
of Rhea, where she is believed to have hidden from Kronos and given birth
to Zeus, was near the shrine of Zeus Lykaios. Only women consecrated to
Rhea were allowed to enter. The celebration, undoubtedly, reinforced maternal obligations to their children.

At Olympia, sacrifices were made to Pelops, the son of Tantalus, himself the victim of a cannibalistic feast (Burkhart, 1983). Also connected with
the Olympic ritual were Zeus and Demeter, the other major figures of the
myth of Pelops. In that myth, Tantalus was punished in Hades, Pelops was
restored to life by Zeus, and the shoulder eaten by Demeter, was later replaced by one of ivory. The rite of Zeus Lykaios was designed to bring the
Arcadians together, just as the Olympic Games united the Greeks through
athletic events. In a series of society-preserving rites, the desire for parental
cannibalism was acknowledged, but shown to be an act which causes the social isolation of the cannibal.

Parental cannibalism is also found in the religious beliefs of the mystical
philosopher Empedokles (circa 493–433 B.C.). In one fragment, for instance, he describes the slaughter of son by father:

> The father lifts up his own son changed in form and slaughters him with
> a prayer, blind fool, as he shrieks piteously, beseeching as he sacrifices.
> But he, deaf to his cries, slaughters him and makes ready in his halls an
> evil feast. In the same way son seizes father and children their mother,
> and tearing out the life they eat the flesh of those they love (Kirk, Raven,
> & Schofield, 1983, p. 319).

The fragment is from Empedokles' poem, *Purifications,* which deals with
the cycle of reincarnations brought about by the primal sin of eating meat.
A man in one life might be an animal in another, slaughtered and eaten by
his own family. Significantly, it is the sacrifice and eating of the son by the
father that Empedokles describes in detail.

Parental cannibalism, however repressed, sublimated, or acted out in an
occasional infanticide, should find an outlet in dreams. The *Oneirocritica* of
Artemidorus (circa late second century A.D.) contains several illustrations. To
dream of Kronos was believed to be inauspicious for marriages and child-
births. Usually, cannibalism dreams are good omens, except for dreams of
eating one's own child, which foretells the death of the child. These are obvious wish-fulfillment dreams, revealing strong infanticidal urges. Another
two infanticidal dreams further illustrate the point. A man dreamed he flayed
his child and made a wineskin out of the body. To Artemidorus, it prophe-

sied the manner of the child's death by drowning. To us, it represents the father's hatred for his son and arouses the suspicion that he might have had a hand, however accidental, in the child's death. A woman dreamed she was drunk and danced for Dionysus. In imitation of Agave and Pentheus, she killed her three-year-old child. Again, the parent's hatred for her child is obvious.

The practice of abortion and infanticide and the celebrations of allegedly cannibalistic religious feasts allowed parents an outlet for their cannibalistic fantasies. The "father-avoidance" nature of Greek society relieved fathers from close contact with their children, possibly as a means of controlling anger. In contrast, as Greek mothers were always at home and in constant contact with their children, their cannibalistic fantasies had to be severely repressed in order for society to survive. Outlets were few. The dream of the woman who drank and danced to Dionysus, however, shows that such feelings did exist.

Dreams of pregnant women are significant. A lion cub, says Artemidorus, reflects the birth of a child. The mother of Perikles dreamed she gave birth to a lion shortly before his birth, a sign of his bold and lion-like nature (Herodotus, circa 484–420 B.C.; Plutarch, circa 50–120 A.D.). The lion cub dream reflects another fantasy. Many Greeks believed that the lion cubs tore their mother's womb with their claws at birth. The parents who dreamed of lion cubs were projecting their aggressive feelings for the fetus onto the fetus itself, thereby justifying their own hostility (Devereux, 1980).

Other pregnant women dreamed they gave birth to a snake, indicating to Artemidorus and the dreamer that the child will become just like mother. In distinction to lion's dreams, Greeks believed that baby snakes are born by eating their way through the mother's abdominal wall, or else, the sides of the mother just burst open (Herodotus; Aelian, circa 170–235 A.D.). The cannibalistic impulses of the parent are here again projected onto the fetus.

Repression of the cannibalistic impulses by mothers can also be seen in the series of maternal bogeys who have populated the imaginations of Greek children from Sappho in the late sixth century B.C., until today (R. and E. Blum, 1970). No extensive mythology is connected to them and they frequently appear as isolated references in literary works. Gello was a girl who died young, and her ghost is said to cause the premature deaths of other children. Mentioned by Sappho, Gello seems to be a local bogeywoman of Lesbos. More frequently attested are the Empusae and Mormo, who kidnap and eat children and young men (Aristophanes, circa 450–385 B.C.; Philostratus, circa 170–249 A.D.). In her beautiful poem, *The Distaff,* Erinna (circa late fourth century B.C.) recalls how she and her girlfriend were terrified as children by stories of Mormo, while Lucian (circa 120–180 A.D.) tells us that Mormo was used to frighten children. Lamia was another maternal bogey cited by Strabo (circa 64 B.C.–21 A.D.) and Lucian as a device to frighten children. According to legend, her children had died and, out of jealousy, she ordered all newborn children slain. Only when she drinks wine or takes her eyes out to go to sleep are children safe (Strabo; Plutarch; Siculus, circa late first century B.C.). The substitution of one oral craving by another satisfies the cannibalistic impulses and anticipates the wine blood substitution of the Christian Eucharist. The removal of the eyes is more complex. Although the eyes can have a passive, feminine quality, here we may be dealing with a screen for the eyes-testicles identification. The female Lamia acts like a devouring male when she can see, but when she takes out her eyes, which equals castration, and goes to sleep, she becomes a passive female (Devereux, 1956).

These maternal bogeys usually have been interpreted as expressions of male fear of mature women or the child's fear of the emotional needs of the mother (Slater, 1974). Interestingly, however, the stories presumably were told to children by their mothers or their nurses. It, therefore, is possible that women adopted and internalized the negative attitudes of the Greek men toward them (Simon, 1978). It seems even more likely, however, that women used voracious, cannibalistic bogeywomen as expressions of their own repressed aggressiveness toward their children.

As with all repressions, some form of ritualized release is necessary lest a woman go mad. One such release was the Dionysian *omophagia,* when the women, at the height of their devotional ecstasy, tore living animals apart and ate the raw flesh. Certain animals were preferred, such as bulls, goats, fawns, vipers, lion cubs, gazelles, and young wolves (Dodds, 1960). Although the sources for the *omophagia* refer to mythological works, we have evidence to show that it was practiced in historical times. It is mentioned in a Milesian inscription dating to 276 B.C. (Milet) in the early second century A.D. Plutarch states that eating raw flesh was a then current religious ritual.

Scattered throughout the sources are occasional references to cannibalism or human sacrifice in the Dionysiac rites. Several Aegean islands, Chios, Tenedos, and Lesbos, practiced human sacrifice to a god, and the Bassares were cannibals as well (Porphyry, circa 232–305 A.D.; Clement, circa 150–216 A.D.). During the height of the Persian War, three Persian youths were sacrificed to Dionysus by the Athenians. Other literary works and many vase paintings depict the Maenads of Dionysus as carrying off babies in a raid (Beasley, 1942).

There are two other sources illustrating the connection between human sacrifice or cannibalism and the *omophagia* of living animals. Near Thebes, an adolescent boy was sacrificed to Dionysus, until the god allowed a billy-goat to be substituted (Pausanius). At Tenedos, a pregnant cow was treated like a human mother. When the calf was born, it was dressed in buskins and then sacrificed to Dionysus, the Mansmasher (Aelian). As a literary device, the Greeks tended to theriomorphize human actions and emotions. It also found application in religion: animals were substitutes for the original human victims of the Maenads (all the evidence points to child victims).

For example, in one instance a billy-goat replaced a boy. A calf became the victim in another. Euripides describes young animals in a more domestic scene in the mountainous wilds outside Thebes:

> Breasts swollen with milk, new mothers who had left their babies behind
> at home nestled gazelles and young wolves in their arms, suckling them.

After the Dionysiac frenzy struck, they swooped down on a field of cattle:

> and then you could have seen a single woman with bare hands tear a fat
> calf, still bellowing with fright, in two, while others clawed the heifers to
> pieces.

Dodds (1960) suggests that eating animals, replacing the earlier human victim, symbolized the eating of the god Dionysus, in order to ingest the god's powers. Another interpretation presents itself when Dionysus takes the role of being the god of married women (Zeitlin, 1982). Forced by social constraints to repress hostility toward their children, the women needed a socially accepted outlet to unleash their pent-up aggressions. Their hostility was sublimated by substitution, as young animals were torn apart and eaten raw by the Maenads. There was further ritualized control as only certain women could become Maenads (Sagan).

According to several legends, those who would refuse to acknowledge Dionysus were destined to suffer the real madness of breaking the constraints of custom and devouring their own children. Best known are the three daughters of Cadmus, who rejected Dionysus, became mad, and eventually killed Pentheus, son of Agave (Euripides). The three daughters of Minyas drew lots among their children and then tore Hippasus apart and devoured him, a ritual lasting to Plutarch's day. The earliest version of the myth of the daughters of Proetus blames their madness on Dionysus as a punishment inflicted on them, having refused to accept the God. They, too, destroyed their children (Hesiod).

This pattern of infanticide was later incorporated into the Roman culture. A poignant papyrus letter from Egypt, dating to 1 B.C. (Hunt & Edgar, 1932), records the tender feelings of a young man separated from his wife and children. He closes the letter, reminding his pregnant wife to care for the baby when it is born, but if it should turn out to be a girl, then she was obliged to destroy it.

A few decades after this letter was written, Christianity began to attract followers, first in Judea and later throughout the Greco-Roman world. One of the distinctions the early Christians took pride in was that, comparing themselves with the pagans, they did not practice abortion or infanticide (Epistle to Diognetus, circa late second century A.D.; Athenagoras, circa late second century A.D.). Christian attitudes toward children were much better than those of most pagans. In the gospels, Jesus frequently commends the innocence of children as an ideal. Even when the child Jesus seems to misbehave, missing his parents' caravan while tarrying in the Temple with the Elders, he is following God's wishes and seems, therefore, misunderstood by his parents (Luke, circa late first century A.D.). In contrast, some of the apocryphal infancy gospels paint a picture of child Jesus misusing his powers to maim, blind, or kill people, sometimes correcting his actions, other times not (James, 1924). The infancy gospels portray a monstrous, aggressive Jesus, the projection of parental aggression onto the Son of Man. The positive attitude is more frequent.

The Acts of Andrew and Matthias, from late antiquity, is a fictionalized account of the journey of the two apostles to the land of the maneaters. An epiphany of the child Jesus foretells the coming tribulations, which include the deaths of the executioners and of the fathers who had urged that their children be eaten in their stead. Despite their positive attitude toward children, the central rite of the Christians was the Eucharist, the eating of bread and wine believed to be the body and blood of Jesus.

The synoptic gospels (Mark, Luke, Matthew, late first century A.D.) record the events of the last supper. In each, Jesus refers to himself in the third person as the Son of Man, and gives the apostles the bread, which is his body, and the wine, which is his blood. Paul (circa mid first century A.D.) reaffirms this identity in *I Corinthians,* though he refers to Jesus as Lord. Although Lord became a common expression, his identity as the Son of Man and the Son of God remained strong. It is found in the epistles of Ignatius (circa early second century A.D.), who was martyred in the reign of Trajan, and in the contemporary *Epistle of Barnabas* (circa early second century A.D.). Though the bread-body and wine-blood identity is ignored in the early manual of Christian instruction known as the *Didache,* Ignatius characterizes heretics as those who do not believe that the Eucharist is the flesh of Jesus.

The celebration of the Eucharist, no doubt, lay behind the pagan accusations of cannibalism. Already in the early second century, Pliny writes Trajan that the Christians he found in Bithynia eat only ordinary food, a hint perhaps of accusations of cannibalism. Allegations of Thyestian banquets and Oedipal unions, that is, cannibalism and incest, followed the cult for the next two centuries (Athenagoras; Tertullian, circa 160–240 A.D.; Minicius Felix). The orator Cornelius Fronto is cited as the source of one of these now considered lurid descriptions. Pagan intellectuals criticized Christianity on a more sophisticated level, using philosophical and theological arguments (Wilkin, 1984). The Christian apologists, however, in bringing up the allegations of cannibalism and incest, often give a detailed description of the crimes of which they are accused, counterattacking with lurid accounts of Greek myths of similar deeds. No pagan intellectual really believed the Christians committed these heinous acts, and the commoners who did believe it probably, could not and would not, read the Christian apologists.

The impression grows that at least some Christian apologists enjoyed retelling the accusations. Tertullian laughs at the magistrate who "found" a Christian who had eaten 100 babies. In the *Octavius,* Minucius Felix writes:

> Details of the initiation of neophytes are as revolting as they are noto-
> rious. An infant, cased in dough to deceive the unsuspecting, is placed
> beside the person to be initiated. The novice is thereupon induced to in-
> flict what seem to be harmless blows upon the dough, and unintention-
> ally the infant is killed by his unsuspecting blows; the blood—oh,
> horrible—they lap up greedily; the limbs they tear to pieces eagerly; and
> over the victim they make league and covenant, and by complicity in guilt
> pledge themselves to mutual silence . . . (pp. 5–7).

The Christians respond with a detailed attack on pagan myths of cannibalism and infanticide, by assertions that they consider abortion and infanticide to be murder, and cannibalism even more foul.

Christian authors, however, reserved their most venemous attacks for the
heretics, who, among other things, did not celebrate the Eucharist properly.
Clement of Alexandria accuses the Carpocratians of celebrating a "love feast,"
where the celebrants had intercourse with anyone. Justin Martyr (100–165
A.D.) tells us that some heretics would arrange to have a lamp fall over in
order to engage in random intercourse and cannibalism. In the confusion,
these became the exact accusations leveled against orthodox Christians. We
find, perhaps, the most imaginative description by Epiphanius of Cyprus,
leveled against the Phibionites:

> When they thus ate together . . . they turn to excitements. The man leav-
> ing his wife says to his own wife: "Stand up and perform the *agape* with
> the brother." Then the unfortunates unite with each other, as I am truly
> ashamed to say the shameful things that are being done by them. . . . The
> woman and the man take the fluid of the emission of the man into their
> hands . . . and pray . . . "We offer to thee this gift, the body of Christ,"
> and then they eat it . . . (Wilkin, 1984, pp. 20–21).

Many scholars are skeptical as to whether such rites were ever cele-
brated; others believe that an occasional libertine Christian sect might have
practiced such rites, which were then accepted as usual Christian practice by
the pagans.

The obsession of some Christian authors with detailing the accusations
made against them, while leveling similar accusations against the heretics,
seems to be two expressions of the same problem. These authors had a deep-
seated guilt, an awareness of the cannibalistic impulse of parents toward their
children. The ostentatious disavowal of any wrong-doing on their part, cou-
pled with their projections of these acts onto their sectarian enemies, illustrates the strength of the urge. Repression of their cannibalistic impulses, in
addition to repressing aggression toward the "neighbor" the Christians are

supposed to love, necessitated a weekly Eucharistic ritual, featuring the eating of the Son of God, who is also the Son of Man.

In conclusion, cannibalistic fantasies by parents are documented in ancient Greece, as they are in many civilizations. The Greeks, still acting out some of their cannibalistic impulses by abortions and occasional infanticides, sublimated others in annual religious feasts, or, in biannual Dionysiaca. Displacing outlets for aggression were available in warfare and athletic events. For the early Christians, the avoidance of abortion and infanticide required frequent enactments of the sublimated cannibalistic feast, the Eucharist.

REFERENCES

Aelian (c. 170–235 A.D.). De natura animalium. In A. F. Schofield (Ed.) (1958–1959). *On the characteristics of animals.* Cambridge: Harvard University Press.

Aeschines (c. 397–322 B.C.). Contra timarchus. In C. D. Adams (Ed.). (1919). *Speeches.* Cambridge: Harvard University Press.

Aristophanes (c. 450–385 B.C.). Ranae. In F. W. Hall & W. M. Geldart (Eds.) (1906–1907). *Commoediae.* Oxford: Oxford University Press.

Artemidorus (c. late second century A.D.). Oneirocritica. In R. White (trans.). (1975). *The interpretation of dreams: The oneirocritica of Artemidorus.* New Jersey: Noyes Press.

Arthur, M. B. (1982). Cultural strategies in Hesiod's theogeny: Law, family, society. *Arethusa, 15,* 63–82.

Athenagoras (c. late second century A.D.). Legatio. In W. R. Schoedel (1972). *Athenagoras: Legatio and de resurrectione.* Oxford: Oxford University Press.

Beasley, J. D. (1942). *Attic red-figure vases.* Oxford: Oxford University Press.

Block, D. (1978). *So the witch won't eat me: Fantasy and the child's fear of infanticide.* Boston: Houghton Mifflin.

Blum, R. & Blum, E. (1970). *The dangerous hour.* New York: Charles Scribner's Sons.

Burkhart, W. (1983). *Homo necans.* P. Bing (trans.). Berkeley: University of California Press.

Clement (c. 150–216 A.D.). In G. W. Butterworth (Ed.), *The exhortation to the Greeks.* Cambridge: Harvard University Press.

Devereux, G. (1953). Why Oedipus killed Laius: A note on the complementary Oedipus complex in Greek drama. *International Journal of Psychoanalysis, 34.* 132–141.

Devereux, G. (1955). A counteroedipal episode in Homer's *Iliad. Bulletin of the Philadelphia Association for Psychoanalysis, 4,* 90–97.

Devereux, G. (1956). A note on the feminine significance of the eyes. *Bulletin of the Philadelphia Association for Psychoanalysis, 6,* 21–24.

Devereux, G. (1963). Sociopolitical functions of the Oedipus myth in early Greece. *Psychoanalytic Quarterly, 32.*

Devereux, G. (1967). Greek pseudo-homosexuality and the "Greek miracle." *Symbolae Osloensis, 42,* 69–92.

Devereux, G. (1970). La naissance d'Aphrodite (The birth of Aphrodite). In Pouillon & Maranda (Eds.), *Echanges et communications.* Paris: Melanges Levi-Strauss.

Devereux, G. (1976). *A study of abortion in primitive societies.* New York: International Universities Press.

Devereux, G. (1978). Ethnopsychoanalytic reflections on the notion of kinship. In *Ethnopsychoanalysis.* Berkeley: University of California Press, pp. 177–215.

Devereux, G. (1980). *Basic problems of ethnopsychiatry.* Chicago: University of Chicago Press.

Dodds, E. R. (Ed.). (1960). *Euripides bacchae* (2nd ed.). Oxford: Clarendon Press.

Engels, D. (1980). The problems of female infanticide in the Greco-Roman world. *Classical Philology, 75,* 112–120.

Epistle of Barnabas (c. early second century A.D.). In K. Lake (Ed.). (1912–1913). *The apostolic fathers.* Cambridge: Harvard University Press.

Epistle to Diognetus (c. late second century A.D.). (See Epistle of Barnabas.)

Erinna (c. late fourth century B.C.). The distaff. In D. L. Page (Ed.). (1941). *Select papyri III.* Cambridge: Harvard University Press.

Eyben, E. (1980). Family planning in Greco-Roman antiquity. *Ancient Society, 11/12.*

Frazier, J. G. (1921). Commentary in Apollodorus. In *The library.* Cambridge: Harvard University Press, p. 393.

Herodotus (c. 484–420 B.C.). In C. Hude (Ed.). (1927). *Historiae.* Oxford: Oxford University Press.

Hesiod, (c. early seventh century B.C.). Theogonia. In A. Rzach (Ed.). (1913). *Hesiodus.* Leipzig: Teubner.

Humphreys, S. (1983). Women in antiquity. In *The family, women and death.* London: Routledge and Kegan Paul, pp. 33–51.

Hunt, A. S. & Edgar, C. C. (1932). *Select papyri I.* Cambridge: Harvard University Press, pp. 294–295.

Ignatius (c. early second century A.D.). (See Epistle of Barnabas.)

James, M. R. (1924). *The apocryphal New Testament.* Oxford: Clarendon Press.

Kirk, G. S. (1970). *Myth: Its meaning and functions in ancient and other cultures.* Berkeley: University of California Press.

Kirk, G. S., Raven, J. E., & Schofield, M. (1983). *The pre-Socratic philosophers.* New York: Cambridge University Press.

Lacey, W. K. (1968). *The family in classical Greece.* Ithaca: Cornell University Press.

Lucian (c. 120–180 A.D.). Philopseudes. In A. M. Harmon, K. Kilburn, & M. D. Macleod (Eds.). (1913–1967). *Lucian.* Cambridge: Harvard University Press.

Lycophron (late fourth century B.C.). Alexandra. In R. Mair (Ed.). (1955). *Callimachus: Hymns and epigrams, Lycophron and Aratus.* Cambridge: Harvard University Press.

Mark, Matthew, Luke (first century A.D.). In H. G. May & B. M. Metzger (Eds.). (1965). *The Oxford Annotated Bible* (revised version). New York: Oxford University Press.

Marrou, H. E. (1964). *A history of education in antiquity.* G. Lamb (trans.). New York: New American Library.

Martyr, J. (100–165 A.D.). Apologia. In J. C. T. Otto (Ed.). (1851–1881). *Corpus apologetarum christianorum saeculi secundi.* Germany: Jena.

Milburn, D. (1982). *Filicide: The mythic reality of childhood.* Washington, D.C.: University Press of America.

Milet (1908). *Sechster vorläufiger Bericht über die in Milet in Didyma ünternommenen Aüsgrabungen.* Berlin: Abhandlungen der Preussischen Akademie der Wissenschaften.

Minucius Felix. (1931). *Octavius.* G. H. Rendall (trans.). Cambridge: Harvard University Press.

Paul (c. mid first century A.D.). *I Corinthians.* (See Epistle of Barnabas.)

Pausanias (c. 150 A.D.). In W. H. S. Jones, H. A. Ormerod, & R. E. Wycherley (Eds.). (1918–1935). *Description of Greece.* Cambridge: Harvard University Press.

Philostratus (c. 170–249 A.D.). In F. C. Conybeare (Ed.). (1912). *Life of Apollonius of Tyana.* Cambridge: Harvard University Press.

Plato (c. 429–347 B.C.). Laches. In N. H. Fowler, et al. (Eds.). (1914–1935). *Plato.* Cambridge: Harvard University Press.

Pliny (c. 61–112 A.D.). Epistles. In B. Radice (Ed.). (1969). *Letters and panegyricus.* Cambridge: Harvard University Press.

Plutarch. (c. 50–120 A.D.). In B. Perrin (Ed.). (1914–1926). *The parallel lives.* Cambridge: Harvard University Press.

Plutarch (c. 50–120 A.D.). In F. C. Babbit, W. C. Helmbold, et al. (Eds.). (1927–1969). *Moralia.* Cambridge: Harvard University Press.

Porphyry (c. 232–305 A.D.). De abscinentia. In A. Nauck (Ed.). (1886). *Opuscula selecta.* Leipzig: Teubner.

Preus, A. (1975). Biomedical techniques for influencing human reproduction in the fourth century B.C. *Arethusa, 8,* 251–256.

Sagan, E. (1974). *Cannibalism.* New York: Psychohistory Press.

Sappho (c. early sixth century B.C.). In D. A. Campbell (Ed.). (1981). *Greek Lyric,* Vol. 1. Cambridge: Harvard University Press.

Siculus, Diodorus (c. late first century B.C.). In C. H. Oldfather, et al. (Eds.). (1933–1967). *Library of history.* Cambridge: Harvard University Press.

Simon, B. (1978). *Mind and madness in ancient Greece.* Ithaca: Cornell University Press.

Slater, P. (1974). The Greek family in history and myth. *Arethusa, 7.*

Strabo (c. 64 B.C.–21 A.D.). In H. L. Jones (Ed.). (1917–1932). *Geography* Cambridge: Harvard University Press.

Tertullian (c. 160–240 A.D.). Apologeticus. In T. R. Glover, G. H. Rendall (1931). *Tertullian: Apology and de spectaculis and Minucius Felix: Octavius.* Cambridge: Harvard University Press.

Timaeus (c. 356–260 B.C.). In F. Jacoby (Ed.). (1926–1958). *Fragmente der griechischen historiker.* Leiden: E. J. Brill.

Wilkin, R. (1984). *The Christians as the Romans saw them.* New Haven: Yale University Press.

Zeitlin, F. I. (1982). Cultic models of the female: Rites of Dionysus and Demeter. *Arethusa, 15,* 23.

Chapter 9

CHILD KILLING AND CHILD RESCUING[1]

Judith S. Kestenberg
Milton Kestenberg

Provided in this chapter is a brief account of the history of infanticide and its derivatives, showing how infanticide and cruelty to children were revived in pure culture not only in the Nazi aggression against alien children, but also against their own children. The genocide of Jews turned out to be a distorted mirror image of the German "drang" (drive) to kill and exterminate their own. This point will serve as a springboard of the revision of Freud's thesis about the origin of Jewish spirituality and morality in the renouncing of patricide. We shall try to show that the renouncing of infanticide, as it is shown in the biblical story of Abraham and Isaac, stamped Jews for all times as rescuers and saviors of children. Finally, we shall postulate that precisely this role of Jews as child-rescuers and child lovers made them the target of those who cannot control their impulses to sacrifice children for the glory of the father and the fatherland.

Modern languages have a term, "widow," to describe the wife of a deceased husband, the term "orphan" to describe the child of a deceased parent. There is no term for one who survives the death of his child. The bereaved parent, faced with a plethora of such deaths through history, either denied his grief or taking fate into his own hand, killed the child himself and declared himself the master of the child's destiny. Religious killing, in which child murder is done at the bidding of gods, is known from the histories of

[1]From the Jerome Riker International Study of Organized Persecution of Children

Egypt, Greece, Rome, the Germanic tribes, and from the Bible. Such sacrifices were ubiquitous in ancient times.

The world of Greek gods is replete with stories of infanticide committed by gods themselves. Uranus, created by Gaea, the earth mother, hated and persecuted his children (Muslin, 1984). His son killed his children as soon as they were born. Fathers slew sons or condemned them to death in order to prolong their own lives and keep these menacing children from killing the fathers. They sacrificed their daughters in gratitude to gods who had favored them in wars and saved their lives and their throne.

Throughout ancient history, warriors would kill other people's children. Ancient mythology is replete with stories of how Hera, Zeus' wife, conspired to kill not only her husband's paramours, but also their children. Both male and female gods were child killers, and only some goddesses turned out to be child saviors. The primordial aggressive mother (Neuman, 1955) has all the hallmarks of a composite man and woman and appears to symbolize the combined strength of parents united against the child. In Greek mythology, goddesses conferred immortality on the infant sons of kings by burning them in the fire at night. The fire in Greek mythology releases us from the bondage of corruption, it likens us to gods, makes us meet with them, and converts our material nature into the immaterial. Death becomes a heroic road to immortality, which we also see in the Germanic Valhalla.

The sacrifice of the first born son was an old rite. Xerxes, marching through Thessaly to attack Spartans, was shown the sanctuary of the Lyphystian Zeus where the oldest male scion of the king's family in each generation was sacrificed to Zeus. Frazer (1890) quotes Plutarch in describing the custom of Orchomenus, where the women of the royal family were drawing lots to determine which woman would sacrifice her child. When the lot fell on Leucippe, she surrendered her son who was torn limb by limb by the rest of the women.

Tacitus described with admiration how the Teutons used to put their newborns into ice water to test whether they would survive and thus prove to be healthy. Children with physical defects were killed. The same practice was known in Greece and ancient Rome. Tacitus criticized the Jews who did not follow this practice but let all their children live. Although Jewish legends refer to ancient ceremonies in which mothers held their babies and jumped over fire, dropping their babies into it as a sacrifice to Moloch, this was condemned in the Torah. A death penalty was instituted for participating in such pagan ceremonies (Kings II 21–6; 23:10 Jeremiah 7:3; 10:5).

Infanticide recurred during the dark hours when Israel fell under the influence of foreign gods. The sacrifice of Jephtha's daughter (Judges 11:30) was evidence of Israel's sad spiritual state and the adoption of foreign customs prevalent at the time (from Maimonides, personal communication by Rabbi Besser). The custom of circumcision adopted by the Israelites suggests that a part of the child was sacrificed in lieu of the whole person (Morgenstern, 1963). Although the ancients not only had the right to kill their own children, and habitually killed the children of their enemies, Moses instructed the Jewish warriors to kill their enemies but not the enemies' female children who have not sinned. Herod, who conspired to kill the infant Jesus, was a representative of Roman rulers and was of Arab descent, although he was proclaimed the king of the Jews and had accepted the Jewish faith. According to St. Matthew ". . . Herod was exceedingly wroth and sent forth and slew all the children that were in Bethlehem and in all the coasts thereof, from two years and under" (Matthew, 2:16).

When the Romans conquered Judea and brought Jews as slaves to Rome, Seneca was the first to discover that the moral values of the slaves were triumphing over the might of the Roman empire. This tradition was maintained and extended by the Christian slaves who were originally Jewish. The influence of the Judeo-Christian religion contributed to the Roman Empire's decision to treat infanticide as a crime (Sagan, 1979). It is likely that population depletion of the Empire through the widespread killing of children and young people in wars was a more important factor in the enactment of a law in 372 A.D., declaring child killing to be murder. Other countries instituted a similar law much later, for example, Germany in the seventh century (deMause, 1974).

Infanticide was the most prevalent crime in the Middle Ages and under the influence of the church, was subject to death penalty. The laws, however, put the entire blame for this crime on the mother who gave birth out of wedlock. In Germany, for instance, the mother who had murdered her infant was placed into a sack with a cat or a dog and drowned in a lake while people observed and sang psalms. Faustus in Goethe's great drama assumed the guilt for seducing Margarethe and fathering her illegitimate child. He decried the doom of thousands of poor mothers who committed infanticide.

To avoid punishment, women would blame witches, Jews, or else, abandon their babies. Jews were accused of killing Christian children to get their blood in order to prepare for the Passover ceremony. Dead children were planted in Jewish homes as described in Heine's poem, "The Rabbi of Bachrach" (1820). Despite the known fact that Jewish laws prohibit the drinking of blood and prescribe that the blood is to be drained from meat before eating it, this accusation of the Jews was readily accepted and exposed them for centuries to pogroms and fraudulent law suits.

The killing of children, which began to abate at the end of the Middle Ages, has been known in almost every part of the world. The 19th century anthropologist W. Frazer (1890) found, in the records of missionaries, that Polynesians killed two-thirds of their children. Frazer quotes Battel who observed that the Jayas, a conquering tribe in Angola, were killing their children so that the women on the march might not be encumbered by babies. Frazer reported on the sacrifice of children by the Wajaggs of German East Africa in the 19th century. To appease the spirits of their forefathers they paid a water tribute by throwing a child of unblemished body into the river to drown. Only then, did they dare siphon into their irrigation channels. Infanticide, particularly of girls, was popular among Arab tribes. Although infanticide diminished as a result of the teachings of the Koran, other forms of cruelty to children persisted (Aries, 1962, pp. 103–104).

Many paintings of the Middle Ages reflected the emotional distance of mother and child even though the introduction of the Marian cult brought the mother-child relationship closer to the hearts of the people. Mary and baby Jesus were depicted as emotionally distant from each other (Aries, 1962). In other paintings, the child was frequently portrayed as a diminutive adult. Aries (1962) suggested that the enormous amount of death among children made parents insensitive to children; they could not dare to form any attachment in anticipation of an imminent death. The Renaissance brought forth a rapprochement between mother and child as could be seen in the tenderness between Jesus and his mother, as in the paintings of Raphael (Aries, 1962). Yet, many of the cruelties of medieval times persisted into this period. Children were still sent away to school at a tender age although the upper class practice of keeping tutors at home became more frequent. Most distance-producing was the custom of sending newborns away to be suckled for two years by a wet nurse in the country. Many times, these children died while in the care of their wet nurses. In Germany, these women were called "Engel-macherinnen" ("angel-makers"). Long after the custom of sending babies away to be nursed subsided in most countries, it continued in Germany. Not only are the destructive wishes of parents expressed in tales such as the Grimm Märchen, in which children are sent to be killed, abandoned, or eaten by witches, but also in 18th and 19th century lullabies, such as these:

> Baby, baby, if he hears you
> As he gallops past the house
> Limb from limb at once he will tear you
> Just as pussy cat tears a mouse
>
> And he will beat you, beat you, beat you
> And he'll beat you all to pulp
> And he'll eat you, eat you, eat you
> Every morsel, snap, snap, snap.
> (Quoted after Piers, 1978)

Several factors seem to contribute to the eventual rapprochement between mother and child and, later, father and child. The Middle Ages were a period of extremely high death rate and a depopulation through wars and plague. Children suffered the most. Perhaps, a fear of losing one's total community prompted adults to entrust their faith to children who would carry on their traditions. The frequent appearance of the Pieta as a pictorial theme may well have reflected the grief for the many children who died. In some family paintings, the dead children were included in the family group as shadowy forms (Aries). It is entirely possible that the Reformation's stress on the Old Testament and the return to biblical themes in Renaissance art reflected a revival of the old biblical values of rescuing, *not* killing children. Luther turned to Jews, whose bible he translated into German, for help in depaganizing papal doctrines. A man of violent temper, however, he turned against the Jews when they did not convert to his faith: he vilified them and called them "vermin," a degrading word accepted readily by the Nazis as a suitable epithet for Jews (*Enclyclopaedia Judaica*, 1976).

Regardless whether accounts of cruelty have been exaggerated by historians (Pollock, 1983), it is reasonable to assume that the improvement in parent-child relationship progressed from cruelty to kindness. Children became increasingly a delight and anecdotes about their cute sayings are quoted. Children were no longer relegated to the sole care of servants; however, with parents assuming more responsibility for them, obedience to parental authority was stressed. Luther himself said that he would rather see his son dead than disobedient. Even though scholars agreed that mothers' milk was best, mothers still sent their children out to nurse. Tucker (1974) states that in Renaissance England, infanticide was still very common with many deaths caused by smothering or bruising, burying alive, and strangling. Most aristocratic children were sent away to grammar school at the ages of six or seven. This practice reflected and, in essence, continued the medieval custom of putting children into service as pages or to be taken to monasteries as oblates. Abandoned and destitute children abounded and the issue of children's welfare was addressed in the Poor Relief Act of 1598. Germany was the last country to deal with the welfare of multitudes of child beggars.

Discipline as a parental duty remained an important theme in the 17th century. Swaddling clothes were still used as a means to keep babies' limbs straight. Children's "random" movement was frowned on. There is reason to believe that outright infanticide of legitimate children was uncommon. In some instances, however, baptism was arranged under such cruel conditions that the majority of the babies died in the wake of such torture (Wirth-Marvick, 1974, p. 283). On the other hand, as the population remained more steady than before, indulgence of children became more frequent.

DeMause's *History of Childhood* (1974) is replete with references to the ambivalence of parents toward their children. One of the authors, J. F. Waltzer (pp. 351–382), stresses this ambivalence in eighteenth century America. By this time, the practice of abandoning newborn children, so common in London that it was institutionalized, was almost nonexistent in America (p. 352). Children, however, were sent away to nurse; it was also common practice for older American children to be sent away to a master for schooling. Parents struggled with the fondness they had for their children. In a contemporary letter, Thomas Rame wrote to John Penn: "You think my fondness for my child will be his ruin? I hope not, for I do assure you I had rather see him dead than to have him when he is grown up, a blockhead" (p. 355).

Beginning with the pilgrims, the American colonists brought with them the Christian ideology that prompted them to regard their children as "seeds," the perpetuators of their own life. We wish particularly to quote Waltzer's (1974) remark that follows this observation as it shows, in an otherwise scholarly book, a prejudicial and unwarranted attempt to take this particular parental value away from Jews: "It has been argued," he says, that "the Jews were the first people to emphasize this idea, although it would be surprising if they really were." The reason for his surprise remains obscure (p. 363).

The philosophy of enlightenment in the eighteenth century and its promise for human happiness became particularly applicable to children through the work of Rousseau. Mothers were encouraged to nurse babies, but in the course of the next 100 years, the practice nearly ceased with wet nurses employed by rich householders in their own home. In some countries, notably Italy and Germany, the custom of sending children out continued through the eighteenth century. As he favored nursing, Rousseau attacked swaddling. We must note here again that German babies were wrapped tighter and longer than French infants; they were called, "Wickelkinder."

During the 19th century, common battering of children was on the wane. In Germany, however, the practice continued for some time; 80 percent of German parents admitted to beating children with canes (Ende, 1981). The castigating of children in schools continued from the Middle Ages; it seemed that the monastic teachers took over this weapon from the parents, and the lay teachers followed suit.

The constraints Victorian children had to endure are well known. Children were to be seen and not heard and were subject to strict discipline. Special attention was paid to constipation and masturbation; children were threatened with dire consequences if they masturbated. The age of reason was confronting the age of puritan ethics. There was a continuous struggle between kindness and cruelty toward children until the twentieth century and the era of the liberated child. Cruelty against children did not cease completely, and parental treatment of children varied from country to country. Otto Corwin told of losing consciousness several times under his father's lash. He believed that his brother was permanently damaged in the process (quoted after P. Robertson, 1974). It does seem that among the enlightened countries Germany was the last to tame its violent impulses against children.

In the nineteenth century, the Brothers Grimm collected Germanic folklore and published folktales in a book for children which was read widely and translated into many languages. These stories still frighten our children as they reveal, with unmistakable clarity, that their parents would like to kill, abandon, starve or eat them. In a charming book, D. Block (1978) reports the fantasies of children which concentrate on fears of infanticide in America today. The ambivalence and resistance to parenthood, especially fatherhood, was described by Muslin (1984). In jest, many mothers express their wishes freely when they say: "I will kill you for that." Many times we have to reassure the frightened children that mother did not really mean to do it

(Kestenberg, 1984). Children displace their fear of their parents onto monsters, and by splitting these vile figures from their mothers and fathers, they can preserve the idealized image of their parents as protective and life enhancing.

By the end of the nineteenth century laws were established for the prevention of cruelty to children. As people became free of oppression, children were freed as well. From being treated like slaves and personal property, like serfs beholden to parents for life, like indentured workers or sadistically persecuted pupils, children were liberated into a freedom which sometimes enslaved the parents and educators. Then, only 40 years after the law protecting children came into being, a massive regression to torturing and killing of children occurred in Germany.

NAZIS' ATTITUDE TOWARD CHILDREN

The most conspicuous precursors of Nazis were the Brothers Grimm, who propagated a nationalism that glorified their descent from cruel Teutonic tribes (Dorson, 1966). It is small wonder, then, that the Grimms' tales were reprinted often in Nazi Germany and admired greatly.

The National Socialists not only killed alien children but had a special way to kill their own. They were infatuated with ancient Germanic rites which centered on fires. Some of their atrocities resembled ancient Teutonic rites.

In the trial of Höchst, the infamous Commander of the Auschwitz camp, a witness testified to the following experience (Rachwalowa, 1946): In 1944, she saw a number of SS officers standing in a circle around the fire. Infants were handed over to each officer who immediately threw the infant into the flames, removed his gloves and threw them also into the fire. With each such action, all SS officers shouted "Heil."

Stories of Nazis throwing infants up in the air and shooting them are well-documented (Keneally, 1983). Babies were thrown like balls into trucks, torn apart, and impaled. But throwing babies into fire alive had a special significance for the Nazis. They taught their own children these rituals, gave them younger children for target practice, and invited them to witness executions.

A woman we interviewed for our study on child survivors of the Holocaust told us the following:

> She and two other women in camp Palamon were put in charge of 30 children, all under 13 years of age, some quite small. They could give the children only little food, but they tried to cheer them up and give them hope that a better future awaits them. One day the camp was surrounded by German troops, armed with guns. A horde of SS men rushed in and screamed that the children be dressed quickly and taken out. To hurry the children, the soldiers beat them. In the middle of the yard, they made a fire. When a mother tried to drag her child away, they threw her

with her child into the fire. The rest of the children screamed in terror. Reassurance was no longer possible. In the middle of this turmoil, our informant fell unconscious, perhaps from the beating administered to her. When she awoke, she was lying on a cement floor with other adults. The children were gone. They had been herded into cattle wagons and taken to Treblinka, one of the extermination camps the Nazis erected in Poland.

This story illustrates the inhuman behavior of Nazis toward children. The inhumanity was not confined to Jews, but it was most pronounced and open in relation to them. Child killing and child torture was inflicted not only on Jewish, Polish, Russian or Czech children, however, but also on German children. It is well known that the National Socialist Party attempted to kill, by euthanasia, retarded or mentally ill German children, confined to institutions. Less known is the cult of death taught to the youngsters in Nazi Germany and the killing of their own German children. By 1945, high school students belonging to the Hitler youth were recruited for various services. One youth (Heer, 1983) was put in the service of helping trainloads of German refugees from the Russian zone. In the cold of winter, he saw transports of these German children, who had traveled in open cattle trains. There were 30 frozen children who had to be taken off one of the wagons; they were all dead. A train with refugees was leaving and a three-year-old was crying miserably for her mother. The youthful helper found her mother and tried to push her child into the car, but the railroad employee closed the door and severed the child's arm. The child had to stay behind. The writer says that these memories haunt him at night and do not give him peace during the day.

Friedlander (1982) demonstrates convincingly how Hitler and his acolytes were fascinated with destruction and loved death. Theirs was a ritualized, stylized and aesthetecized death, a pagan feast. The dead continued to march with the living in one of the marching songs of the Hitler youth. Killing was glorified, and one's own death was the supreme sacrifice to the Führer. We see, then, the resurgence of a father who wants to kill his own children; he sends them to their death to conquer lands for him and in his name.

In order to conquer and dominate the world, the father also advocates the birth of many children dedicated to him as well as the theft of children from other nations who will be raised to give their lives for Hitler. A Führer worship substitutes for religion and its God. Belonging to the Führer is the substitute for belonging to a family. The killing of "vermin" that can contaminate the superior Germans and the enslavement of Slavs elevates the German people into "Herrenmenschen." Alas, even the elevated Herrenmenschen had to die. Reminiscent to the heroic stories of their fathers who fought in World War I, the Hitler youth sang:

Do you see in the east the red of the dawn?
A sign to freedom, to the sun.
We stick together, for life or for death;

Whatever comes, it may come!
(Translation of authors quoted after Friedlander, 1982)

German youths, born in 1925, 1926, and 1927, were thrown into the fighting at the front after a brief period of training. Some were still students in high school when they went to war. To avoid the bombs of the Allies, children were sent to camps and separated from their parents. Some of these children were sent to the eastern lands that were invaded. In the spring of 1945, when the Red Army conquered all of eastern Europe, the unhappy camp children were surrounded by the chaos of the front. Taken by surprise in their "safe" camps, they fled, chased by their caretakers, and, sometimes, abandoned by them. The children remained separated from their parents long after the war was over. Some of the children died and some who returned did not find their homes (Klose, 1982). It may sound that we are describing Jewish or Polish children. We are not. This happened to German children who lived for the glory of their Führer.

Obsessed with the need to make the Jewish people an obsolete nation whose remainder could be seen only in the museums of the German Reich, Hitler was out to degrade and annihilate them. He was out to destroy the German people as well, by glorifying them as the sadistic beasts of prey, superior to the rest of the world while the Jews were inferior to all.

The destruction began not only with the glorification of death, but with the degradation of intellectuality, the burning of books, and the conscious attempt to eradicate thought and make action the eternal weapon of people whose "untaming was planned systematically" (Rauschning, quoted after Klose, 1982). Thousands of years of domestication were to be undone by the education of Germanic youths to become exploiters and slave masters.

In our study of Nazi atrocities committed during their reign, we came to suspect that all of Hitler's wrath was in some way directed against children. The adult Jews and the adult Slavs, whom he subjugated, were reduced to the status of children. They lost power over their own bodies. They had to eat what was dished out to them, be dirty, full of lice, or suddenly cleaned by disinfectants at the behest of their "caretakers." They could not come and go as they pleased. Their work brought no income. They could only speak when spoken to. They had to obey. The Nazis sought to destroy family feelings, to make murderers out of their victims. They especially enjoyed forcing a Jewish parent to kill one of his children to save another. When they felt sufficiently rewarded in their endeavors, they laughed. It gave them satisfaction to sever family ties, and make children out of adults. Religious people, be they Jews or priests, were their special targets. They tried to rob them of their dignity, as keepers of ethics. They were out to destroy moral principles on a wholesale basis. This destruction of values, however, encompassed their own children.

How could such a wholesale turning of aggression against oneself be accomplished? Melitta Maschmann (1963) describes her German mother, who expected that her children obey her with the same unquestioning compliance that she received from the maid and the chauffeur. Melitta, 15 years old, felt like one of the oppressed masses to whom Hitler promised work, equality, and a sense of belonging and worth because they were German. The model Nazi youth Quex was sired by a communist father who, nevertheless, beat the oppressed mother every week when he received his unemployment check and became drunk. He beat his son senselessly and cruelly. Quex had to oppose his father and go over to the archenemy, the Hitler youth, who gave him a feeling of superiority, worth, and a possibility for advancement of which he never dreamed. Recklessly giving his life by exposing himself to the communist who took revenge on him, Quex became a hero for all other youth. Bravery, fearlessness, (Schenzinger, 1932) something more than courage, was praised. The marching and singing alone created the illusion of grandeur, of being aligned with many like oneself as if they were one step, one breath, only subordinated to a leader who was close to them and led them to victory or death.

There were three highly successful methods introduced into the psychic economy of the deluded and betrayed German youth. A great deal of self-directed aggression was diverted to "inferiors," Slavs, Gypsies, and Jews. The self-destructive wishes were neutralized by an enormous increase in group and individual narcissism, fed by slogans and false scientific evidence about the superiority of the Nordic race. The amalgamation of the exalted, overgrown self-esteem with the desire to die, produced a unique grandeur in which death was narcissistically invested as an ideal.

It has been said repeatedly that Hitler's philosophy was based on a competition with the Jewish God who chose the children of Israel as his preferred offspring, and gave them the confidence of their being superior to others. Their superiority, however, lay in their morality and wisdom and in their ability to subordinate the wish to live forever to an immortality, based on the continuation of their seed in their children. Hitler's ideas about how Jews could be defeated and how their chosenness could be usurped by the Germans were rather simple. No longer were morality and wisdom, intellectuality, and the teaching of God's laws the ideals of the chosen. Intellect was demeaned as a sign of weakness; the body was elevated as the symbol of greatness by which one was chosen. Giving in to impulses and becoming like an animal was sanctioned. Darwin's thesis of the selection of the fittest was extended to the human being. Those who were fit would kill to survive and destroy those who weakened the race. The previously degraded simpleton, the Goliath who could be slain by little David, became the hero while David became a worthless creature destined to die ignominiously. Through the enormous increase in narcissism in the masses of German youth, Hitler and his cohorts saved them from their cruel oppressors, their parents and teachers. They could feel superior to them and did, indeed, feel free to denounce and have them killed if they opposed them. At the same time as he became the savior of German children, Hitler prepared them for death. He was their rescuer and destroyer. He gave them "freedom," self-esteem, grandeur, ideals, and a desire to live and he used all these aggrandizing features to promote death.

Psychoanalytic Tthoughts on the Conflict Between Child Killing and Child Rescuing

Having discovered murderous wishes toward parents, psychoanalysis neglected to deal systematically with the murderous wishes of parents toward their children. In recent years, Devereux (1953) began to pay special attention to the Oedipus saga in the light of the Laius complex. Devereux's central thesis was that Oedipus' own impulses were stimulated by the behavior of his father. In myths and stories, the theme of the killing of a child ordered by kings or parents who feared their own children's deeds, is recurrent. Sometimes we encounter a queen, usually a stepmother, who sends her stepchild to death for fear of competition, as in *Snow White,* where the threat was shifted from the idealized mother to the stepmother. In the following considerations, we shall confine ourselves mostly to the killing of children by men, with the full understanding that wishes to kill children are evident in both sexes.

Ubiquitous in the human psyche is the child killing complex that is counterweighed by a powerful impulse to rescue. Even in Nazi time, there were Christians who risked their lives and their children's lives to rescue Jews whom they had to treat as if they were children (Fogelman, 1984; Oliner, 1982; Tec, 1982). In modern literature, the father's aggression against the infant is treated with indulgence. This is because the modern father uses his aggression to harden the child and help him grow (Ross, 1984; Kestenberg et al., 1982) rather than torture or kill him. Fathers have progressed from killing their potential rivals to using their aggression to help the children grow. How did this transformation come about?

Throughout history, outright killing was replaced with sending children away from home, starving, or overworking them. Stringent, cruel laws against killing of illegitimate children by their mothers were expressions of externalization on the part of the pious lawgivers of their own murderous impulses. Up to this day, the question of infanticide is paramount in people's mind, especially as regards the question whether abortion constitutes child killing. But, nowhere in history did we see the accumulation and idealization of child killing as was to be seen in the regression during the Nazi reign.

Freud 1964), who wrote his paper on Moses and monotheism a few years after the Nazi regime sanctioned and organized the persecution of Jews, speculated that Moses, as an Egyptian prince, had chosen the Jewish people to revive the monotheistic religion he cherished. The Jews whom he rescued from Egyptian bondage, however, rebelled against him and killed him in the desert. Freud looked on this idea as a historical truth and assigned credence to it based on the Christians' accusation that Jews have killed Jesus. He disregarded the fact, however, that the accusation relates to the killing of the son and not the father. The people who abolished killing in their commandments and condemned the sacrifice of children were accused of killing the son of God and of ritual murder of Christian children.

We have some evidence that Freud had difficulty admitting his own wishes directed against his sons, especially the oldest. He emphasized the son's wish to kill his father and never discussed the father's wishes to get rid of the future rival. In his book on dreams (1900–1901), Freud discussed the following dream: It became necessary in the city of Rome to remove children to safety and two boys were brought to a father, the elder clearly Freud's own son. One of Freud's associations was that he was in a strange city and passed a shield bearing the words "Dr. Herodes. Consulting hours." He remarked to his companion: "Let us hope that our colleague does not happen to be a children's doctor." The obvious reference was to the slaughter of the innocent by King Herod. As his associations continue, Freud puts emphasis on the wish to have a child and does not recognize the wish to hurt one.

Freud (1953b) pointed out with great clarity that the prohibition of image-making in Judaism produced spirituality and an emphasis on intellect. He spoke of the narcissistic pride that follows the renunciations of instinct and of the elevation of self-regard when there are advances in intellectuality (pp. 116–117): "An advance consists in deciding against direct sense perception in favor of what are known as the higher intellectual processes—that is memories, reflections and inferences" (p. 117). He led us to the inference that through the introduction of the monotheistic, only, invisible God, the child was acknowledged as descendant of his father. The love of a father for his child could be accepted because children were the seeds of the father. Children were no longer the usurpers of the mother's affection, no longer potential threats to the supremacy of the father whom they will kill and dethrone. Children allied themselves not only to respect their elders but to refrain from taking advantage of their peers.

Freud, for unaccountable reasons, spoke of Abraham's covenant with God through circumcision as a "particularly clumsy invention." In his view, it obscured the fact that circumcision was borrowed from the Egyptians and introduced by Moses. By ignoring the importance of Abraham's covenant with God, Freud also looked away from the internal struggle of Abraham who, when ready to send both his son to death, saw them rescued by angels, who were messengers from God.[2] The two voices in Abrahams's conflict were represented by two forces: God himself (a father figure) and God's mes-

---

[2]The Bible confirms Freud's speculations in *Totem and Taboo* (1913) that it was the youngest son who triumphed over the older. God seems to help the younger one, as in the story of Isaac and Israel, as in the case of Jacob, in which the younger was helped by the mother to usurp the birth right of the elder. The implication is that the baby is favored, as later on Joseph and Benjamin were favored over others.

senger (a son figure). The conflict was resolved, the young animals remained the scapegoats for children, and Abraham was elevated to an exalted fatherhood over many nations, whose laws many will admire and follow. Fatherhood is exalted into a kind of immortality through a multitude of righteous descendants, and children are saved (see especially Zeligs, 1974).

The essence of Jewish morality and the backbone of its laws consist in the renunciation of killing and the reconciliation between father and son, so they can live in peace. Circumcision in lieu of a sacrifice of a child to an almighty father-god distinguishes the chosen people from those who are not chosen by God; circumcision is the external sign of the covenant with God. In the accepted circumcision prayer, the father promises to teach the child the laws of the Torah, to find a wife for him, and redeem him (Gerard, 1976). He is also required to teach him a trade and as some rabbis propagated, to teach him how to survive, as exemplified in showing him how to swim.

Although the word "love" with regard to children is mentioned rarely, there is a great deal of evidence of this love in the numerous discussions about child care which cemented the relationship (Gerard, p. 61). According to Gerard, Rabbi Jonathan interpreted Ecclesiastes 3:2: "he has set the world in their heart" to refer to the love of the children which God put into the heart of men (p. 61).

Since biblical times, every son renews the father's covenant with God and, through the learning of the Torah, continues Jewish wisdom and morality onto generation after generation. Kanerfogel (1985) studied the attitude of Jews to children in the medieval society. Contrary to what has been described for the rest of medieval society, Jewish children were never treated like miniature adults or mocked. Their manner of speaking, their mannerisms were not ignored, and Jews were interested in furthering the development of their children from infancy through toddlerhood and into adulthood which began at age 13. Education in the Jewish home began at seven and proceeded along adult lines of instruction. The three year old was trained by an understanding regimen with the aim of keeping the child calm. Contrary to the mores of the times, even the poorest families employed tutors for their children rather than sending them away to schools. If children had to be sent away, this did not occur before the age of 13. Asked about the occurrence of infanticide in the Middle Ages and about the custom of sending children out to be nursed by women in the country, Kanerfogel replied that he knew of no Jewish legislation against infanticide and assumed that such a crime was a rarity among Jews.

It was common practice to keep Jewish and Christian wet nurses, but they stayed either in Jewish homes or in the same town in which the family lived. The death of children who were sent away for nursing, prevalent at that time, was not an issue in Jewish families. No child in a Jewish family is seen in the same light as the household help. The child's wisdom is propagated and praised. Judging from the accusations made against Jews that they ritually murdered Christian children, it seems that the antisemites who hate Jews strive to negate *the* achievement of the Jew: he has overcome primitive temptations to kill children and has become, instead, a proud father and a wisdom loving intellectual and promoter of just laws.

Jews are continuously accused of sins they have overcome already through their covenant with God and his emissaries. In the Christian religion, the reconciliation between father and son consists of another kind of morality whereby both can be Gods and the son dies as redeemer. In the Jewish religion, the son is also a redeemer, but he does not have to die. He can redeem by being just, law abiding and by spreading the gospel of the Torah to his children and children's children.

SUMMARY

The impulse to kill one's children and commit genocide on one's own people is not easy to conquer. From time to time, it becomes more virulent and tempting than in others. Its repression reversed itself during the Nazi regression to barbarism. To undo the commandments of Jews against infanticide and the protection Jews gave to children, the Nazis had to annihilate their opponents and kill their children cruelly in front of their eyes. Ridding themselves of the Jews, as saviors of children, freed them to commit mass murder on their own.

REFERENCES

Aries, P. (1962). *Centuries of childhood*. New York: Vintage Books.

Block, D. (1978). *So the witch won't eat me: Fantasy and the child's fear of infanticide*. Boston: Houghton-Mifflin.

deMause, L. (1974). *The evolution of childhood*. New York: Psychohistory Press.

Devereux, G. (1953). Why Oedipus killed Laius. *International Journal of Psychoanalysis, 24*, 132–141.

Dorson, R. M. (1966). Foreword. In K. Ranke (Ed.), *Folktales of Germany*. Chicago: University of Chicago Press.

Ende, A. (1981). Battering and neglect: Children in Germany, 1860–1978. In *Journal of Psychohistory, 7*, 281–288.

Fogelman, E. (September/October 1984). Social psychological study of the rescuers. *Martyrdom and Resistance*, p. 8.

Frazer, J. G. (1959). *The new golden bough*. New York: Criterion Books. (Original work published 1890.)

Freud, S. (1953a). The Interpretation of dreams. In J. Strachey (Ed. and Trans.), *The standard edition of the complete psychological works of Sigmund Freud* (Vol. 5, pp. 339–610). London: Hogarth Press. (Original work published in 1901.)

Freud, S. (1953b). Totem and taboo. In J. Strachey (Ed. and Trans.), *The standard edition of the complete psychological works of Sigmund Freud* (Vol. 13, pp. 1–162). London: Hogarth Press. (Original work published 1913.)

Freud, S. (1964). Moses and monotheism. In J. Strachey (Ed. and Trans), *The standard edition of the complete psychological works of Sigmund Freud* (Vol. 23, pp. 3–137) London: Hogarth Press. (Original work published 1934.)

Friedlander, S. (1982). *Reflections of Nazism: An essay on kitsch and death.* New York: Harper & Row.

Gerard, J. H. (1976). *Children in the Aggadah.* Thesis. New York: Hebrew Union College, Jewish Institute of Religion.

Heer, H. (1983). *Als ich 9 jahre alt war, kam der krieg (When I was 9 years old, the war came).* Reinbeck: Rohwolt Verlag.

Heine, H. (1820). *Rabbi von Bacharach—Collected poems.* Leipzig: Hesse Publishers, p. 177.

Heller, J. E. & Mordechai, A. (1972). Martin Luther. In *Encyclopaedia Judaica* (Vol. 11). Jerusalem: Keter Publishing, p. 585.

Kanerfogel, E. (1985). Attitudes toward childhood and children in Medieval Jewish society. In D. Blumenthal (Ed.). *Approaches to Judaism in Medieval times, (Vol. 2.).* Chico, CA: Scholars Press, pp. 1–34.

Keaneally, T. (1983). *Schindler's list.* New York: Simon and Schuster.

Kestenberg, J. S. (1984). Center for parents and children. Unpublished manuscript.

Kestenberg, J. S., Marcus, H., Sossin, K. M., & Stevenson, R. (1982). The development of paternal attitudes. In S. H. Cath, A. R. Gurwitt, & J. R. Ross (Eds.), *Father and Child.* Boston: Little, Brown.

Klose, W. (1982). *Generation im gleichschritt: Die Hitlerjugend Generation in goosestep: The Hitler youth).* Oldenberg.

Maimonides, M. (1965). *Guide for the perplexed* S. Friedlander (trans.). New York: Dover Publishing.

Maschmann, M. (1963). *Facit. Mein weg in der Hitlerjugend (My road in the Hitler youth).* Munich: Deutscher Taschenbuch Verlag.

Morgenstern, J. (1963). *Rite of birth.* Hoboken, NJ: Ktav Publishing.

Muslin, H. (1984). On the resistance to parenthood: Considerations on the self as the father. In S. Cohen, B. J. Cohler, & S. H. Weissman (Eds.). *Parenthood. A psychodynamic perspective.* New York: Guilford Press, pp. 315–325.

Neumann, E. (1955). *The great mother.* New York: Pantheon Books.

Oliner, S. (1982). The need to recognize heroes of the Nazi era. *Reconstructionists, 6,* 7–14.

Piers, M. (1978). *Infanticide: Past and present.* New York: W.W. Norton.

Pollock, L. (1983). *Forgotten children.* New York: Cambridge University Press.

Rachwalowa, W. (1946). Höchst trial testimonies. *Auschwitz Archives, 38,* 106.

Ranke, K. (1966). *Folktales of Germany*. Chicago: University of Chicago Press.

Rauschning, H. (1973). Quoted after W. Klose (1982). *Gespräche mit Hitler (Conversations with Hitler)*. Vienna: Europaverlag.

Robertson, P. (1974). Home as a nest: Middle class childhood in nineteenth century Europe. In L. deMause (Ed.), *The history of childhood*. New York: The Psychohistory Press, pp. 351–382.

Ross, J. M. (1982). Oedipus revisited: Laius and the "Laius Complex." *The Psychoanalytic Study of the Child, 37,* 169–200.

Ross, J. M. (1984). The son of the father: Notes on fathers, aggression, and pathogenesis. In E. J. Anthony & G. Pollock (Eds.), *Parental influences*. Boston: Little, Brown.

Sagan, E. (1979). *The lust to annihilate*. New York: Psychohistory Press.

Schenzinger, K. A. (1932). *Der Hitlerjunge Quex (The Hitler boy Quex)*. Berlin: Zeitgeschichte Verlag.

Tacitus (1942). *Germany and its tribes*. New York: Random House. (Original work published 1898.)

Tec, N. (1982). *Dry tears*. Westport: Wildcat Publishers.

Tucker, M. J. (1974). The child as beginning and end: Fifteenth and sixteenth century English childhood. In L. deMause (Ed.), *The history of childhood*. New York: The Psychohistory Press, pp. 229–258.

Waltzer, J. F. (1974). A period of ambivalence: Eighteenth century American childhood. In L. deMause (Ed.), *The history of childhood*. New York: The Psychohistory Press, pp. 351–382.

Wirth-Marvick, E. (1974). Nature versus nurture: Patterns and trends in seventeenth century French child-rearing. In L. deMause (Ed.), *The history of childhood*. New York: The Psychohistory Press, pp. 259–302.

Zeligs, D. (1974). *Psychoanalysis and the bible*. New York: Bloch.

Chapter 10

TO FIND A GOOD ENOUGH ENEMY

The Psychological "Fit" Between
The United States and The Soviet Union[1]

Howard F. Stein

INTRODUCTION

This chapter explores the group psychodynamics of the *boundary* between one's own group and that of the enemy through the study of a historical "case example," that of the relationship between the United States and Soviet Union. Attention is given to the intolerance of any ambiguity over the demarcation; that is, the need to keep inside distinct from outside, "us" distinct from "them," and the accompanying fear of contamination from the outside. An American child recently said suspiciously to psychiatrist John E. Mack (1985), "You're trying to get us to see the Russians as human beings." To admit that the historical enemy could, in any way, be human would mean that we would have to accept all which has been split off, externalized, projectively identified and projected onto the enemy, as perhaps being part of ourselves.

Inter-group hostility and war play out in the "outer" world those dramas and inner splits, which in more sophisticated settings, are enacted psychosomatically and in inter-personal pathology. *Metaphorically* speaking, internalized "implosions" within the body and in the family are paralleled by

[1]Portions of this chapter were previously published as "Psychological Complementarity in Soviet-American Relations" in *Political Psychology*, volume 6, No. 2, pp. 249–261. Copyright © 1985, Plenum Publishing Corporation. Used by permission.

externalized "explosions" of disowned affect now targeted on one's historic enemy. Such enemies magically re-embody what one has ejected from one's own "body politic." How can we describe the way in which such adversaries as the United States and the Soviet Union see themselves and each other?

The representation of the enemy is that of a distinct, "solid" object, but one, which is imbued with many of one's own traits. Each nation dreads the possibility of having its boundaries violated. A cycle of projection and introjection intensifies hatred for the enemy, which must be differentiated as outside the boundary of safety.

In this dyadic relationship, the United States and Soviet Union constitute the two poles of the conflict, poles or positions which imply each other. Locked in this reciprocal "paranoid" position, the two opponents cannot resolve their conflict. The only "solution" each sees is the vilification of the other. Magically, each opponent believes: "If you die, then evil dies: and since I am not evil, I live." The relationship is seen in exclusive idealizing/demonizing terms. One is either enemy or ally.

The alternative solution, discussed later in this chapter, is a relationship more inclusive than the two poles, one which transcends duality, one in which the world can be experienced as multiple varieties of being human, and one in which erstwhile adversaries, together, create a new, common world, one in which the enemy is admitted into "humanity" because one has been able to accept the "humanity" of one's own group.

The Historic Dyad of the United States and the Soviet Union

In modern history, the United States and Soviet Union have been opponents, World War II notwithstanding, since 1917. One would think that with sufficient good will and effort, the inveterate conflict by now would have been resolved and the two adversaries reconciled. Where there is failure in resolving a conflict, one has a right to suspect the participants have a vested, if unconscious, interest in the perpetuation of enmity, even as they ardently pursue peace. Indeed, one may plausibly argue that peace-making often serves as a red herring to decoy and legitimate the underlying fantasy aim of war.

American diplomacy follows from what George Kennan calls "the image of the Soviet regime which has come to inform American policy. It is an image of unmitigated darkness, with which we are all familiar . . ." (1983, p. 44). The American midwest connotes a spaciousness of "friendly spaces," "where seldom is heard a discouraging word," while the great Russian plains and central Asian steppe connote a foreboding vastness. The proverbial Russian patience and mystical timelessness contrast equally with the proverbial American impatience and exuberance. In this chapter I explore the many underlying meanings of this Soviet "image" and the corresponding "American" image among Soviets.

We tend to act toward the Soviet Union as though it were unruly, projecting on it that which we find unacceptable in ourselves. How can we solve the problems of international diplomacy when we consistently fail to distinguish between others' problems and ours, when, at best, our solutions have the quality of treating others for our own "disease." In fact, how can we *afford* to solve problems when we depend on their *irresolution* for our own internal stability?

There is then a psychological "fit" between the United States and Soviet Union as adversaries. Group self-definition and cohesiveness are achieved by contrast with and opposition to an historic enemy which is perceived through projection as embodying disavowed characteristics of one's own group. The availability of an enemy is an important feature of a group's own internal self-regulation. Conflicts between groups, each of which sees itself to be the victim of the other, cannot be solved when intragroup stability is purchased through intergroup hostility, and one group's knowledge of the other is largely governed by projection. A bona fide solution can only come from a refusal to take sides and to embrace all participants to the conflict.

What Would We Do Without the Russians (and Vice-Versa)?

On the face of it, no question appears more preposterous. How much better off we would be, we insist, if only the Soviets were peace-loving (as we aver we are) for then we could turn our attention to pressing domestic issues. As the aftermath of the Soviet destruction in 1983 of the Korean Air Lines passenger jet suggests, the Soviets not only threaten our national security, but *the Soviet availability as a menace is indispensable to that national security.* Much as we wish the Soviets to change, we depend on them *not* to change because the prospect of peace would eliminate their availability as the externalized focus and symbolic object of anxiety.

In terms of object relations theory, a "good enough enemy" is a separate object that is used as a reservoir to store and absorb all of one's own negated elements. It is heir to all "environmental failure" in our early family environment and is selected by those around us to represent all the intolerable persecutory material from those early object relations. The enemy is experienced as embodying all that one *must* rid himself of, yet simultaneously *cannot* do.

A "good enough enemy" is one which is capable of stabilizing the internal group-world by serving as an available repository for group-externalizations. It cannot be emphasized too often that not just any object or group representation will do, in Volkan's phrase (1983), as a "suitable target of externalization." Good enough enemies must be cultivated and courted painstakingly. "Outer" must be provoked, coerced, into corresponding with inner in order that externalizations "come true."

Scholars, not unlike political and military strategists, spend entirely too much time and effort dividing the nature and characteristics of the adversary and devote virtually no time or effort into exploring the relationship between adversaries, together with the investment that each participant has in that relationship. Although many complicated and sophisticated ideas are condensed into the concept of "enemy," at a fundamental level, our enemy is our pretext. To address the relationship, and our (as well as their) tacit collusion in that relationship, is to deprive ourselves of that vital pretext.

Soviets and Americans, alike, denounce each other, although each is unaware that the face of the enemy bears the mask on which we may discern the secret of our own hearts. Each, likewise, is unaware that national unity (a shibboleth and goal in both) depends on the indispensable enemy. Such enmity is essential to our national defense.

Us and Them

Over the years, a number of writers have commented on the human proclivity to subdivide the human species into "us" and "them." Erikson (1968) wrote of each group's tendency to view itself as a virtual "pseudo-species" and other groups as less than human. Malefijt (1968) wrote a compendious survey of how foreign and alien groups are viewed as varieties of Homo monstrosus throughout history. Jerome Frank wrote of the ubiquitous "image" and "face" of the enemy (1967, 1968, 1980):

> This image is remarkably similar no matter who the conflicting parties are. Enemy images mirror each other—that is, each side attributes the same virtues to itself and the same vices to the enemy. We are trustworthy, peace-loving, honorable and humanitarian; they are treacherous, warlike and cruel (1980, p. 951).

At a recent conference of the Group for the Advancement of Psychiatry (April, 1983), Volkan titled his presentation, "The Need to Have an Enemy." The psychodynamics of this need is seen in the historical enmity among many nationalities, as well as antagonistic pairing within the social fabric.

Self-definition, then, in all these instances, is achieved largely by contrast with one (or those) whom one is decidedly *not*. In an allegorical account of "The Day the Soviet Union (Mysteriously) Disappeared," psychohistorian Henry Ebel refers to the "indispensable bogeyman" who enables each "to *focus* their sense of paranoid endangerment" (1983). This should enable us to account for the seemingly insuperable obstacles to the achievement of human siblinghood (despite Schiller and Beethoven). So long as the enemy is seen as wearing the mask we have superimposed on it, we inevitably must see a face we despise when we look at the enemy.

Often, the "right" enemy must also be *perceived* to be powerful enough so as to constitute a real threat. A good enough enemy may be felt to endanger the very survival of one's own group, or it may be felt to be the source of humiliation for one's group; in either event, the enemy must be experienced as capable of succeeding in its menace.

Although it is true that the need for an enemy is part of a universal we/they split, certain adversaries are, so to speak, better than others. For instance, although the Soviet Union and the United States were allies against the Axis powers (Germany, Italy, Japan) during World War II, this alliance was only a temporary aberration in a mutual distrust that has dated to the Revolution of 1917 (see Henry, 1963). To put it formulistically: the best enemy is the one which best mirrors and embodies the "negative identity" (Erickson, 1968) of the group, the one that can best focus and embody the "not-me."

In an intriguing interpretation of the psychohistorical "fit" between the United States and the Soviet Union, Schmookler (1985) cites the projection onto the Soviet Union of disavowed ruthlessness and the lust for power, unacceptable impulses of impiety and rebellion, and repudiated collectivist dependency wishes among Americans. This, however, is not yet the end of the story, for it is *reciprocal* disassociation and exteriorization that keeps this international system going. One must likewise inquire of the Soviets: What makes the United States such a suitable target for them? For only an enemy which will serve as a willing partner—as a reflecting mirror and absorber of one's own projective identifications—is a truly "good enough" enemy.

The national ideologies of both the Soviet Union and the United States are founded upon revolution against monarchies, and Soviets and Americans, alike, view each other as an autocratic threat to those freedoms for which their revolutions had been fought.

At yet another level of analysis, one can identify the "symbiosis" of American anti-communism and Soviet anti-capitalism: "communism" being the American counter-dependent bogey, and "capitalism" being the Soviet counter-individuative menace. (Might this account for the American revulsion toward and fascination with George Orwell's *1984*?) Each embodies the threat which masks the disavowed wish.

There are yet other fateful equivalences that fuel Soviet-American psychological complementarity. What Professor Nina Tumarkin (1983) calls the Soviet "fear of disorganization" finds as its complement the U.S. fear of totalitarianism. The Soviets, who prefer an *external* locus of control, fear the presence of *too little* outer authority; while Americans, who espouse an *internal* locus of control, fear the presence of *too much* external authority. In a shared language of metastatic cancer, both people fear the "corruption" of the body politic by infiltration from the adversary. Although, as Professor Tumarkin (1983) argues, the Soviets view themselves as "bad little children" in relation to the United States, which they view as the "bad parent" (punitive), one likewise could argue that the United States almost too eagerly accepts the delegated role of scolding, ridiculing parent, and, at the same time experiences the Soviets to be ominous parental figures who threaten their often adolescent-style freedom (see Erikson, 1963). It quickly should be added that, although at the level of secondary process this appears to be a contradiction, at the level of the unconscious an object can symbolize apparent opposites (parent/child), and there are no negatives to prevent the alternation or condensation of images.

Now, as Spiegel (1971), Devereux (1967), and Stein (1985) have written, no culture's values are altogether self-consistent. Among the manifestly placid Pueblo Zuni of New Mexico and the Mountain Arapesh of New Guinea, witchcraft abounds. Russians piously bow to tsarist and Soviet authority, yet admire the defiant spirit of the Cossacks. Americans prize individualism, self-reliance and egalitarianism, yet maintain undiminished fascination with au-tocratic bosses of politics and industry. As Devereux writes: "Every highly cathected pattern or belief has also a less elaborated contrary manifestation ('man's best friend'/'dirty dog'). Man affirms on one level what he denies on another level" (1978, pp. 381 and 397). What makes for the dangerous "fit" between the United States and the Soviet Union is that what is highly ca-thected by one is counter-cathected by the other—and projected outward as a despised attribute of the enemy.

In inter-group perceptions and conduct, as in family life, one cannot al-together part with one's externalizations. To keep the horror of "going soft on communism" inflamed, we must tenaciously affirm the "specter of com-munism." Yet, that very "specter" remains a continuous source of fascina-tion as well as dread.

From Freud, we learned to suspect that a disavowed, forbidden wish may be present where a great fear or prohibition exists. It is trite to say we hate our enemies, although the hatred is unmistakable. It is more psychody-namically apt to say that we need to hate our enemies—and likewise have enemies to hate—in order that we do not despise and destroy ourselves. We can see the symbiotic and complementary quality of these adversary rela-tionships. I also would add that in focusing on the enmity itself, we observ-ers and interpreters often overlook the importance of the *relationship* cultivated and preserved: in enmity, one maintains, through the "other," a relationship with parts of oneself and early objects.

Projective "Knowledge" of the Adversary

We "know" the Soviet Union principally through images of what Soviets represent to us, and conversely, they know us in the same way. International prognostication is a form of magical divination; our "experts" are largely those whom we appoint to mirror our fantasies and defenses. After long cultivation, the Soviets to us, and we to them, are now an image-become-fact.

Our obsessive dread that the "Red Tide of the Russians" will overtake us, or imperialism them, is psychologically the fear, itself containing a wish. The face of the enemy is one's own disavowed face. Solutions to insecurity only compound insecurity by heightening the danger. To safeguard group boundaries (to shore up repressions and inner splits), each adversary em-barks on an expansion of its boundaries (for example, invasions, allies, etc.).

Disrespecting others' boundaries in order to protect one's own, each accuses the other of disrespecting boundaries. Ideologies of supra-ethnic and supra-national secular messianism rationalize the offensive: the Soviets accuse us of imperialism, we accuse them of communism. The more each fears the threat of being overwhelmed by what the other represents, the more each feels compelled to expand its boundaries in order to protect the vulnerable core: after all, if I can expand to become the world (merger fantasy), there will no longer be any danger from outside, because *there will at last no longer be an outside or other.*

Resistance (in the psychoanalytic sense) to peace, resistance to rapprochement, thus can be understood as a fervent defense of externalizations and projections. From an eminently practical viewpoint, those engaged in international diplomacy must not only contend with the real and imagined threats which the enemy poses, but must also address *the threat which the prospect of an enduring peace would pose* to the participants to international conflict.

Victim and Attacker Identities

Victim-identities among historical adversaries are widespread, if not universal. *Attacker-identities,* it would appear are almost invariably *avenger-identities* recoiling from *victim-identities.* Through the new identity, history is reversed and undone; the passive suffering associated with the historical hurt is transformed via narcissistic rage into the active, outward discharge of aggression.

Victim-identities and their warrior-successors abound throughout the ethnographic record, primitive and modern, small-scale and complex. The Pueblo societies of the American southwest perceive themselves as peaceful, harmonious, cooperative, kindly, and historically at the mercy of invader-marauder Navaho-Apache tribes, who are "employed" psychologically by these Pueblo groups to embody their own disavowed aggressive impulses. According to Zuni logic, for example, since no real Zuni could harbor hostile feelings toward another Zuni, let alone practice witchcraft against another fellow tribesman, if a Zuni is hostile, he must not be a Zuni! Russians, contemporary and past, cite the litany of invasions from the east, northwest, and west as justifying their defensiveness, secretiveness, and military touchiness. Although a sprawling massif that reaches across two continents now, the Russia of the nineteenth century and the Soviet Union of the twentieth century experiences itself as a small, vulnerable, fragile, yet dangerous, infant, helpless in the face of a menacing world that is forever plotting against it.

Attacker-identities appear to involve flight from victim-identities at the same time that they rationalize and court further suffering. Victimization is later used to rationalize and court further suffering and to rationalize violence against one's erstwhile persecutors or their symbolic successors. What seems clearly called for in furthering our understanding of Soviet-American relations and inter-group conflict is an understanding of the role played by victim-identities and their subsequently "justified" aggressions.

Problems Which Cannot Be Solved

> For this truth must be before us: Whatever America hopes to bring to pass in the world must first come to pass in the heart of America. (Eisenhower, 1953).

In recent years, I have become intrigued with what I would call "problems which cannot be solved within their current framework," this despite the conscious good intentions and presumed good will of all participants. From difficult doctor-patient dyads, to inflexibly patterned family systems, and finally to international relations that always threaten to escalate into something more out of control, I have become convinced that the same underlying processes govern these very different social structures and are implied both in etiology and perpetuation of conflict-irresolution. What is more, I have come to conclude that the question we usually ask, namely "Which side should I take in the dispute?" only further contributes to the problem in the guise of appearing as a solution.

Bateson (1972), for instance, discussed the conflict between the "imperialist" Romans and the "downtrodden, exploited colony" of Hebrews in Palestine around the time of Christ. He concluded:

> I do not care, here, about defending the Romans or defending the Palestinians—the upper dogs or the underdogs. I want to consider the dynamics of the whole traditional pathology in which we are caught, and in which we shall remain as long as we continue to struggle with that old conflict. We just go round and round in terms of the old premises (p. 433).

Dealing in two polar dyadic situations makes the problems impossible to solve because one pole always implies the other. There is need for the development of greater maturity on the part of both poles or "enemies" before they can give up the interactive games based on their necessity to maintain the underlying split-mother internalization. Past utopian attempts, even the League of Nations, were conceived still too rationally to be meaningfully sustained by the more emotional nerve centers of the individual members involved.

It is our continued hope that with patience and greater insight these seemingly insolvable problems will yield to solution. By throwing light on the necessary process, this chapter is an attempt to begin movement in this direction.

REFERENCES

Bateson, G. (1972). Conscious purpose versus nature. In *Steps to an ecology of mind*. San Francisco: Chandler, pp. 432–445.

Devereux, G. (1967). *From anxiety to method in the behavioral sciences*. The Hague: Mouton.

Devereux, G. (1978). The works of George Devereux. In G. D. Spindler (Ed.), *The making of psychological anthropology*. Los Angeles: University of California Press, pp. 364–406.

Ebel, H. (1983). The day the Soviet Union (mysteriously) disappeared. Unpublished manuscript quoted with permission.

Eisenhower, D. (1953). *The inaugural address*.

Erikson, E. H. (1963). *Childhood and society*. New York: W. W. Norton.

Erikson, E. H. (1968). *Identity: Youth and crisis*. New York: W. W. Norton.

Frank, J. D. (1967). *Sanity and survival*. New York: Random House.

Frank, J. D. (June 1968). The face of the enemy. *Psychology Today*, 24–29.

Frank, J. D. (1980). The nuclear arms race—Sociopsychological aspects. *American Journal of Public Health, 70* (9), 950–952.

Freud, S. (1953). The interpretation of dreams. In J. Strachey (Ed.), *The standard edition of the complete psychological works of Sigmund Freud*. London: Hogarth Press.

Henry, J. (1963). The United States and the Soviet Union: Some economic and social consequences of a twentieth-century nightmare. In *Culture against man*. New York: Random House, pp. 100–123.

Kennan, G. (October 3, 1983). Reflections: Breaking the spell. *The New Yorker*, 44–51.

Mack, J. E. (1985). *Defense mechanisms in children*. Paper presented at conference on Mechanisms of defense: Arms and the man, psychological aspects of the nuclear arms race, Washington, D.C.

Malefijt, A. (1968). Homo monstrosus. *Scientific American, 219*(4), 113–118.

Schmookler, A. G. (1985). U.S.–U.S.S.R.: Are we angling toward a shoot-out at the OK Corral? *Political Psychology, 6*(2), 275–290.

Spiegel, J. (1971). *Transactions: The interplay between individual, family and society*. New York: Science House.

Stein, H. F. (1985). Values and family therapy. In J. Schwartzman (Ed.), *Macrosystemic approaches to family therapy*. New York: Guilford, pp. 201–243.

Tumarkin, N. (1983). Presentation at the Second Annual Esalen Institute Symposium on the Psychology of the U.S.–Soviet Relationship. Esalen Institute, Big Sur, Calif.

Volkan, V. (April 1983). *The need to have an enemy*. Manuscript presented at the Committee on International Relations, Group for the Advancement of Psychiatry meetings, Cherry Hill, N.J.

Chapter 11

TERRORISM AND THE NUCLEAR BOMB

An Ominous Threat of a New Social Order

Gerard G. Neuman

In the *U.S. News & World Report* of July 8, 1985 an article titled, "The Rise of World Terrorism" includes two graphs which describe the increase of incidents of terrorism which grew to 3,525 by 1984. The article stated, "according to Risks International, Inc., of Alexandria, Va., terrorists struck 22,171 times from 1970 until the start of this year, killing 40,394 persons and wounding 24,588. Americans or their property were targeted 3,032 times. In 91 percent of attacks since 1970, terrorists appeared to have accomplished their objectives."

As to types of incidents, we continue quoting, (*U.S. News & World Report,* July 8, 1985) "there were 37 maimings, 142 hijackings, 1,027 kidnappings, 3,774 assassinations, 6,884 attacks on facilities, and 10,207 bombings."

World news about terrorism evokes in each of us increasing anxiety related to terror of the unknown, inability to protect ourselves, and, despite "courageous" statements, inability to find any way to control what is happening around us. What is happening to even the so-called civilized world, to all of us?

Our political leaders have no answers when it comes to protecting the citizens of the nation, and our police forces cannot protect us individually. Why this deterioration of social and political structure? Before we can find any answers, we need to understand the phenomenon in terms of how the changes in the social order are the reflection of the changes which have occurred within ourselves.

This may be one of the saddest chapters in this book. The message of the book is that the human species went through experiences in the beginning which made it necessary to develop special aggressive capacities to survive. In the specific evolution of the human species there was insufficient preparation to carry this necessary aggression, which was later experienced as over-aggression. All culture, civilization, and changing individual development are mankind's attempt to convert, or at least, control, this over-aggression, which threatens to destroy the world and ourselves. So far, we have not been successful in accomplishing this. From early victims, we developed into killers and destroyers. We have not made much headway in healing the basic split between restitution in creativity, scientific rationality and beauty, and the lurking violence underneath.

Just as we asked in a previous chapter, how could a country that produced Goethe, a Beethoven, a Thomas Mann, follow a Hitler with impulsive total abandon, so we ask in this chapter, how can a world dedicated to increasing communication, individual growth and human comfort through increasing standards of living find itself controlled by a handful of terrorists? The greater technological product, designed to increase our comfort and protection, also produces atomic devices which threaten to destroy us. Billions of dollars and millions of man-hours cannot protect us from a few individuals who, willing to sacrifice their lives for a fanatic (psychotic) idea, express a part of our own personality. Trying to keep our own hidden impulses under control, we are, like Hamlet, weakened and unable to react effectively.

As has been developed in other chapters, there are two basic dangers to the individual animal or man. He can be killed or harmed by a stronger animal outside his own group. Within the group, there is the *alpha versus beta* contest between males, or *male-male* contest between humanoids. He can also be killed or devoured by his infanticidal mother. In other chapters in this book, we have developed the animal and prehistoric examples.

There are two corresponding defenses against these risks: stronger male (paternal) protection, or finding ways of strengthening the maternal protection by integrating the individual experience into a meaningful larger whole which will support both the frustrated aggressor as well as the victim.

Before we think of solutions, however, let us understand what is happening on the social and political scene. Shortly after the conclusion of World War II, we entered a transitional period. Even though the "forces of evil" such as Nazi Germany, Fascist Italy, and Japan had been decisively defeated, it was done at such tremendous costs in resources and human life (twenty to forty million dead), both during the war, as well as in post-war reconstruction, that the costs of victory could not be rationally justified.

Of all the smaller wars that followed, with a few exceptions such as the Falkland Islands war, a branch of terrorist activity, guerrilla forces, became more effective than big armies for West and East (Vietnam and Afghanistan). A big army is the backbone of national defense. Have big powers become the Goliaths to more effective forms of new Davids?

A number of less tangible, but more basic, changes could be sensed below the surface. The previous forms (Gestalts) of society began to lose their focus as their boundaries faded and blurred. In the economic sphere, corporations developed loyalties on an international level, often overshadowing loyalties to their own country. In the early 1950s, outer space became a significant part of our experience, introducing a whole new point of view, which we are still trying to integrate. Flying in orbit with tremendous speed tends to make national borders seem insignificant.

To better understand our situation today, let us quickly review the evolutionary development of society up to this point. About 400,000 B.C. awareness was gained that a hunting group can be a protective mechanism; by 40,000 B.C. families and small work groups began to have a maternally protective significance; by 10,000 B.C. clans or tribes became sedentary, agriculture found its more permanent roots, and land became invested with maternal security.

City walls protected the still fragile social unit. We move from Jericho (9000 B.C.) to Jerusalem (1000 B.C.), Athens (600-700 B.C.), and finally Rome, where the Alexandrian overextension of the city remained the focal symbol of "world empire." As that city became overextended, the dark period of the early Middle Ages initiated a transitional period comparable to the present time. Religion filled in the lack of meaning of the crumbling Gestalts of antiquity. Fortunately, this transition was a "social and cultural regression in service of the ego." The Renaissance reestablished the pride of self-confidence lost by the "decline of the Roman Empire." The new Nation State with a secure king at its helm (Louis XIV, Henry VIII, etc.) set the standards for the new political maternal Gestalt. Most countries wanted to unify their separate parts along the lines of this model. The later the unification occurred, the less the cohesion and maturity of its parts. Germany and Italy were particular late-comers, a fact which was a contributing factor for fascism to develop so virulently in those two countries.

This form of social order, painfully achieved in its struggle with the religious forces, was soon (early nineteenth century) to be challenged by the "have-nots" searching for an international order under the various slogans of "democracy," "socialism," "communism," etc. The idea of a boundaryless world of the "have-nots," first proclaimed in Russia, almost immediately was lost to the prevailing power model of the national state. Even a revolutionary society could not accept the anarchist within its borders. Even today, the terrorist, most like the anarchist, without clear-cut political purpose, is anathema to the Soviet Union.

Are we now seeing the beginning of the end of the social order resting on the cultural and territorial foundations of the national state? Although we have accepted the basic outlines of the *motherland* headed by a political father, the specific content was never secure.

Models moved from dictator, to benign ruler, to balanced alignments of population groups (mostly ethnic or religious) to attempted democracy, without ever achieving true democracy in any country. True democracy has never been achieved because old, divisive loyalties preclude mature integration.

The same pattern of dissolution of Gestalts, which blurred boundaries, created insecurity, and opened the field to excessive solutions, can be traced for internal political and cultural forms. Stable institutions such as the family, moral beliefs, legal systems, "patriotism," loyalty to work units, sense of home, religious values, all have lost a bit of their previous stable Gestalt qualities.

Psychologically, lack of Gestalt with secure boundaries makes for less security in personal identity and, therefore, lack of security in one's life adjustment. As we became less secure in personal identity, we sink to less mature levels of functioning. It has been my experience in working with adolescents or in mental hospital settings that the less adjusted the group, the sicker will be the leaders they elect. The same is true of criminal groups. Hitlers and Khadafis are no accident. In the splitting of the Gestalt, the dictators become the devils to the democratic gods.

As boundaries become blurred, personal identities are weakened even more. Now, the actors on the stage are either prop-supported egomaniacs or hooded anonymous figures. The superego and the id combine forces for criminal or irrational action, while the ego sits helplessly by, feeling weak and impotent, unable to react to what it can merely observe.

Dictators eventually kill themselves or get assassinated, but there is no redress for the omnipotent infant, the terrorist.

If one trait is related to increased violence, it is *anomie* (Durkheim, 1897) in social terms or anonymity in individual terms. We easily can become killers of individuals we do not know.

It is not only the terrorists who are anonymous. The victims usually are anonymous, too. The demand or cause is more important than the individual targeted for attack. Since human life is important to a civilized society, the psychopathic terrorist will always have the upper hand, as violence is the goal, and in the terrorist's anonymity of feelings, it makes no difference whether the victim is a person, museum, hospital, or anything else. Since his own life has little value, there is no way in which normal human interaction, even the Golden Rule, can find useful application.

What are the psychological dynamics for acting out the role of a terrorist? On the deepest level, it is the only way left to make contact with something that has meaning to someone, as in *Taxidriver,* a movie that schizophrenic John Hinckley, schizophrenic, would-be presidential assassin, could relate to so well. The assassin makes the last possible contact with another human being through a violent implement such as a gun, which he believes may meet the approval of some fantasy mother, religion, or political or philosophical movement. He is still not completely isolated, as deranged as the cause for the action may be.

Are there any rationally understandable elements in this? There is one, if we accept the premise of necessary power struggles. As long as it remains within a political framework, terrorism is cheaper. Atomic warfare, or even conventional warfare, has priced itself out of the market.

If a country can train a handful of terrorists who can force political changes, it is an inexpensive replacement for organized military action. Terrorism, however, being only one step from anarchism, has regressed to almost the earliest beginnings of mankind's attempt to control its own over-aggression. The important question remains, is there enough rebound left for this to still be considered regression in service of the social ego? Social orders usually change when externalized aggression cannot be controlled adequately by the existing order. New institutions take the place of recently less sufficient ones.

What are the outlines of such an emerging order? We observe that even though their causes are very different, terrorists of one country are closer to terrorists of another than with groups within their own country. Just as water seeks its own level, so emotional behavior finds its own level in relationships. Sometimes, a rationalization of have-nots versus haves, or religious versus irreligious, or victims versus oppressors in the world can still be made. Sometimes, it becomes just one violent person understanding another.

In this climate of violence, little rational stability can be offered anywhere. The violent person, to "feel at home," destroys any symbol of stability and is attracted by "things on the move" or between "homes." This is why hijackings are exercised on planes or, in the earlier days, trains, or, in still earlier times, caravans. Travelers become child-like more easily and, therefore, are frightened more easily. This fright can be used more easily to brainwash and control them. Terrorists instinctively sense the success of the "Stockholm effect," where the victim, the weak, and the child, will almost instinctively subscribe to the cause of the victimizer to "survive." Explanations of this, in terms of "identifying with the aggressor," usually are too advanced. The rule is fear.

In character, it may resemble the earliest days of rape and bride-stealing. At that time, however, it was a step along the path of developing new human interactions, whereas in terrorism today, we are losing social cohesion.

Violence, having become international, only can be controlled by international efforts in intelligence and police action. The picture has changed from the world of "1984," where big, integrated superstates were fighting each other. Such a superstate requires firm boundaries, while worldwide terrorism operates around the world at will. It is not a world of fight of all against all, but rather, a world of fear of all of all. Communication can no longer be trusted, even previously trusted relationships of friends, family, or other intimate bonds, fall by the wayside, and security, as we earlier knew it, is gone.

This sounds like the most pessimistic scenario. I hope that it is just a description of the worst case that might occur.

Before addressing the subject of what to do, we have to look at why we have such difficulty in doing anything. We believe that an orderly world with justice and fairness is the norm desired by all. In other words, we assume that everybody else in the world has gone to the same Sunday School we have, or, if not the same, at least to a related one. There are some, more sophisticated, individuals who would call this notion naïve, but even the term naïve does not give the whole story. We are emotionally "defended" against seeing a different world picture. Why? Because we have to believe that others are like us in their values, or there is the danger that we have to recognize the unacceptable aggressive roots within ourselves. Being an honorable victim is less threatening than being an effective survivor.

Most terrorists only understand the street morality of the rule of power. The Israelis, for example, who are closer to that understanding, immediately follow up terrorist action with a show of power, while we, as well-brought up gentlemen and ladies, will probably shake the hand and thank the hijacker when he finally releases us. This, of course, means to the hijacker that he can repeat the procedure and extort his price at will. In the past, from early history on, the societies that survived were the ones who did not rely on the good will of others. It is often argued that if we act like a criminal, even in selected instances, we are bound to become criminals ourselves. Perhaps some of us would, but if our civilization has any roots at all, the difference between acting in self-defense against a criminal attack and being brought down more permanently to a lower level should be very clear.

Many argue for a nonviolent Gandhi-like approach as an answer to terrorism. Nonviolent methods are only successful where we find a social order incorporating values built on guilt. Against terrorists or governments supporting terrorist activity, nonviolence would be useless. It is still not clear whether the methods avowed by Gandhi or the threat of the power of the masses of deprived Indians in revolt defeated the English.

To deal successfully with terrorists, the following rules become necessary

1. Standards of civilized human behavior, as contrasted with terrorist acts, need to be clearly stated and enforced. A terrorist act is always outside morality and the law, even if committed in the context of a social or political problem. Under no circumstance is it to be seen as an extension of diplomacy or war.

2. Trained experts need to watch potential criminals and act with appropriate speed and expertise.

These rules already are well understood by many. The difficulty lies in the fact that we are hampered by our unwillingness to understand our own internal defenses and rationalizations.

What reactions would be required on a day-by-day basis? In order to rationally solve a problem, it needs to be understood. In general, there are three basic personality structures on which terrorism rests. These types can be found among the terrorists, as well as in the politicians or even the religious leaders who encourage them.

1. The religious or political fanatic is one type. Unfortunately, a part of

us identifies with his sacrificing himself for some "good," and we fail to see the underlying psychosis. We have a spot in our heart for him as we identify with the illusion. For many of us, life is only tolerable with illusions of our own. There are illusions that do not interfere with other people's well being, however, and there are others that are, or border on the criminal, if violently executed.

We tend to identify with the "doing" involved in revolutionary activity, as our own country emerged by revolution against the established order. We were mature enough to integrate our anger and guilt into rapidly building a bigger and better motherland, however, using the freed energy to expand and fill in from one ocean to the other.

The less successful revolutionaries stay on the dyadic level of endless revenge, creating untold misery to others and themselves.

In the dyadic relationship before *Oedipus* (Sophocles, 430–415 B.C.) was written, Greek drama depicted members of family clans killing one another in alternation, taking revenge in endless success. The chorus on stage, an as yet very ineffectual superego, could only keep repeating, "Isn't it terrible, isn't it terrible, this is the fate of the world." Oedipus broke this pattern by plucking out his eyes. For the first time, the tragic patricide looks into himself and, by finding part of his own guilt, is able to break the psychotic pattern. He, thus, moves through what Melanie Klein (1952) calls the depressive position into a more advanced neurotic pattern allowing for possible cure. The pre-oedipal pattern is best discussed by Wolfgang and Ferracucci in their *Subculture of Violence* (1967), which is still the best reference for understanding aggressive and criminal behavior.

To summarize: the illusion that violent acts can bring salvation remains just that, an illusion. The psychotic understructure cannot find closure.

2. Most terrorists belong to a second type, based on what has been variously diagnosed as character disorder, psychopathy, sociopathy, and is best described in a book by Cleckley (1976) called *The Mask of Sanity*. The title suggests that sanity is only in the mask, while psychosis is behind it. It is a character structure which flourishes in the transitional world that we have entered. The mask is so concealing that it usually takes an expert to see through it. This type appears in many forms and on many social levels, including the highest professional and political levels. Even as eminent a sociologist as Hannah Arendt (1963), covering the Eichmann trials in Jerusalem, thought that many of the Nazi leaders, including Eichmann, were not criminal but "banal," carrying out their duties not too differently than an American businessman. Since Rorschach records are available of these leaders and of Eichmann, we restudied their personalities. In restudying the Rorschachs, we found there was little "banal" about Eichmann. Hitler was a revenge fanatic (Type 1); Eichmann was a very skilled and refined servant, with sociopathic understructure (Type 2).

Cleckley defined his sociopathic type as an individual who has developed in such a way that parental and social standards have never been internalized. This type is found from among hardened criminals on one extreme, to superficially charming, alert, well-informed, pleasing, good talkers, with good intelligence on the other.

Many of them are very successful. They are not restricted by either guilt or anxiety and are able to outguess the behavior of their opponents. The opponent usually is limited by his conscience structure, partly based on guilt and defenses against inner anxieties.

What all such individuals have in common is lack of depth of feeling, and a lack of lasting commitment or even beginning loyalty. Such people make excellent imposters and are often excellent politicians, as they instinctively can react to the nuances of the political atmosphere. They generally are not psychologically treatable, even though they may feign to desire treatment if they feel that somebody would be pleased enough and would be fooled by them. Since they cannot be reached, due to lack of anxiety or a sense of guilt, the best that can be done with them is to "humor them out of town."

When experts in the field discuss the transferences in describing how to negotiate with such a terrorist, they are missing the point, as this type is unable to form any transference at all. The only language he understands is that you are one step ahead of him and that he, therefore, cannot fool you and had better be concerned with his own survival. Negotiating implies a framework of human values.

Although we still have the stereotype of the poor, uneducated revolutionary terrorist, in reality, there are many more of the character disorder type.

Statistics give a picture of the "typical terrorist," which is an average drawn from many thousands of terrorists studied. Typically, he is 20 to 23 years of age, usually male, is single or separated, from a middle or upper class urban family, often recruited at a university, has an average of 2½ years of college and by profession is a lawyer, government worker, student, nurse or sociologist—hardly the image of a poor revolutionary, but more likely, a "trained professional of terrorist activities." To avoid being influenced by emotional or tricky negotiations is part of his or her professional terrorist training. Obviously, the "negotiator" or assigned counter agent has to be very skilled in distinguishing between the fanatic and the sociopath. Here, specially trained psychologists would be helpful. It takes substantial clinical experience to make the distinction.

3. There is a sprinkling of "neurotic" terrorists. This type can be distinguished from the first two by the fact the victim's identity is either known or can easily be imbued with familiar, usually familial identities of the terrorist. Here, transference implications are most successful in negotiations. The guilt of the neurotic, however, will contribute to his own early demise and, thereby, provides for only a short, and not very successful, career from the terrorist point of view.

I would like to close with a speculation concerning both terrorism and the nuclear bomb, both in the title of this chapter. We can talk about the aspects of anonymity of both, the blurring of boundaries implied by both, the dehumanizing aspects of both, the difficulty of limits for both. Could it be that on a deep, unconscious level, however, the dehumanized terrorist symbolizes the last macho revolt against the mother-witch symbol of the all-devouring nuclear bomb? On the ultimate diffuse level, the life-giving and supportive mother cannot be differentiated anymore from the totally killing and destructive maternal image.

The world is moving into a contest between the threat of the destructive and the restitutionally creative and empathic mother image. Let us do everything in our power to support and internalize the latter mother image.

REFERENCES

Arendt, H. (1962). *The origins of totalitarianism.* New York: Meridian.

Arendt, H. (1963). *Eichmann in Jerusalem.* New York: The Viking Press.

Ayolon, O. (1980). Coping with terrorism: The Israeli case. In D. Meichenbaum & M. Jahnko (Eds.), *Stress prevention and management.* New York: Plenum Press.

Becker, J. E. (1978). *Hitler's children: The story of the Baader-Meinhof gang.* London: Granada.

Bell, J. B. (1975). *Transnational terror.* Washington, D.C.: Hoover American Enterprise Institute.

Blanner, R. (1964). *Alienation and freedom.* Chicago: University of Chicago Press.

Cleckley, H. (1976). *The mask of sanity* (5th ed.). St. Louis: C. V. Mosby.

De Grazia, S. (1948). *The political community: A study of anomie.* Chicago: University of Chicago Press.

Durkheim, E. (1951). *Suicide.* J. A. Spaulding & J. Simpson (trans.). New York: The Free Press. (Original work published 1897.)

Evans, A. E. (October 1976). Aircraft hijacking. *American Journal of International Law,* pp. 641–671.

Feierabend, I. K. (1970). *Social changes and political violence: Cross-national patterns.* New York: Bantam Books.

Finster, A. W. (1972). *Alienation and the social system.* New York: John Wiley & Sons.

Freud, A. (1966). *The ego and the mechanisms of defense.* New York: International Universities Press.

Friedlander, R. A. (1976). The origins of international terrorism. In *Israel yearbook on human rights.* Tel Aviv: Tel Aviv University.

Hacker, F. J. (1976). *Crusaders, criminals, crazies: Terror and terrorism in our time.* New York: W. W. Norton.

Hamburg, D. A. (1974). Coping behavior in life threatening circumstance. *Psychotherapy and Psychosomatics, 23,* 13–25.

Jacobson, S. R. (1973). Individual and group responses to confinement in a hijacked plane. *American Journal of Orthopsychiatry 43*(3), 459–469.

Kissinger, H. A. (September 8, 1975). Hijacking, terrorism and war. *Department of State Bulletin, 73,* 360–361.

Klein, M. (1952). *Developments in psychoanalysis.* London: Hogarth Press.

Lifton, R. J. (1967). *Death in life.* New York: Random House.

Miale, F. R. & Selzer, M. (1975). *The Nuremberg mind.* New York: Quadrangle.

Milgram, S. (1968). Some conditions of obedience and disobedience to authority. *International Journal of Psychiatry, 6,* 259–276.

Miller, A. H. (1980). *Terrorism and hostage negotiations.* Boulder: Westview Press.

Ochberg, F. M. (1977). *The victim of terrorism: Psychiatric considerations.* Paper presented at the Fourth Seminar on Terrorism. Evian: The International Center for Comparative Criminology.

Ochberg, F. M. & Soskins, D. A. (1982). *Victims of terrorism.* Boulder: Westview Press.

Schreiber, J. (1978). *The ultimate weapon: Terrorists and world order.* New York: Morrow.

Selye, H. (1956). *The stress of life.* New York: McGraw-Hill.

Sophocles. (1968). Oedipus the king. In M. Kallich, A. Macleish, & G. Schoenbohm (Eds.), *Oedipus myth and magic.* New York: The Odyssey Press, pp. 3–46. (Original work written in c. 430–425 B.C.)

Stevenson, W. (1976). *90 minutes at Entebbe.* New York: Bantam Books.

Strentz, T. (1981). A terrorist organizational profile: A psychological role model. In Y. A. Alexander & J. Gleason (Eds.), *Behavioral and quantitative perspective on terrorism.* New York: Pergamon Press.

U.S. News and World Report (July 8, 1985). The rise of world terrorism, p. 27.

Walter, V. (1964). Violence and the process of terror. *American Sociological Review, 29,* 248–258.

Wolfgang, M. E. & Ferracucci, F. (1967). *The subculture of violence.* London: Travistock.

Chapter 12

POTENTIAL FOR TRANSFORMATION

Gerard G. Neuman

There are many forms of aggression in nature. We are concerned here with *human* aggression, which takes specific forms, new in the process of evolution.

This chapter deals with the origins of human aggression, how it differs from the aggression found in nature, and what can be done about it; in other words, how we can deal with this basic problem of mankind.

Since the universe did not start with man, our behavior has its roots in earlier species of the animal kingdom. We believe that there are two basic evolutionary roots leading from animal evolution to its present human expression, the older female infanticidal root, and the male-male power root.

Aggression as Based on the Maternal Infanticidal Root

Infanticide, as applied to human fears and aggression has caused deep emotions during the last century as to whether it comes to us naturally through the animal world or whether we have learned it in response to the increased frustrations of human life.

Seeing ourselves as an integral part of evolution contains, in itself, dyadically polarizing components. We are either victims of our own more primitive instincts or we follow the "altruistic" view of evolution as described by Eibl-Eibesfeldt (1971), Ashley Montagu (1976), and a number of other anthropologists. Our evidence shows that we are both and neither. As a product of evolution, we participated in both trends. Our specific prehistory, however, created a new species with its own vicissitudes.

More recently, we find attempts to show that we can see lethal aggression in the higher apes, some aggressive monkeys, some mammals such as lions and wild dogs, kittens, puppies, and foals, and definitely in lower life forms such as birds and fish. Sharks, for instance, often eat their siblings in the maternal womb. Certain species of flies eat mother's inside before they are born. Male fish often eat eggs they have fertilized. When food is scarce, parent birds may abandon their eggs or even their nestlings. The black eagle often begins incubating the first egg several days before laying the second. When the second chick hatches, its older and stronger sibling will peck it to death. (This is parental infanticide displaced into fatal sibling rivalry.) Birds are monogamous usually. Occasionally, however, a polyandrous female will kill the brood of a male and add this male to her harem.

Many researchers believe the sexual hypothesis of increasing fertility or achieving genetically more adequate offspring would explain animal infanticide. Alternate research and observation, however, could not find this hypothesis as being central. Still, others have spoken of infanticide as a means of birth control, to assure group survival. Our observation shows that aggression is part of normal survival for both the individual and the group. The built-in conflict between the survival of the species and the survival of the individual becomes adjusted during millions of years of evolution toward the most workable compromises. The *human* problem remains that we did not have the evolutionary necessary time to do this. A total of 3 to 4 million years is little when compared with 20 to 50 million years and more allowed to other species. In addition, our unpreparedness, because of this shortness of time, produced a panic which led us into more self-destructive behavior such as cannibalism, with consequent addictions and necessary defense mechanisms, which, in their insufficiency, often increased the panic described in other chapters of this book.

Now, let us develop the infanticidal, maternal root as it affects our species collectively and, thereby, each member individually. As we remember from our prehistoric discussion, many million years ago and lasting into the beginning of the Pleistocene, we had to leave the trees due to overall deforestation and lack of food, to become an unprotected, bipedal, hunting and gathering group. We developed the ability to hunt-at-a-distance with our eyes, now based on horizontal vision, rather than a sense of smell, when searching the horizon for food. This new form of initially unprotected and, therefore, frustrated life left an understructure of rage which could only partially be sublimated by new forms of hunting. Also, for the individual infant, the distance between lap and breast became increased due to the new erect posture, thereby creating an experience of personal distance resulting in another "empty space" which had to be filled. In addition, the erect posture did not allow the birth canal to expand, so that we had to be born within nine months, rather than the 1 to 1½ years which would have been, and still would be, more adequate to develop most of the necessary faculties for independent living while still in the womb. Now, barely 40 percent of brain development takes place inside the womb and the rest of physiological development takes place postnatally at a time which has to be shared with the beginning of social learning. As we remain helpless and dependent for years, the substratum of rage is further increased. Not only are we more dependent as infants, with the overall human growth of upper cortex development, maternal instinct increasingly gives way to more emotionless rationality just at a time when mother love and understanding are most needed. Mothers, being a link in the chain of this newly evolving process, repeat in each birth their own birth experience, so that rage begets rage and more defenses have to be erected to keep mankind from demise.

But, even the shortened period of pregnancy did not achieve easier birth. The human, due to the increasingly large size of the infant's head, experiences the most difficult and hazardous birth process among all the mammals, again, increasing the substratum of rage for both infant and mother.

Having been deprived first of the supporting tree, then the supporting prairie, the easily reachable supportive breast, then the all-supportive womb, and the relatively more comfortable birth process, the newborn infant seeks mother's love at any cost. Ambivalence in the mother about the birth of a new child cannot be understood by the infant. Depending so totally on mother, he has to keep her in the picture at any cost. He must, therefore, first deny his rage and then convert it into self-blame (original sin). If he senses any problem, it must have been "caused by him"; he, as an infant, probably was not lovable enough or, possibly, not well enough behaved, thereby causing difficulties and risks for mother, etc.

This initial impression becomes reinforced by holding infants and toddlers to standards of behavior beyond their integrative capacities and general motor facilities. The consequences of what has become to us "normal" pregnancy, "normal" birth, and "normal" childrearing fill our institutions such as hospitals, clinics, and jails. Every other hospital bed is filled with a mental patient while ambulatory medical patients contain 60 percent emotional components to their illness. Each case of homicidal or otherwise aggressive behavior, psychosis, neurosis, as well as every other form of illness seen daily in our practices, represents a microcosm of that situation in our own society as well as the experiences of the world as a whole. By the time one half of the population in city, nation, or the assembly of nations on earth supports the other half, we, as a species, have a serious problem.

As indicated before, our more deep-seated problem relates to our evolutionary similarity to other mammals as compared to our uniqueness as human beings. We will explore the over-aggression developed as a new species in relation to the first root of aggression—the infanticidal maternal root.

As far as all animals are concerned, nothing more traumatic can happen in their development than separation from mother earlier than nature prescribes. We saw, in the first chapter, how isolation from mother can make ordinary rats into "killer rats." At the Wisconsin Primate Laboratory, innumerable studies have been conducted since 1939 under the direction of Harry Harlow and his wife (1979), related to the better understanding of "mother love" and the consequences of the deprivation of it. We have learned much from these studies. We know that the needed relationship to mother is not primarily related to food, as most had thought; not exclusively to touch; not to any senses *per se,* but in some sense to all of these. The partial deprivation of this relationship is partially reparable by relationships with peers and surrogates, but the total loss of mother love is irreparable. We see in the deprived monkeys many of the reactions we see in humans, such as later appearing symptoms of aggressive acting out, depression, or other forms of illness.

Where humans are different is in their overreactions; carrying grudges and the need for revenge over a longer time, sometimes to the "seventh generation," as well as being more savage, more inventive in cruelty and destruction. Although consequences in the animal world relate to individuals, in the human species not only individuals, but the species itself, is affected by destruction against the self. In the animal world, the greater power of abstraction has not led to organized destruction beyond the life sustaining unit; in the human, it has, *ergo* world wars and atomic bombs. On the positive side of human love, we have not distanced ourselves as far from the animal, (elephants have meaningful courtships), as we have on the destructive side.

Now let us consider some of the human issues of the maternal root. Just as in the animal world, sex and aggression are often hard to separate. Brain specialists (MacLean, 1973) point out that centers of aggression and centers of sex in the limbic system are spatially quite contiguous, so that many interactive responses are not surprising. For instance, a differentiation of sex and aggression in rape is very complex. The same is true of "lust murder," and the sexual excitement many sadistic or masochistic individuals experience in torture. Most sexual perversities also have strong, aggressive components.

There is a general belief in the social sciences that incest is a universal human taboo. In our experience, this universality leaves a lot to be desired. Most clinicians hear of seven or eight cases of father-daughter incest a year; mother-son incest is less frequent; sibling incest is much more frequent than that. The many people now being discovered of committing various forms of "sexual abuse," with and without aggression, do not seem to be sufficiently impeded by this "universal" taboo.

In history, we read that certain people in Egyptian times, the Mitanis for instance, were proud of their incestuous practices, (Nefertiti came from Mitanic origins). It is, therefore, likely that the incestuous world of Akhnaton was not such a surprise. A number of scientists, notably Velikovsky (1960), believe that Akhnaton's family is the prototype of the Greek Oedipus myth. A study of the origins of the Greek myth show that both the myths and the tragedies based on them are related more to the male-male aspects of the relationship of Laius to his son Oedipus as predicted by "fate," rather than on the incestuous marriage of Oedipus and his mother. Freud, trying to find sublimation for the aggressive roots of his theory, was more attracted to his libidinal interpretation of the Oedipal theme, which emphasized the upper cortical brain levels of the possible oedipal interpretations. He followed the anthropological thinking of his day, which viewed the origin of marriage and family as arising out of the incest taboo.

It appears that the fear of incest is not a consequence of social phenomena, although it is socially reinforced, but rather relates to the more basic fear of being incorporated, submerged, "devoured" by mother. Mother-son incest, although more destructive to family development on the social level, involves, on the most basic emotional level, her male offspring trusting a friendly, sexual orifice and the dark empty space beyond, if he is not to lose his penis, perceived as castration on the highest oedipal level, or his diffusion to a totally undifferentiated self on the lower levels of his state of consciousness. Other women he chooses (or overwhelms, as in earlier days), not mothers, or maternal totem mothers, are safer, because he attempts to control them rather than be controlled by them. Although there is obviously an evolutional background for exogamy to advance the species, the transition to the human species, as mentioned earlier, has been relatively recent. Consequently, most social learning related to this new family construction is also of short duration. We are still confused in our knowledge about it and, therefore, rituals of marriage, child care, and sexual behavior are far from institutionalized.

Freud, in his striving for a personality theory, started with the confusion about whether early parental sexual seduction had actually occurred or was only a wishful construct in the minds of patients. After almost 100 years, this question still divides the adherents and opponents of Freud. We believe that even though there is likely to be some truth in both positions, Freud's contribution of building a diagnostic and therapeutic system of depth psychology is of greater benefit to mankind than a black-and-white answer to a question which has no simple answer. It is interesting to us, however, that Freud, just as Sophocles before him, finds the sexual construction a useful defense against the less acceptable aggressive understructure. As unacceptable as wanting to sleep with mother is, wanting to kill her is even less acceptable. Killing the leader of the primal horde (*Totem and Taboo*), or Moses, in his later years (Freud, 1946), is still a way of preserving the fantasy of a life-supporting maternal figure. It took Melanie Klein (1954) to move into pre-oedipal territory to discuss the dynamics of the "good and bad" breast (a part object) of the as yet unintegrated maternal figure. The interactive process of projection and introjection helps the basically paranoid or schizoid infant to integrate the underlying aggression into a whole object, which can be maintained by advance of object cathexis toward greater object constancy.

Melanie Klein posits the paranoid-schizoid phase each infant experiences, but never explains why all of us start life so sick, and, if sick, why schizoid and paranoid—other animals do not. In the same way, other analysts before and after Klein talk about "archaic levels," which produce "inhuman" fantasy, delusion, and dream products; the archaic, however, is not explained and does not reach any clear sense of reality.

Also, since life in the womb had been assumed to be emotional pre-life, physiologically paradisaically pleasant, no emotional origin of personality, as related to this ontological pre-birth world, entered the thinking of the theorists. Not paying attention to the vicissitudes in the womb, the question of why there should be greater difficulty in the human womb never entered their thinking. As far as we can tell, this question has not even been raised by more sophisticated fetologists today.

We find traces of this common human heritage in each individual, especially as it relates to schizophrenic, psychotic, psychopathic, and many psychosomatic phenomena. These traces, however, are not necessarily predictive, as they are often too diffuse, but rather, indicate potential danger when defenses are not built to contain them. The "good-enough-mother" not only protects the child against present hazards, but also contributes to keeping the deeper, "archaic" roots under control. The traumatic history of the human species has put us into a developmental hole from which we have to lift ourselves, first with parental help, then by ourselves in internalizing this "good-enough-mother" image, if we want to overcome our deficits.

A sense of communion through good-enough, ideal mother-infant relationship then fills this "elemental empty space," which previously had been absorbed with rage. We will discuss the elements of possible transformations toward becoming our own good enough parent later in this chapter.

Aggression as Based on the Paternal, Male-Male Power Root

The other root, the male-male or paternal also has its origins in the evolutionary past. Nature's ecology is so designed that each inhabitant on our planet eats other living beings to survive, and in turn becomes food to stronger or more efficient survivors. At the same time, nature gives each species ways of defending itself in order to help sustain life for this species.

In the higher mammals, it usually becomes the task of the strong male, the so-called *alpha* animal, to define the hunting territory and protect the group. This exalted position is striven for by a constant game of king-of-the-hill, resulting in a pecking order of strength which structurally protects the group, the individuals within the group, and later, sub-groups, families, etc. As discussed earlier, the humanoid group leaving the trees toward a new life style in the prairie had to biologically dip back into the earlier hunting mammal species structure to become competitive with the other hunters; the wild dogs, hyenas, vultures, etc., found in the prairie. The life-style in the trees over millions of years had bred out those qualities, so they needed to be reestablished. These immediately needed patterns based on the fight-flight structure in the mammalian nervous system, achieved in a more precipitous manner than normally is allowed for in the evolutionary process, caused a poorly modulated transition to the level of aggression now necessary for survival. The resulting overaggression had to be dealt with through the development of the various defense systems we find enumerated in our textbooks. Defenses like denial, dissemblage, depression, and displacement, we share with the animal world. Some controls of oral/anal aggression we learned as *Homo erectus* types. The major "human" additions came during Neanderthaler days when, based on magic, dreaming, and various forms of fantasy formations, we invented reaction formation, which later led to many symbolic ways of sublimatory activities. As brain and fantasy life enlarged, we learned to use symbols of all kinds, making culture, art, religion and science possible. But just as we were liberated somewhat by gaining distance from anxieties through symbols, the higher abstractions could not eliminate the original aggressive sources which, in more and more disguised ways, grew within the seemingly effective symbol, like a disguised cancer. Many defenses, only supported by our narcissistic illusions, and often delusions, usually were not sufficiently integrative, and remained in the organism like time-bombs, to later explode into either psychosomatic or overt mental illness, acting out behavioral symptoms, or psychosomatic phenomena.

Let us return to our more specific discussion of the male-male root. The animal world, in general, has found a way to integrate the proverbial *alpha* bull with the effeminized *beta* bull without killing the weaker beta bull. Man, on a more basic level, has not. In our progress toward greater power, we grew from killing small mammals to large animals to our brethren, and became addicted to human flesh, livers, brains, which, after we had reached the point of diminishing return, had to be symbolically ritualized into our various forms of religion, art, law, regulatory social forms, science and culture, in general. But even these restitutional defenses could not transform the aggressive components sufficiently, so that the human species today is left with a great number of addictive behaviors in order to suppress the underlying aggression at all cost, through obsessive-compulsive mechanisms. If not alcoholism and drugs, then work, fanaticism in health, obsessions of many varieties, pornography, sexual perversions, and other minor addictions, too numerous to mention obviously. It is better to work too many hours than to drink or smoke too much, but the basic aggressive energy is still wasted in attempted compulsive suppressions, rather than allowing for pleasureful living.

How did we handle the *alpha-beta* bull root? Most would agree very poorly, up to the last few hundred years. We began to deal with it symbolically during the invention of bear cults during Neanderthal days. As we remember from the chapter on pre-history, we learned to make the cave bear into a "superhuman" creature or a god, moving aggression into the spiritual realm and, by way of reaction formation, we transformed the "feared horrible" into the "desired and respected holy." The words for sacred in the earlier languages still hold both meanings. The earliest written source, the

Iliad, still does not have any good restitution for male-male aggression.

The early books of the bible try to stay the killing hands of fathers and brothers by giving the responsibility for judgment to Jahwe, whom we begged to accept us as good children. Unfortunately, as the text above shows, we could not keep our part of the covenant and in "primary masochism" fashion, punishment in the form of death or defeat in battle overtook us many times.

In our religious activities, we are substantially offering the same hopes and prayers as the founders of the various belief systems 2,000 or more years ago. The gods we created in our image seemingly remained as inefficient in reaching utopia as we, the creators. Some of us are now quite skilled at analyzing the roots of religious beliefs and artistic, cultural, and scientific endeavors, but not very good at drawing salubrious conclusions from such analyses, nor becoming able to do something of a more effective nature about it.

After promoting our enemy/friend cave bears to godlike creatures, we slowly developed enough societal structure to translate small group aggression into armies and wars, coinciding with new forms of living as required by the demands of agriculture and urbanization. The individualized peripatetic hunter became the organized warrior of the newly stationary community. It usually overlaps the age of recorded history, from the early Egyptian, Sumerian, Babylonian days to World War II. We may have reached the limits of this kind of warfare. The technical products of our more highly abstracting brain structure may have become so sophisticated in the means of organized warfare, we are understandably panicked that nuclear means will take the place of "conventional" means of killing.

Another aspect of the male-male interaction, which still remains in our psyche, relates to as yet untransformed homosexual behavior. The *beta* human, effeminized by forced rectal intercourse, became so angry that alternating killings between tribes was repeated up "to the seventh generation." We have numerous pieces of evidence for this, not only in early Greek literature, but in the earliest myths and ballads of many peoples. Not only do we find it phylogenetically in pre-oedipal cultures, but it appears ontologically, as well, in Melanie Klein's pre-oedipal infant, and in the case material of many an individual patient.

In Greece, between 600 B.C. and 400 B.C., we find early transitional forms leading from aggressive male-male interaction to a positive value-laden, idealized societal form. Strong male tutors of heterosexual makeup would educate deserving young males academically, as well as pass the wisdom of the semen to them in anal intercourse. This was approved, not only by the youngster's family, but by Greek society as a whole. Platonic love, friendship, and loyalty tried to intellectually integrate sex and aggression as part of a philosophically based ideal society. In a similar *tour de force,* the myth makers tried to hold their gods to these high "human" standards, but more often than not, did not succeed. This procedure, however, allowed the mortal Greek to identify with a rather benign superego, thereby establishing an achievable balance between their ideals and their image makers, often with the skilled help of humor.

The Nordic myths, also compromised in a similar fashion, though aggressive trickery usually took the place of humor. The Romans, who did not know too much about humor, found it permissible for a father to kill his recalcitrant son on the spot. This, by itself, was minor compared to the disastrously paranoid male-male, even including female power relationships, which, in addition to killing thousands of humans, killed the great Roman Empire itself.

Christianity saved the medieval day of totally degenerate male-male relationship by establishing new standards between bishops and priests, as well as kings and knights, and, later, between dukes and tradesmen. The original mammal pecking order which had worked so well became reestablished for these three basic realms of society.

Sublimation toward blood brotherhood is based on reaction formation of the aggressive roots. Here, two males, who swear loyalty toward one another for an idealized goal of possibly patriotic or religious conviction, literally open their veins and let the blood combine in a previously dug hole in the ground, to serve as a symbol of this eternal friendship and loyalty. In the Viking culture, for instance, this split is reified in their cultural value system. It was expected of a good Viking warrior that he be totally cunning toward the enemy and totally loyal to a friend. This would not have been too difficult to achieve if enemy and friendship relationships would have remained stable. But as in today's national and international politics, friends and enemies changed roles too frequently to adhere to such a standard without conflict.

The aggression of the male-male root could be sublimated originally with some success. After the Greek tutorial system broke down, however, it was no longer possible for the sexual part of the male-male root to be integrated, and it, therefore, had to be suppressed. As the Middle Ages deteriorated in structure, sexual "abominations" were treated more severely.

In all religions today, homosexuality has been condemned, giving sanction to the inherent fear of most males that their own feminine part will break through and that they will not be considered, or consider themselves, sufficiently masculine; an underlying fear seen in many male patients in clinical situations. In a world of masculine values, lesbianism never presented a similar threat.

There is another aspect derived from the "paternal" root. This is the rage related to the weak father. This, in its major application, is an exclusively human reaction. The expectation of the strong *alpha* male who can protect the group comes from the animal world. In the human world, fathers are not only expected to protect the group and family but, if there is insufficient maternal relationship, fathers are given an opportunity to offer a second chance of giving the youngster a better "maternal" relationship. If he does not offer it, the earlier rage toward the insufficient mother, evoking the archaic mother-witch image in the youngster, is transferred toward the now insufficient father. Outbursts of that rage are observed especially during transitional periods such as adolescence.

As a matter of fact, the rage toward the weak parent, evoking the earlier archaic prototype, usually is more severe than the rage against a dictatorial, controlling parent. A child usually can forgive the parent almost anything, with the exception of weakness. Protection and survival still remain the basic instincts.

In terms of the two genders, a relationship with a weak father does not free the young male from the threatening enveloping or incestuous involvement with mother, and gives him no role model for his future. For the female child, the lack of a strong father also fails to free her to move in the direction of heterosexuality, again leaving her to struggle with the unresolved conflicts related to her "mother-witch" introject. Our textbooks and clinical practices are filled with many examples of this and their implications for mental health.

We usually obtain examples for the male-male root from males. How does the female experience it? We, unfortunately, do not know as much about it, but let us mention a few issues.

In the clinically observed female, the male is often feared as a rapist-killer, belittled as an immature boy, or, on the other side of the coin, experienced as an over-idealized protective "father," sometimes even divinely overvalued. Prehistorically, the male-female post-instinctual "relationship" in the human took on the form of rape, partially for sexual reasons, but more often, to steal and conquer property. Women, seen as property, could be used for serving the male in any form convenient to him. It is our theory that part of the reason for frontal sexual intercourse in the human relates to the female's only chance of dissuading the intemperate male, superior in physical strength and running power, by trying to establish a relationship with him, even if it had to be built on seduction, ruse, and deception. Later the male, also seeing some value in a more human relationship, learned the origins of empathy from his female victim.

The myth of Samson and Delilah depicts a stage where the converted male expresses his rage about female deceit. For the male, woman was split into whore or saint, for the female, male was split into rapist and killer, on the one hand, or idealized protector on the other. There are many examples of attempts to fuse this polarized dichotomy of each of the two roots.

Our mythologies, fairy tales, novels, plays, movies, and everyday life as seen on the street and in the clinic, give us examples of mostly unsuccessful attempts at fusion. All our defense mechanisms of denial, displacement, idealization, etc. have not been of lasting help. There is insufficient stability in split (dyadic) relationships. We will have to triangulate our ways from thesis and antithesis to a synthesis, a new, transformed, all-inclusive relationship.

If we look carefully, we still can see both roots, maternal and paternal, represented in practically all our symbols of aggression. Going up the ladder of weapons, sticks and bones, the pre-symbolic detached penis, has as yet no female (maternal) aspect connected with it. The spear enters the body, mirroring the sexual encounter. The sword is sheathed and unsheathed in addition to spearing the body. Later swords and sabers have, in addition, two loops ornamenting the grip, often incorporating the symbol of the cross, giving symbolic protection to the aggressor. The gun and the bigger gun, cannon, carry bullets in their womb to be expelled, similar to an explosive birth and similar to a penis baby ready to enter the enemy like a penis. DeMause (1982) described the similarity of feeling between the birth process and the "outbreak" of war.

Even the most advanced missiles shot from a cannon-like container never leave their penile form. But, just as the symbols of aggression have both roots, so do the symbols of love. Cupid's arrow does not hide it, but even red roses have thorns, if we care to look more closely.

So, for both sexes, there are ultimately two roots of origin of aggression, the maternal infanticidal, and the paternal male-male competitive.

The human species has three problems to solve:

1. It has to prevent the reawakening of the deep killer overaggressive roots through "good enough" maternal and paternal supports in the earliest child rearing, based on the degree of maturity the parents themselves have reached.

2. It has to find fusion of these two roots on all levels, from the bodily to the highest symbolic cultural levels.

3. It has to build on these fusions toward transformation into integrated group and individual life-styles for, at the minimum, survival, and, on higher levels, to make more meaningful living possible.

Potential for Transformation

Our story begins with the "elemental empty space," unique to the human, which can either be filled with projected rage or with the first symbolic and then experienced introjected "good-enough" mother image. We recall that this space was first created by distancing our horizon as we started to walk erect and by distancing the breast from the infant for the same reason. Our helpless life depended on being held for a much more extensive and much longer period than that for which we had been evolutionarily programmed. No one book would be large enough to describe the myriad ways in which we have tried to fill this empty space. All symbolic forms, all religion, art and science, owe their existence to these basic human need fulfilling attempts.

In summary, we can say that all attempts at symbolizing the threats of experiencing the aggressive emotions became restitutional "schizoid" attempts of distancing, compensating us through the mechanism of reaction formation with "truth, beauty, and goodness we hold so dear." Our organic brain development followed the course of this distancing. The evolutionary development of the lower brain centers (cerebellum, brain stem, and limbic system) helped this distancing split by becoming more separated from the newly developing upper-cortical brain structures.

On the experiential level, we observe the movement from magic to religion to art to science, leading to the "abstract" realities of higher mathematics and theoretical physics. Having outstripped perception by way of direct sense experience, a most significant shift occurred when in the humans, and the humans only, symbols could relate directly to other symbols without relating back to our limbic system (Geschwind, 1965), which all other mammals have to do. The development of prepositional features in our languages made this possible. It opened a new world of left hemisphere dominated thinking, a world of technical miracles, but lost us the biological humanity of basic "truth" and meaningful object relationships in the process. We became "angels" or "devils," neither of which exist, outside of the inventional areas of the new human upper cortex brain structures. The danger is that if we progress to squeeze the final elements of emotion out of those artificial symbols, we will literally become "robots," possibly graduating into a new species.

The development of our frontal lobes, the part of the brain which is in direct contact with all the other parts, still may prevent this if we can overcome the fears which make distancing schizoid defense structures necessary. We will not find our "self" for which we so desperately look, by further distancing abstractions, but by finding ways of dealing with the fears to make the defenses unnecessary. This was the dream of Freud and all the other pioneers of dynamic psychology.

The search for the protective parent is so preemptory of other activities that we are willing to give up our "rational" sense of security. Eisenbud (1982), in his lifelong attempt at understanding "parasensory" experiences, comes to the conclusion that basic human motivation of "finding mother" at any cost is still the best explanatory paradigm for many seemingly "unexplainable" forms of behavior.

While seeking aggression such as war, revolution explosions, may be illogical, it may allow the lower brain centers to equal the experience to "a mother," which left us in similar experiential chaos. It is still better to fill the empty space with a mother-witch or papist father introject than to have no parent at all. This also offers one explanation for our "Escape from Freedom," of democracy to autocrats, (Fromm, 1969), the sado-masochistic course of our war and peace-dimensional history, and our inability to find real peace. "Real peace," as the antidote to war and aggression, is still a schizoid unreality. It will not help us in coping with the demands of a biological world, let alone allow us to reach the plane of meaningful feedback called "creative living." But let us see what we can do as individuals.

As has been mentioned earlier, as long as we study human life and experience only post-natally, we are entering the scene in the third act of the play. The resolution does not make sense without knowledge of the antecedent forces of impact. Those forces are the prehistoric travail of the pre-human and human species, the womb experiences, and the origins of the individual personality, leading to the specific coloring of the postnatal stages.

All theorists, thus far, have started postnatally. Sigmund Freud opened the field of meaningful modern personality research. In another major milestone, Melanie Klein led us further in the direction we are pursuing. She focused on introjection and projection as moves toward the "depressive position" and the achievement of "whole object" construction. Her work built the bridge to Winnicott's (1951) "transitional object," making the transition to the "true" self from the "false" self possible.

Winnicott, better than anyone, attempts to deal with this empty space by filling it with "transitional objects," thereby making it into a "transitional space."

Going back to what is usually considered the first human sensate experience, namely the beginning resolution of the mother-infant symbiosis into a *me* and *not me* infant, Winnicott postulates three factors: the perception of the external part object; the expectation of the internalized inner object of the breast; and, as his unique contribution, the intermediate area of "experiencing" the experience. The infant creates the breast as he finds it, and finds the meaning of it only as he creates it. We can better experience it with both brain hemispheres participating, than understand it with left brain logic alone. The "illusory" part of this experience is uniquely human and provides the basis for increasingly higher abstractions. It is human because it is different in quality from objects instinctually expected in the animal world. Although animals can deal with "concrete" objects and learn any combinations of them, they cannot deal with prepositional properties. The illusory quality of the symbol is outside an animal's field of experience. His self is always an animal-experienced true self, while the human self always hovers between the "as if" experience of the false self and the honest experience of the "true self." Jung (1952) and Kohut (1977), among others, also provide shades of the development of the self.

Winnicott (1951) often says about the "transitional" situation that there is no infant without a mother and no mother without an infant. Being capable of being alone implies a good-enough internalized mother, just as we can feel completely isolated, even being in the company of others.

The movement toward capacity for creativity, autonomy of self and empathy derive from the quality of this transitional experience. Melanie Klein's self is based on reactions to the instinctual forces which are assumed as inborn givens. Jung's self is based on individuation guided by the "creative unconscious," which has been given to all of us. Kohut's mirroring has too much of the external interaction to highlight the essence of Winnicott's self-creating "experiencing."

As we understand Winnicott's basic prototype, we can see how "playing" rather than "hard reality" on the one hand, or disconnected fantasy on the other stays within the vitally creative transitional space, out of which therapy, education, art, and any other meaningful human activity can develop. The inner and outer world is a playful, flexible, ever-changing field of increasingly meaningful experiences, rather than a static, rigid, defense-oriented phenomenon. The concept of "illusory" has many versions. It can be a displacement and become the world of "science." It can be a schizoid displacement and become the world of emotional and mental illness, or it can playfully become a constructive creative phenomenon.

Winnicott does not write much about aggressive or destructive problems. He remains the optimistic, congenial, helpful, paternal, psychoanalytic extension of his own creative pediatric background. He keeps loving children and their mothers. A few times, however, he touches on the origin of "mother-love." He explains that the mother who can stand and stay the youngster's rage will allow the child to convert this rage into love for mother's persistence. I was interested to see much of his clinical material related to the symbolism of strings and ropes, which he correctly relates to processes of separation and connectedness. He never relates it, however, to the important cord, the umbilical cord. If he had, this may have led him into the world of transition from the womb through the birth process and given new and possibly additional meaning to his transitional field.

It is our experience with clinical cases of emotional problems, behavior disorders, and psychosomatic syndrome that we have more success when we can make contact with primary rages, fears and frustrations, and by helping the patient to briefly reexperience his pain so that energy becomes freed toward the restitutional transformation. Our own inner empty space, originally filled with rage, exchanges this rage for hope enhancing life-giving input. We find the same true for individuals in therapeutic groups. The group becomes the maternal womb and the individuals achieve a new emotional birth. Just as in the pathological group, war can break out simulating birth, so in a mutually enhancing group, the participants enter into new lifestyles supported by a restitutional group leader and by constructive experience distilled from the cooperation of the other members.

Social implications of this will eventually become a formula for dealing with the issues of war and other social problems. Wars in the past were facilitated by the interaction of charismatic, emotionally sick leaders with masses whose deep unconscious forced them to participate in structurally formless groups of sado-masochistic need systems. The explosions of war or social disorganization allowed them to reexperience the mother-witch related fears. The explosion served to release an increasingly unbearable inner tension. Meaningful group interaction becomes the helpful antidote to the anomie of human-like creatures, hiding their rage and fear behind the mask of anonymity, making human slaughter of all kinds possible.

Meaningful group interaction, as an antidote, leads to individual autonomy based on self-reliance, freeing energy for both flexible and integrative behavior. This, in turn, allows for constructive creativity and meaningful relationships based on true empathy, providing the basis for transformation from a fear-ridden existence into joyful living—that is, if we work hard on not allowing the "false self" to defeat us again.

REFERENCES

deMause, L. (1982). *Foundations of psychohistory.* New York: Creative Press.

Eibl-Eibesfeldt. (1971). *Love and hate.* New York: Holt, Rinehart and Winston.

Eisenbud, J. (1982). *Paranormal foreknowledge.* New York: Human Sciences Press.

Freud, S. (1946). Moses and monotheism. In *Collected Papers.* New York: International Psychoanalytic Press.

Freud, S. (1950). *Totem and taboo.* New York: W. W. Norton.

Fromm, E. (1969). *Escape from freedom.* New York: Holt, Rinehart and Winston.

Geschwind, N. (1965). Disconnexion syndrome in animals and man. *Brain, 88,* 237–294; 585–644.

Harlow, H. F. & Mears, C. (1979). *The human model: Primate perspectives.* Washington, D.C.: V. H. Winston & Sons.

Jung, C. C. (1952). Symbols of transformation. In *Collected Works,* Vol. V. New York: Pantheon Books.

Klein, M. (1954). *The psychoanalysis of children.* London: The Hogarth Press.

Kohut, E. (1977). *The restoration of the self.* New York: International University Press.

MacLean, P. D. (1973). The triune concept of brain and behavior. In T. J. Boag & D. Campbell (Eds.), *Hicks memorial lectures.* Toronto: University of Toronto Press.

Montagu, A. (1976). *The nature of human aggression.* New York: Oxford University Press.

Velikovsky, I. (1960). *Oedipus and Akhnaton.* New York: Doubleday.

Winnicott, D. W. (1951). Transitional object and transitional phenomena. In *Through pediatrics to psychoanalysis.* New York: Basic Books, pp. 229–242.

Chapter 13

EPILOGUE

Slaying the Dragon

Gerard G. Neuman

Having analyzed the origins and history of our aggression and thrown some light on the defense mechanisms which either help us ignore it or project it into inimical people, objects, or circumstances, in order *not* to find out that "the enemy is us," the question arises as to what we can do to deal with this situation.

In therapy, usually after a period of defining the problem, the same question is reached and the process of "know thyself" is started. We obviously are dealing with a complex problem and may need to learn many more specific things to facilitate progress. The one thing we can say right now is that whatever we have been doing so far has not been successful. We may draw the conclusion, therefore, that we should *do* less rather than more, and try first to understand and then develop the courage to face the factors involved. We have the knowledge to develop the necessary facilities to help in the process of this "understanding." Reason and rationality, faith and conviction, preaching and teaching, although helpful at times, in an overall sense, do not seem to suffice.

The problem, in its complexity, resembles sometimes a play with mirrors. The elements of aggression seem to sneak into all the attempts at finding rational solutions. There is no end of promising political theories, social models, and simple utopias. Tao the Way, the Sermon on the Mount, the promises of messiahs and promised lands, of classless societies, and the eternal Third Reich, have left us on the brink of disaster, swept along by our seemingly unstoppable race toward a self-destructive, uninhabitable planet, and the horrors of the nuclear bomb.

I call it a game of mirrors because the institutions don't seem to change, just the inmates. Previous victims become the next killers, and revolutions, seemingly providing new hope, usually end in having reduced the chances of ever achieving that hope. The same has been true of every war fought.

There do not seem to be any quick solutions. Can we accept that? We often feel so panicky. We are learning from both group and individual therapy that in moments of panic, it is most efficient to move ahead with speed commensurate to the organism's ability to integrate. Thereby, we avoid the failure of being seduced into either acting out the aggression precipitously, or "acting it in" through either actually killing ourselves, developing serious psychosomatic conditions, or in finding other symbolic ways of self-destruction. Moving with appropriate speed, we have a better chance to become individually and societally sufficiently mature to fill the "empty space" and to finally become our own "good enough parent." We need to develop further the implements of our individual group and mass restitutional activities, including art and motor activities. Then, the newly achieved introject of becoming our own good parent will allow us to become our own effective, autonomous self, being able to look the "false self" in the eye and, finally, stop the game of mirrors.

The process of integrating our three brains and truly knowing ourselves, which is often painful, remains the only worthwhile hope.

Many a cynic tells us that "analyzing" each individual, or even groups of individuals, is impractical and impossible. Again, the impulsive, anxiety-laden approach of "What do we do about it at this very moment since it is so late already," only tends to block the progress we can make. Roosevelt, with one statement, "We have nothing to fear but fear itself," introduced a modern mental health concept, transforming the panic of the failing economic situation of his day. Unfortunately, Hitler, Mussolini, and the Japanese warlords, living in the same world of economic disasters, had not gone to the same Sunday school. We shudder to think about what the result might have been, had the depression in this country resulted in a power grab by one of our own frustrated fanatics.

We will not need to "analyze" everybody. Through successful guidance, many of us can become mature enough to provide like-minded leaders and, thereby, create for ourselves a higher degree of maturity and wisdom at the guiding levels of our society—locally, nationally, and, ultimately, internationally.

What can give us additional hope? As we learn more about ourselves, our history, and our society, we will be able to make more mature choices. This book's aim is to highlight some of the more recently discovered relevant facts necessary for individual and societal transformation. For instance, Lloyd deMause's fantasy analysis of leaders and groups is one of the more hopeful developments in creating preventive warning systems. There are a number of other ideas along similar lines.

Naked aggression is the "dragon," but the seduction through promises of socially perfect or philosophically paradisiacal societies creates an almost equal danger by giving false hope, to be followed by disappointment, leading to depression, thereby, renewing the vicious downward cycle of the "mirror game." In order to save the Holy Land during the Crusades, we killed millions; in order to create a classless society, we killed millions; in order to make the world safe for democracy, we killed millions. Let us for once face it. The "ideal" is just a reaction formation of unacceptable aggression. None of the shamans and prophets of the past, perhaps somewhat helpful in their day, have been able to help us find our way out. Nobody but *ourselves* can do it ultimately. Both aggression toward and dependence on anything outside ourselves are just opposite sides of the same coin. The most difficult lesson to learn is that we cannot really control the behavior of another person, group, or country. We have to start with ourselves, not arrogantly, but also not guiltily.

For example, as we mature, we find that we stop at a red light and go on green, not because we are afraid of a ticket, but because life on the road becomes safer and more comfortable for every driver. We interact without need to control aggression or to need the threat of the law. As our emotional defense systems become less driven, and as we become more mature, we may be able to move from problems of adaptation or adjustment, only a form of "existing," to modes of creative and empathic "living." Some will reach it earlier, others will follow in time, and gradually, we will be able to turn things around.

The "dragon" can be slain by blinding him with the light of true understanding. The dragon within us can be transformed into new aspects of "living," based on empathy and creativity.

INDEX